The Ex-Offender's Re-Entry

Assistance Directory

Selected Books by the Author

99 Days to Re-Entry Success Journal

201 Dynamite Job Search Letters

America's Top 100 Jobs for People Without a Four-Year Degree

America's Top Internet Job Sites

America's Top Jobs for People Re-Entering the Workforce

The Anger Management Pocket Guide

Best Jobs for Ex-Offenders

Best Resumes and Letters for Ex-Offenders

Blue-Collar Resume and Job Hunting Guide

Change Your Job, Change Your Life

The Complete Guide to Public Employment

Dynamite Cover Letters

Dynamite Resumes

The Ex-Offender's 30/30 Job Solution

The Ex-Offender's Job Interview Guide

The Ex-Offender's New Job Finding and Survival Guide

The Ex-Offender's Quick Job Hunting Guide

Get a Raise in 7 Days

Give Me More Money!

High Impact Resumes and Letters

I Can't Believe They Asked Me That!

I Want to Do Something Else, But I'm Not Sure What It Is

International Jobs Directory

Job Hunting Tips for People With Hot and Not-So-Hot Backgrounds

Job Interview Tips for People With Not-So-Hot Backgrounds

Jobs for Travel Lovers

Military-to-Civilian Resumes and Letters

Military-to-Civilian Success for Veterans and Their Families

Military-to-Civilian Transition Pocket Guide

Nail the Cover Letter!

Nail the Resume!

No One Will Hire Me!

Overcoming Employment Barriers

Quick Job Finding Pocket Guide

The Re-Entry Employment and Life Skills Pocket Guide

The Re-Entry Personal Finance Pocket Guide

The Re-Entry Start-Up Pocket Guide

Re-Imagining Life on the Outside Pocket Guide

Savvy Interviewing

Savvy Networker

Win the Interview, Win the Job

You Should Hire Me!

The Ex-Offender's Re-Entry Assistance Directory

Public and Private Support Programs for Making It on the Outside

Ronald L. Krannich, Ph.D.

IMPACT PUBLICATIONS
Manassas Park, VA

Warning/Liability/Warranty: The author and publisher have made every attempt to provide the reader with accurate, timely, and useful information. However, given the rapid changes taking place in today's re-entry scene, some of this information will inevitably change. The information presented here is for reference purposes only. The author and publisher make no claims that using this information will guarantee the reader re-entry success. The author and publisher shall not be liable for any losses or damages incurred in the process of following the advice in this book. Please see pages x, xi, and 221 for information on updating entries.

ISBNs: 978-1-57023-367-8 (paperback); 978-1-57023-380-7 (eBook)

Library of Congress: 2015913910

Publisher: For information on Impact Publications, including current and forthcoming publications, authors, press kits, online bookstore, additional websites, downloadable catalogs, and submission requirements, visit the left navigation bar on the front page of the main company website: www.impactpublications.com.

Publicity/Rights: For information on publicity, author interviews, and subsidiary rights, contact the Media Relations Department: Tel. 703-361-7300, Fax 703-335-9486, or email: query@impactpublications.com.

Sales/Distribution: All distribution and special sales inquiries should be directed to the publisher: Sales Department, IMPACT PUBLICATIONS, 9104 Manassas Drive, Suite N, Manassas Park, VA 20111-5211, Tel. 703-361-7300, Fax 703-335-9486, or email: query@impactpublications.com. All bookstore and eBook sales are handled through Impact's trade distributor: National Book Network, 15200 NBN Way, Blue Ridge Summit, PA 17214, Tel. 1-800-462-6420.

Quantity Discounts: We offer quantity discounts on bulk purchases. Please review our discount schedule for this book on page 228, at www.impactpublica tions.com, or contact the Special Sales Department, Tel. 703-361-0255.

The Author: Ronald L. Krannich, Ph.D., is one of today's leading career and travel writers who has authored more than 100 books, including several self-help guides for people in transition and those with not-so-hot backgrounds. A former Peace Corps Volunteer, Fulbright Scholar, and university professor, Ron specializes in producing and distributing books, DVDs, training programs, and related materials on employment, career transition, addiction, anger management, criminal justice, life skills, and travel. He can be contacted at ron@impactpublications.com.

Contents

Preface .... **viii**
- Tough Challenges viii
- Helping Hands.. ix
- Words of Hope and Caution... ix
- Annotated Entries... xi
- Thanks.. xi

1 A Leg Up, A Hand Down **1**
- Welcome to the Free World... 1
- Hope for Better Days 3
- Primary Audience.. 3
- Legs Up, Hands Down 4
- Run With Wise and Empathetic People 4
- Attitude, Motivation, and Personal Growth............................ 5
- The Hard Work of Being Alone 7
- An Awesome and Troubled Correctional Complex 8
- Coming Changes 11
- Community-Based Re-Entry Resources 12
- Evidence-Based Laboratories of Re-Entry Success................... 16

2 Gateways to Community Re-Entry Mazes............................... **18**
- Welcome to the Great Churn... 18
- Joining the Marginalized.. 19
- Second Chance Communities 20
- Welcome to a Maze of Community Players.............................. 21
- Gateway Programs and Services.. 24
- Foundations, Institutes, and Nonprofits 45

3 Documentation: IDs, Rap Sheets, and Online Reputations............... **55**
- What You Need ASAP 56
- Acquire Acceptable IDs 58
  - Birth, Marriage, Divorce, Death Documents.......................... 59
  - Social Security Card/Number 60
  - Driver's License.. 61
  - Valid Passport.. 63
- Know Your Rap Sheets... 63
- Consider Online Reputation and Repair Strategies................... 65

4   Release and Re-Entry Programs 66

- The Recidivism Issue and Argument 67
- What Works in America's Many Re-Entry Laboratories 67
- Today's Re-Entry Landscape 69
- Federal Re-Entry Programs and Activities 70
- State and Local Re-Entry Initiatives 72

- Alabama	73	- Montana	118
- Alaska	75	- Nebraska	120
- Arizona	77	- Nevada	122
- Arkansas	79	- New Hampshire	124
- California	80	- New Jersey	124
- Colorado	84	- New Mexico	127
- Connecticut	86	- New York	129
- Delaware	88	- North Carolina	133
- District of Columbia	88	- North Dakota	135
- Florida	89	- Ohio	136
- Georgia	92	- Oklahoma	140
- Hawaii	94	- Oregon	143
- Idaho	95	- Pennsylvania	145
- Illinois	96	- Rhode Island	151
- Indiana	98	- South Carolina	152
- Iowa	101	- South Dakota	154
- Kansas	102	- Tennessee	155
- Kentucky	103	- Texas	157
- Louisiana	105	- Utah	160
- Maine	106	- Vermont	161
- Maryland	108	- Virginia	164
- Massachusetts	110	- Washington	167
- Michigan	112	- West Virginia	169
- Minnesota	113	- Wisconsin	170
- Mississippi	116	- Wyoming	173
- Missouri	117		

**5   Re-Entry Handbooks, Workbooks, Directories,
    Curricula, and Databases..174**

- Standard Contents 174

- Downloadable Re-Entry Guides and Online Databases 175

    - Nationwide 181   - Massachusetts 187
    - Alabama 183   - Minnesota 188
    - Alaska 183   - Mississippi 188
    - Arkansas 183   - Missouri 188
    - California 184   - New Jersey 188
    - Colorado 184   - New Mexico 189
    - District of Columbia 184   - New York 189
    - Florida 185   - North Carolina 190
    - Georgia 185   - Oklahoma 190
    - Hawaii 186   - Oregon 190
    - Idaho 186   - Pennsylvania 190
    - Illinois 186   - South Carolina 191
    - Indiana 186   - Texas 191
    - Kentucky 187   - Virginia 192
    - Louisiana 187

- In-House Curricula and Resources 192

Appendices 195

- A Collateral Consequences of Convictions:
     State-by-State Restrictions 196
- B Your Re-Entry Success IQ 199
- C Re-Entry Preparation Checklist 208
- D Weekly Goal Setting and Achievement Activities 213
- E My Re-Entry Success Contract 216
- F Weekly Job Search Performance and Planning Report 219
- G Recommended Re-Entry Resources 221

Re-Entry Resource Center 222

Preface

IT'S NOT SURPRISING – most people in transition face numerous challenges to getting ahead. Encountering a variety of taxing re-entry "games," ex-offenders have to first figure out the **rules** and understand any **barriers** before they can become serious **players**. Lacking such knowledge is a sure way to experience frustration and failure with the whole transition process.

Tough Challenges

Ex-offenders must handle many difficult transition issues as they move from the darkness of prison to the sunshine of freedom. Unlike newly minted college graduates, transitioning military, relocating spouses and clergy, or retirees flush with resources for enjoying a jobless life, ex-offenders face a variety of legal, financial, and social barriers that can cloud their future. For many, dark clouds seem to follow them everywhere.

Not used to making decisions on their own, most ex-offenders are **mentally unprepared** for what comes next. After all, they've just completed a rather chilling and costly gig behind bars as an "inmate" where they experienced a combination of fear, distrust, fragile hope, boredom, grief, and depression. They are now newly released "ex-cons" with all the baggage that label implies. Their correctional experience was all about **survival** inside the prison walls rather than preparation for success in the free world.

Indeed, most ex-offenders need help from Day One in making it on the outside. Being released with only the clothes on their back, $10 to $200 in gate money, a few sketchy relationships, unstable housing and employment, most ex-offenders now face costly housing, inconvenient transportation, lack of money and credit, a discriminatory job market, and a highly digitized world requiring Internet access and skills. Saddled with questionable resumes and rap sheets, ex-offenders experience numerous **rejections** that can lead to failed re-entry experiences.

It's not a pretty picture as many ex-offenders, including incarcerated military veterans, quickly join America's marginalized population of poor and homeless people who more or less manage to live a desperate existence on the edge of society. What they most need are helping hands to get them through their first 99 days of re-entry challenges to jump-start their lives rather than become another recidivism statistic.

Helping Hands

Helping hands are what this directory is all about. Designed to assist ex-offenders and re-entry professionals with critical transition **decisions**, it introduces users to a fascinating re-entry world focused on:

- Documentation
- Housing
- Employment
- Transportation
- Food
- Clothing
- Health and wellness
- Mental health

- Substance abuse
- Education
- Parenting
- Personal finances
- Life skills
- Relationship building
- Victim restitution
- Tattoo removal

Filled with names, addresses, phone numbers, websites, and download-able resources of key government agencies, nonprofit groups, and faith-based organizations, this directory is designed for anyone involved with re-entry programs and resources as well as for those interested in developing their own "what works" programs.

Words of Hope and Caution

This directory identifies major efforts at tackling one of today's most daunting problems – how to ensure the safe and productive integration of the more than 700,000 individuals who annually leave prisons, along with the nearly 12 million individuals who circulate in and out of jails and detention centers. Identifying major players, it reveals what is actually being done state-by-state at the street level to better deal with the vexing problems of recidivism and collateral damage in America's dysfunctional criminal justice system. As such, this directory offers a snapshot of the state of re-entry in America as of 2016 with these major highlights:

- 39 gateway websites focused on everything from housing to employment
- 1,000+ re-entry assistance programs operating in each state

- 50 free downloadable re-entry handbooks and curricula designed for use in 28 states and nationwide

Compiling a directory rich in names, addresses, telephone numbers, and websites is a risky and sometimes funny business. And doing a directory that primarily includes government agencies, nonprofit groups, and faith-based organizations is doubly risky. While I have attempted to ensure the accuracy of the entries, nonetheless, many of these players will change locations and some will go out of business in the coming months. Indeed, while conducting research for this directory, several organizations changed addresses and telephone numbers, discontinued websites, or changed critical resource linkages. One nonprofit in Iowa was even raided by the FBI soon after receiving a $1.5 million government contract for delivering re-entry services (that one didn't make this directory)! Others changed addresses and modified their missions, because they recently experienced funding cuts, which is a common experience with nonprofit groups and faith-based organizations that are greatly dependent upon government largesse to fund their activities and operations. Living contract-to-contract or grant-to-grant is a very risky business that creates a great deal of uncertainty about the future of many well-intentioned organizations designed to work with marginalized populations.

When you find an inoperative website, telephone number, or mailing address, I recommend you do the following rather than contact me or the publisher with a "it doesn't exist" or "it's a bad entry" complaint:

1. Look for the organization by searching for it in two different ways:

   - If the website address doesn't take you to the site, try searching for it again by entering the organization name, address, and/or phone number.

   - If the web address has an extension beyond the web suffix, which is often the problem, shorten it to the initial domain address, which will end in .com, .org, .net, or some other website suffix.

2. Search for the organization on the Internet by using more than one **search engine**. Your best results will come from these search and meta search engines:

- Google
- Bing
- Yahoo

- Ask.com
- DuckDuckGo

- Dogpile
- iSeek

3. If you only use one web browser, try switching to an alternative **web browser** that may yield better web searches:

- Google Chrome
- Mozilla Firefox

- Safari
- Opera

- Internet Explorer

4. Complete the "Recommended Re-Entry Resources" form (Appendix G) and fax or email it to me for my reference (Fax 703-335-9486 or ron@impactpublications.com). Please do the same if you come across re-entry resources that are not listed in this directory but which you feel should be included in future editions.

Annotated Entries

I've purposefully not annotated the re-entry entries in Chapter 4 since most of these organizations are well represented on their websites, which are identified in most cases. Annotating such entries would be redundant and most likely misleading. After all, many of these organizations will change their focus and emphases as their missions and funding change accordingly.

Thanks

I especially want to thank the many ex-offender re-entry players featured in this directory, particularly those representing gateway organizations in Chapter 2 and developers of the many re-entry handbooks, workbooks, directories, curricula, and databases featured in Chapter 5. These organizations are literally working America's re-entry trenches with many helping hands designed to transform the lives of ex-offenders in transition. Many have developed programs and products that can serve as **models** for others interested in the re-entry process.

Many thanks go to three individuals who spent numerous hours engaged in often mind-numbing and thankless tasks – checking the accuracy of entries, proofing for errors, and deciphering my almost illegible handwritten notes and sometimes difficult instructions on what goes where: Carol Cable, Ruth Sanders, and Mardie Younglof. However, any errors of commission or omission are solely my responsibility.

Finally, I want to thank my many readers who are passionate about creating more effective re-entry policies and practices. They understand the tremendous human and economic costs of a criminal justice system that is primarily designed to "catch and release" individuals with little thought to the collateral costs of its actions nor the importance of developing powerful re-entry approaches for marginalized individuals and vulnerable communities. May they continue their good works in offering helping hands to those in need of special friends and mentors.

Ron Krannich

1

A Leg Up, A Hand Down

WHETHER THEY ADMIT IT or not, ex-offenders need help in navigating the next stages of their lives. Moving from depressing concrete and steel cages to unfamiliar roads that fork in many different directions, these hopeful souls search for renewed freedom and independence in a not-so-friendly and often unforgiving world that values trust, stability, predictability, and workplace skills. In many cases, they leave prison as destitute, disturbed, and delusional people who also appear to be risky losers saddled with questionable rap sheets and debilitating financial obligations. Feeling hopeful but encountering numerous barriers to success, their future is anything but certain.

Welcome to the Free World

Facing the sunshine of freedom with a recent history of daily lockdown, many ex-offenders enter the free world with only the clothes on their back, some measly gate money ($10 to $200), a few sketchy relationships, and, often, not much love. Most are unprepared for an increasingly digitized world. They face a costly housing market and a demanding job market focused on skills, accomplishments, and learning. Many newly released ex-offenders begin their journey to freedom with a ride on a Greyhound bus to, hopefully, a more promising future. If they're lucky, they may encounter some good samaritans willing to extend helping hands with housing and employment, the two most immediate needs of ex-offenders.

Welcome to the real world where living a free life can be hard, disappointing, and filled with barriers to getting ahead.

What happens next is anyone's guess. It could be good, but it's often disappointing for everyone involved. Welcome to the real world where living a free life can be hard, disappointing, and filled with barriers to getting ahead. Indeed, according to an Urban Institute study of soon-to-be-released state prison inmates, many ex-offenders enter the outside world with several strikes against them:

- 75% have substance abuse problems
- 70% are high school dropouts
- 50% are functionally illiterate
- 21% have a work-related disability
- 18% have Hepatitis C
- 15% have a mental illness
- 12% report a vision or hearing problem
- 7% have a tuberculosis infection
- 4% show signs of PTSD
- 3% are HIV-positive or have AIDS
- 3% participate in work-release programs

Within three years, nearly 70 percent of ex-offenders don't make it on the outside primarily because of parole violations. After all, many ex-offenders re-enter society with limited education, few marketable skills, negative attitudes, mental health issues, and scary rap sheets. They are in desperate need of a **support structure** on the outside.

On their own, many ex-offenders look and behave like losers. Unfortunately, most soon expand their rap sheets as they return to jails and prisons to do more mind-numbing and expensive taxpayer-sponsored time. This **revolving door** is not a pretty picture for a troubled criminal justice system ostensibly tasked with dispensing justice and transforming lives through rehabilitation. Indeed, it's a classic broken system mainly run by and for broken people.

Welcome to the re-entry world where **hope** is often the latest victim of a treacherous system gone awry. The best way to navigate this system is to take advantage of the many helping hands featured in this user-friendly directory. As you increasingly become street-smart in the free world, you may well be able to keep hope alive and never again return to another house of cages. In so doing, you will begin **building**

a support system that will truly set you free and help you create a new and meaningful life of joy, love, and accomplishment.

Hope for Better Days

Expected to stay clean and pull themselves up by their bootstraps, these newly minted freedom-seekers all of a sudden find life on the outside to be somewhat bipolar – simultaneously exciting, interesting, unfamiliar, and scary. Regardless of which road they take, ex-cons find most pathways filled with challenges, paved with potholes, lined with quicksand, and punctuated with dead ends, rejections, and hopelessness. Faced with numerous barriers to re-entry success, they soon realize that navigating this road can be rough and tough. They could use some help along the way.

Most pathways for ex-cons are filled with challenges, paved with potholes, lined with quicksand, and punctuated with dead ends, rejections, and hopelessness.

As many newly released inmates discover, the free world is anything but free, especially if you don't know where you're going or whom to trust! Navigating this road requires smart decisions for moving ahead in the right direction. Above all, successful re-entry demands new knowledge and skills as well as a **changed mindset** about how the outside world really operates.

Primary Audience

While this directory will be widely used by re-entry professionals and others who are in the business of helping ex-offenders transition to the free world, it's first and foremost designed for ex-offenders and their families in need of helping hands. As such, it speaks to ex-offenders' most pressing street-level needs: jobs, housing, food, clothing, transportation, health care, education, counseling, documentation, and services related to substance abuse, mental health, child care, banking, and financial planning. For in the end, it is these ostensibly resurrected souls who will benefit the most from the many pages of re-entry information and advice found in this book.

Legs Up, Hands Down

Making it on the outside requires both legs up and hands down. The **legs up** come from **you** and the **hands down** come from **others**. Prerequisites for re-entry success include these three things you'll need to do on a routine basis:

1. Project a persistently positive attitude
2. Engage in purposeful hard work
3. Acquire support from others

While this directory may not help you much in projecting a positive attitude and instilling purposeful hard work (two legs up) – both of which are within your control – it does show you how and where to get assistance from others who can provide you with a helping hand (a hand down) on your road to independence and freedom.

The following pages are all about developing a powerful **support network** to get you through the important initial stages of your re-entry transition. This book is your connection to the outside world of helping hands. Whatever you do, don't try to do this re-entry stuff on your own. **Lone wolves** can become very isolated, lonely, frustrated, and angry when things don't work according to expectations or when they encounter seemingly insurmountable barriers to success. At the same time, you don't want to be a beggar who becomes totally dependent upon others for assistance. Ideally, your job is to find the best resources to help you jumpstart your transition to the free world where you will eventually become independent of such assistance as well as later provide a helping hand (mentor) to others who find themselves in similar re-entry situations.

Run with Wise and Empathetic People

Wisely use the resources outlined in this directory. In so doing, you should be able to significantly shorten your re-entry adjustment time and, in the process, meet some really wonderful people who sincerely want to help you become the very best person you can be. They are different types of people than you may be used to encountering – people exuding great empathy, character, and purpose. You'll find these people in many places – in churches, synagogues, mosques, government agencies, schools, civic groups, nonprofits, charities, next door, down the block, etc.

Most of these groups and people understand your situation and want to help you. Few are naive do-gooders. Many will **listen** and **empathize** with you and your situation. Some know your journey very well since they, too, have similar red flags in their backgrounds – they've walked your walk as ex-offenders. Some are actually re-entry success stories themselves who will not be too judgmental or critical of you – they've been there, done that, know your situation well, and can really talk your talk. Many are very **street smart** – they give great insider tips on the what, where, and how of re-entry. Some may become your **mentors** and lifelong **friends** – they are positive and trustworthy people you need to hang around with in the future. They will help you succeed in several key re-entry areas – employment, housing, transportation, health care, family, and community – that can make the difference between re-entry success and re-entry failure.

> *You want to run with winners who are known for their intelligence, character, and willingness to help and who have high expectations for you.*

You need to quickly connect with such groups and people and work with them in becoming another re-entry success story to be shared with others who follow in your footsteps. Above all, you want to **run with winners** who are known for their intelligence, character, and willingness to help, and who expect you to be trustworthy, responsible, and take initiative and ownership of your future.

Attitude, Motivation, and Personal Growth

Not surprisingly, after being locked up in a cage for many months and years, your attitude, motivation, and overall mindset have probably taken big hits. If you were lucky early on in your incarceration, you worked through Ned Rollo's self-help book, *A Map Through the Maze: A Guide to Surviving the Criminal Justice System*. It would have mentally prepared you for your correctional experience and showed you how to turn an inherently dysfunctional environment into one of personal growth. If you didn't use this book, you may have taken the negative path and acquired lots of psychological baggage that comes with this type of territory.

Worst of all, you may have been psychologically traumatized by your correctional experience and thus now exhibit these 25 feelings and behaviors:

- You lack direction, purpose, and motivation.
- You have difficulty getting and staying motivated.
- You often feel worthless, hopeless, and helpless.
- You are afraid of failing and the future.
- You sometimes have suicidal thoughts.
- You tend to be very aggressive and physical with others.
- You get angry and sometimes go into a rage.
- You experience difficulty in making decisions on your own.
- You frequently experience fear, anxiety, guilt, and boredom.
- You worry about everything and often don't know what to do next.
- You avoid taking responsibility, frequently blame others, and make excuses.
- You lack initiative, drive, persistence, and follow-through.
- You often feel isolated, lonely, and depressed.
- You have bad thoughts about yourself and others.
- You are suspicious and distrustful of others.
- You look for the worst rather than the best in others.
- You have bouts of stinking thinking and negativity.
- You lack a sense of reality and frequently appear delusional.
- You are impulsive and tend to make mistakes.
- You easily become addicted and have difficulty changing habits.
- You fail to regularly take prescribed medications affecting your mental health.
- You have experienced many problems and tragedies in your life.
- You seem to attract bad luck – a black cloud constantly follows you.
- You want to be free, but you're scared of re-entering the free world.

Indeed, you may have classic characteristics of Post-Traumatic Stress Disorder (PTSD). After all, the system is ostensibly designed to separate, isolate, and punish you both physically and psychologically and thus ensure your complete compliance. It's a no-brainer system that keeps you off the streets and tax rolls.

As you may have already learned, attitude is key to your mental health. You'll have to work on your **attitude** in order to get it to work to your advantage. If you can reboot it, your attitude will help give you **purpose and drive** – two key elements of personal success. In other words, you need to examine and change your **mindset** – from a negative and defeatist mindset to a positive and goal-oriented mindset.

> *You need to examine and change your mindset – from a negative and defeatist mindset to a positive and goal-oriented mindset.*

You have to get yourself motivated for the tasks ahead, and that involves **developing a positive, can-do attitude**. If you need help with re-orienting your attitude, hang around positive people. By all means, avoid negative people who will drag you down to their level. You don't need such negativity in your life. Better still, check out a few of these "must have" positive attitude and motivation building books, which may be in your local library:

- *7 Habits of Highly Effective People* (Stephen R. Covey)
- *100 Ways to Motivate Yourself* (Steve Chandler)
- *Attitude is Everything* (Keith Harrell)
- *Awaken the Giant Within* (Anthony Robbins)
- *Change Your Thinking, Change Your Life* (Brian Tracy)
- *Goals! How to Get Everything You Want* (Brian Tracy)
- *How to Win Friends and Influence People* (Dale Carnegie)
- *Little Gold Book of YES! Attitude* (Jeffrey Gitomer)
- *Magic of Thinking Big* (David Schwartz)
- *Mindset: The New Psychology of Success* (Carol Dweck)
- *Power of Positive Thinking* (Norman Vincent Peale)
- *The Success Principles* (Jack Canfield)
- *Think and Grow Rich* (Napoleon Hill)
- *Wishcraft* (Barbara Sher)

The Hard Work of Being Alone

The hardest work you may ever do is striking out into the unknown to simultaneously locate stable housing, find a good job, arrange daily transportation, use health services, report to a probation officer, and re-introduce yourself to family and friends. Most challenging of all, you must become a **multitasker** who juggles many balls at the same time. While just looking for a job should be a full-time job, add to that task the critical housing and transportation decisions that go along with job finding and you have more things to do that you may feel up to, especially since you've spent a great of time not making your own decisions.

So where do you go, what to you do, and how do you handle **rejections**? This will be hard, hard work – hours and days, and maybe even months of rejections, disappointments, frustrations, and anger in not being able to do everything simultaneously. You'll struggle. You'll have difficulty keeping a positive attitude. At times, you'll want to give up and give into some really bad temptations that can take you back to the house of cages. But that's part of the process. Here's a not-so-well-kept secret: you're not so special. Life in general is filled with numerous rejections, disappointments, and frustrations that have nothing to do with being an ex-offender. That's just life!

> *Here's a not-so-well-kept secret: you're not so special. Life in general is filled with numerous rejections, disappointments, and frustrations that have nothing to do with being an ex-offender. That's just life!*

If you work hard at this – get up early every day and work at least eight hours on your re-entry plan and collect your 20 "no's" for the day (remember, "yeses" are just a few more "no's" away) and manage to deal with rejections as "part of the game" – you will eventually succeed. But it will take time, persistence, and a changed mindset. While you may not know where the road is going, at least you're on the road and headed in the right direction. Stay positive and stick with it. And along the way, seek support from many of the sources outlined in this directory. Don't try to do re-entry on your own.

An Awesome and Troubled Correctional Complex

The United States operates the world's largest, costliest, and most dysfunctional criminal justice and incarceration systems. Representing nearly 5 percent of the world's population, the U.S. is home to nearly 25 percent of the world's prison population. It also houses 33 percent of all female prisoners in the world. It arrests and locks up more of its citizens than any other country in the world. With 77 million citizens having an arrest record and millions circulating in and out of correctional facilities each year, America could be rightfully called an "Arrested Society" and "Incarcerated Nation." Viewed from another perspective, criminal justice and incarceration are **big businesses** in the United States. It's especially big business for private prison operators, the bail bond industry, and prison suppliers and procurement industry. As such, it's very difficult to change such a large, vested, and dysfunctional system.

The U.S. correctional complex is simply enormous, with nearly 12 million people circulating in and out of prisons, jails, and detention centers each year. Within that complex, at any one time, 2.4 million people are housed in 1,719 state prisons, 102 federal prisons, 2,259 juvenile correctional facilities, 3,283 local jails, 79 Indian Country jails, and several military brigs and confinement facilities. Over 200,000 people are locked up in federal prisons, 1.3+ million in state prisons, nearly 800,000 in local jails, and nearly 55,000 in juvenile detention centers. Each year over 700,000 ex-offenders are released from state and federal prisons; another 9 million are released from fast revolving jails. Over 5 million Americans are on parole or probation, but annually 33 percent of all prison admissions are parole violators.

All totaled, the estimated direct costs of operating the American criminal justice system are $250 billion a year; the cost of incarceration alone is $80 billion a year. But the larger and more long-term **collateral costs** to individuals, families, and communities are simply incalculable – think trillions of dollars!

Federal and state prisons, which normally house between 500 to 5,000 inmates, are homes to a disproportionate number of immigrants, violent criminals, the mentally ill, and really bad people – the so-called losers – you don't want to associate with. Over 25 percent of federal prisoners are noncitizens, and nearly 8 percent are serving time for violent crimes. Over 50 percent of inmates in state prisons are convicted of violent crimes. Somewhere between 20 to 50 percent of inmates suffer from mental illness. Some of the largest and most notorious prisons include the largest maximum security prison and "Alcatraz of the South" – Louisiana State Penitentiary in Angola (5,000 inmates); San Quentin State Prison (3,302 inmates); Attica Correctional Facility (2,150 inmates); Folsom State Prison (1,813 inmates); U.S. Penitentiary Marion

(1,000 inmates); Leavenworth Federal Penitentiary (2,000 inmates); and Sing Sing (1,700 inmates).

The **churn** or **circulation rate** of prisoners is highest at the city and county levels where jails continually process two types of short-term prisoners in and out of their facilities – those awaiting their day in court, who are either denied bail or cannot post bail (mainly poor people charged with crimes), and individuals sentenced to less than 12 months behind bars. A Vera Institute of Justice report in 2015 made this sobering observation about the class and health nature of the American jail system:

> U.S. jails have largely become warehouses for the poor, mentally ill, and addicted who lack the financial means and mental capacity to post bail which may be as little as $200.

While going to jail or a detention center for less than one year is disruptive to one's life and relationships – leading to job, housing, and financial losses as well as strained and broken relationships – people detained in these facilities are more likely to quickly bounce back in the free world than those serving longer prison sentences. Therefore, the need for re-entry services are greater at the federal and state prison level than at the city and county jail levels, although they are still necessary for jails that release the largest number of inmates back into communities.

Jails can be **massive and depressing operations**, larger than most prisons, and operating as small towns or cities requiring all the basic services of large communities, huge boot camps, or recruitment centers. These can be large and complicated culinary and transportation centers similar to military encampments. Indeed, some jails serve over 50,000 meals a day and spend a disproportionate amount of time transporting hundreds of inmates back and forth to courts. Indeed, the five largest jails in the United States, with a total population of nearly 65,000, are found in Los Angeles County (20,000 detainees); New York City (Rikers Island complex with 10 jails housing 14,000 detainees); Harris County (Houston), Texas (10,000 detainees); Cook (Chicago) County (9,900 detainees); and Maricopa (Phoenix) County, Arizona (9,300 detainees). Los Angeles County alone transports nearly 1,600 inmates to court each day. While these metropolitan jail populations have either declined or plateaued in recent years, recent major increases in jail populations have been in exurban and rural areas, according to a recent study by the Vera Institute of Justice.

This is also a very **expensive operation**. The high incarceration rates in the U.S. are largely due to changes in sentencing practices and the "war on drugs" that resulted in quadrupling the prison population from 1980 to 2003 in the name of getting tough on crime. Sentencing practices that lengthened prison time, such as mandatory minimum sentencing, "three strikes" laws, and ending of parole and early release, have been extremely costly and largely ineffective in lowering crime and recidivism rates. Such ill-conceived public policy changes, which were largely divorced from research and reality, have been a boon to the legal and prison industries but an expensive public funding exercise that has also created collateral damage for individuals, families, and communities. The end result is that it's much more expensive and inconsequential to incarcerate nonviolent criminals ($25,000 to $200,000 per year) than to send them to an elite college. Increasingly, progressive politicians and taxpayers ask these performance questions:

> *"What's wrong with this picture, especially when it produces just the opposite results – more crime and increased costs? Does anyone really know what they are doing or what works when it comes to crime and punishment?"*

Now, add to this the need to develop re-entry programs and services to assist ex-offenders in overcoming the collateral damage caused by the incarceration experience, and communities have a very expensive task ahead.

Coming Changes

California's recent attempt (2014), through passage of Proposition 47, to reduce the high cost of the state's criminal justice system is encouraging. California is beginning to significantly reduce its prison population and collateral damage by redefining nonviolent felonies (especially minor drug offenses) as misdemeanors and thus fundamentally altering sentencing guidelines. This change has significantly reduced the state's prison population and freed up more prison space for violent offenders. As California saves millions of dollars in incarceration costs as well as experiences declines in recidivism, such reforms will most likely be copied by many other states that are clamoring for major changes in their costly criminal justice systems.

Re-entry programs and services are most needed for individuals serving the longest time behind bars – the more than 1.5 million people in federal and state prisons. While nearly 95 percent of these individuals will eventually serve their time and return to society, they also are the least prepared to re-enter society. Many are destitute, disassociated from friends and family, and in need of mental health services as they try to re-establish their lost lives on the outside. Those serving five or more years in prison face greater challenges than short-term prisoners who serve less than 12 months in jails and other correctional facilities.

As California saves millions of dollars in incarceration costs, their sentencing reforms will most likely be copied by many other states clamoring for major changes in their costly criminal justice systems.

Community-Based Re-Entry Resources

The following pages pull together some of the most important community-based resources for re-entering the free world, from housing, employment, and documentation to transportation, health care, and education. They are designed to help you navigate today's re-entry maze and make sure you stay out for good!

Since **re-entry** is now a hot topic in correctional circles, and more and more financial resources are available to develop pilot re-entry programs, several new initiatives are taking place in the public and private sectors, with nonprofits such as the Goodwill, Prison Ministries, Delancey Street Foundation, Potter's House, Mercy Corps, Dismas Charities, and Catholic Charities playing important roles in delivering re-entry programs and services. These initiatives coordinate information on re-entry resources as well as develop innovative re-entry programs that help ex-offenders better integrate into communities with jobs, housing, and other supports.

Indeed, for the uninitiated, there appears to be a jungle of re-entry information and services available in the free world. The re-entry track records of states and communities are at best spotty, with some states and communities making major efforts to develop effective programs. Others lag behind – at the end of their sentences, offenders are set free on the streets with little or no re-entry training or basic supports beyond some gate money, a "goodbye, good luck" farewell greeting, and some information on government and nonprofit support services. Lacking re-entry resources, prison officials appear preoccupied with the daily intake of new inmates to be processed, caged, controlled, and managed until they serve their time and are then put out on the street ("released") to cope with their new-found re-entry realities.

To be most effective in re-entering the free world, you need to quickly discover the who, what, where, and how of re-entry resources. The good news is that many such resources can be quickly accessed online. If you don't have Internet access, you should be able to access the Internet for free through your local library, community centers, and several community organizations, including churches. In the next chapter, I'll review some of the gateway re-entry websites for getting the process underway.

One of the brightest spots for ex-offender re-entry are several initiatives taking place within state departments of corrections and rehabilitation. Many have been mandated and funded to develop comprehensive re-entry programs and services. In fact, more and more state departments of corrections are building useful gateway databases for accessing community-based re-entry resources online. Take, for example, the state of Ohio which has been addressing the whole issue of re-entry by implementing *The Ohio Plan for Productive Offender Reentry and Recidivism* which was issued in July 2002. Known as the "Ohio Plan," it literally prepares offenders for release by requiring them to participate in an institution-based re-entry program. One of the major accomplishments of the Ohio Department of Rehabilitation and Corrections has been the establishment of the Reentry Resource Center. Its M.U.S.C.L.E. resource guide (**M**aking **U**se of **S**ervices **C**an **L**ead to **E**mpowerment) offers a comprehensive listing of community resources that can be accessed geographically by clicking onto an interactive county map of the state. Here's how the Reentry Resource Center describes the M.U.S.C.L.E. program:

> M.U.S.C.L.E. is a centralized guide for Department staff, offenders, families, and community partners that provides assistance in locating community resources and information to foster strong, safe communities. The Reentry Resource Guide is a collection of county by county fact sheets that provides vital information to assist offenders'

reentry into society. Areas include social services, human services, local, county, state, and federal agencies, and other service agencies such as libraries, substance abuse programs, mental health counseling, veterans services commissions, educational opportunities, faith-based agencies, food, clothing, and job training and placement.

The Ohio program is designed to be used by six major groups concerned with offender re-entry:

- Offenders and individuals with a prior criminal history
- Families and friends
- Volunteers and mentors
- Community partners and social service agencies
- Case managers, parole, and probation officers
- Residential and non-residential program providers

By clicking onto the county map, users gain instant access to re-entry information and services available in the particular county for which they are targeting their search:

www.drc.ohio.gov/web/reentry_resource.htm

The next page shows what this online directory looks like.

Virginia, on the other hand, has a much less developed re-entry program. At present the Virginia Department of Social Services and local departments of social services provide a variety of support services to ex-offenders and their families. The state government is currently in the information gathering and study stages – trying to figure out what to do next. In fact, given the fragmented nature of re-entry, the state of Virginia lacks comprehensive information on current re-entry initiatives at the state and local levels. But much to its credit, the state government recently completed a major report on what to do in order to reduce Virginia's recidivism rate, especially after having abolished parole in 1996 and having lived with two decades of "getting tough with criminals" by locking them up for at least 85 percent of their sentencing time. Not surprisingly, one of the disappointing results (ouch!) of such a sentencing policy has been the following, which was incorporated in the first recommendation of the December 5, 2015 report to to the Governor's Commission on Parole Review entitled *"Final Report and Recommendations"*:

Click on a county to locate resources:

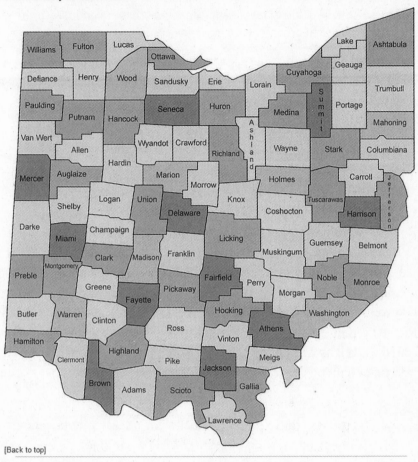

[Back to top]

Click County for Listings

Adams	Fairfield	Licking	Portage
Allen	Fayette	Logan	Preble
Ashland	Franklin	Lorain	Putnam
Ashtabula	Fulton	Lucas	Richland
Athens	Gallia	Madison	Ross
Auglaize	Geauga	Mahoning	Sandusky
Belmont	Greene	Marion	Scioto
Brown	Guernsey	Medina	Seneca
Butler	Hamilton	Meigs	Shelby
Carroll	Hancock	Mercer	Summit
Champaign	Hardin	Miami	Stark
Clark	Harrison	Monroe	Trumbull
Clermont	Henry	Montgomery	Tuscarawas
Clinton	Highland	Morgan	Union
Columbiana	Hocking	Morrow	Van Wert
Coshocton	Holmes	Muskingum	Vinton
Crawford	Huron	Noble	Warren
Cuyahoga	Jackson	Ottawa	Washington
Darke	Jefferson	Paulding	Wayne
Defiance	Knox	Perry	Williams
Delaware	Lake	Pickaway	Wood
Erie	Lawrence	Pike	Wyandot

The incarceration of nonviolent offenders and individuals that do not pose a threat to the safety of the community have been found to increase criminal behavior (Nagin, Cullen, & Jonston, 2013).

For a revealing look at recidivism, criminal justice failures, and enlightened recommendations on what needs to be done in Virginia, you can read this special report online:

> https://parolecommission.virginia.gov/resources/final
> report/2015-12-04-parole-commission-final-report.pdf

Virginia's current statewide re-entry program consists of a few regional offices spread throughout the state and operated by Virginia CARES, Inc. as well as a network of nonprofit organizations, such as Boaz & Ruth (www.boazandruth.com) of Richmond and OAR of Fairfax (www.oarfairfax.org), involved in helping ex-offenders re-enter individual communities and rebuilt their lives. In the case of Virginia CARES, ex-offenders are advised to submit an application form within two weeks of release to request some basic re-entry assistance relating to finding food, clothing, housing, transportation, and forms of identification as well as employment assistance, counseling, and peer support. Information on this operation can be found here:

> www.vacares.org

A few prisons attempt to prepare inmates for release by operating in-house re-entry programs (see pages 192-193 on Virginia).

Evidence-Based Laboratories of Re-Entry Success

Other states are at various stages of developing re-entry programs and services. The trend appears clear: more and more states now realize the high costs of recidivism and the failures of their criminal justice and incarceration systems. They are beginning to understand the concept and costs of **collateral damage**.

In the coming decade, we can expect a greater focus on effective re-entry programs as well as a re-examination of the criminal justice system, especially on what does and doesn't work to reduce the high long-term costs of crime and recidivism. The unanswered question is this: Will we also provide adequate resources to make successful re-entry a street-level reality? In the meantime, the remainder of this book outlines what is currently going on in the world of ex-offender re-entry. When adequate resources meet these realities, significant change may take place.

The following pages point in the direction of hopeful signs for the future. What is really exciting is to see states and localities involved in developing innovative re-entry programs that function as **experimental laboratories** on what more or less works in reducing recidivism. What should emerge are several evidence-based models of effective re-entry programs and services.

2

Gateways to Community Re-Entry Mazes

IF YOU'VE JUST BEEN released from prison, chances are you're simultaneously elated, anxious, and needy. You might also be realistic since this may not be your first time in an incarceration/release maze and could become a disappointing merry-go-round. Unfortunately, the odds are probably against your success (70 percent) since you're entering the world with many strikes against you and without a lifeboat to keep you afloat: unstable housing, no job, little education, limited work experience, addiction issues, child support and restitution payments, anger issues, and maybe no ID. And you probably don't look like you're headed for success by the way you dress, conduct yourself, and display some questionable body art. Big smile, good eye contact, and firm handshake? What limited gate money you received will probably be gone in no time on transportation, cigarettes, and other expenses. Welcome to the free world where life can be tough.

Welcome to the Great Churn

Life may initially appear free, but it can be very hard and frustrating for those who must struggle over the basics of daily living. Indeed, you may soon get caught up in the **great churn** of the criminal justice system: failing to follow the rules governing your release (parole/probation) or unable to handle life on the outside, you soon succumb to temptations of your old neighborhood and circle of dubious friends that result in you returning to jail or prison.

You become another recidivism statistic, and confirm once again that you are part of a dysfunctional criminal justice system. It's an old pattern, and unfortunately it plays out every day in hundreds of communities, jails, and prisons across the country. We're not sure what to do, but a lot of people are certainly making a lot of money doing things that don't really work, even though they are into the so-called evidence-based movement with all its questionable numbers.

Joining the Marginalized

As you'll quickly discover, re-entry programs and services are both widespread and fragmented throughout the United States. What's amazing is how many such programs and services actually exist, with most designed to assist America's growing underclass of poor and needy people. Indeed, many are organized for marginalized populations who are on the edge of being destitute and homeless; who are largely resource-poor and unbanked people; who are escaping from abusive relationships; who struggle with mental illnesses; who frequently have run-ins with the law; who encounter a not-so-friendly criminal justice system and its draconic bail bond system; and who are more likely to have a shocking rap sheet than an inviting resume. Some are really bad people, sociopaths who probably need to stay locked up and thus permanently separated from society. But others need some help to get them up and running in the right direction.

> *Forget the other re-entry stuff for now. Just get that job! It will make other re-entry challenges more manageable. Whatever you do, avoid becoming a marginalized person preoccupied with daily survival.*

Yes, life is tough. But life could be much easier if you could find a decent job. You should spend most of your re-entry time looking for a stable job. Failing to quickly do so may send you right back to prison as a "parole violator" – the only time in America where one can end up in prison for not finding a job! Forget the other re-entry stuff for now. **Just get that job.** It will make other re-entry challenges more **manageable** . . . and keep you out of prison.

Living on the edge, these marginalized people often pursue desperate lives in constant search for food, clothing, shelter, and money. They routinely use soup kitchens, food banks, homeless shelters, clothing/donation centers, and free clinics. They don't have much time to find a job. Not surprisingly, many of these people get entangled in the criminal justice system because of their nuisance and illegal behaviors. Because of their visual presence and lifestyle on the streets, it's not difficult for them to get into trouble with complaining citizens and law enforcement.

Life can be difficult if you navigate the world as a needy and marginalized person who is preoccupied with daily survival. This is America's unwanted population that middle- to upper-class communities would rather see disappear from their streets, parks, and neighborhoods; become invisible or out-of-sight; or relocate to other more "receptive" communities somewhere down the road.

Your task is to build and float your own lifeboat for the next several weeks and months as you transition from being a prisoner to being a productive taxpaying citizen who quickly moves through the ranks of the poor and needy and thus avoids the struggles experienced by those who live on the margins of society. Hopefully, some day in the future you will be able to look back and offer a helping hand to those who could use your empathy and assistance. Indeed, such "payback" can be a very meaningful and gratifying experience.

Second Chance Communities

Don't let anyone tell you that no one cares about you and your future or that most people will be critical and judgmental about you rather than listen to you. That may have happened frequently in the harsh command-and-control structure and lockdown culture of prison or jail. But you're now navigating different waters and operating within a new circle of concerned individuals.

In fact, there are lots of caring people "out there" who give renewed meaning to the notions of second chances, forgiveness, redemption, and transformation in the organizations and programs they operate for ex-offenders and their families. While many of these people work in church food pantries, clothing centers, and affiliated faith-based charitable organizations that may also want to save your soul, others just want to help others in need, because doing so gives their life deeper meaning and purpose. Many of these helpers also are empathetic ex-offenders who wish to "give back" to communities that assisted them in rebuilding their lives. You can learn a lot from these helping hands.

Welcome to a Maze of Community Players

The largest concentration of re-entry programs and services is found in major metropolitan areas, such as New York City, Philadelphia, Boston, Washington, DC, Baltimore, Atlanta, Miami, Chicago, Denver, San Francisco, Los Angeles, San Diego, Phoenix, Dallas, and Houston. These cities are magnets for many ex-offenders who return to their former neighborhoods – many of which are in high-crime districts – to begin rebuilding their lives. Within a few months, they learn to either sink or swim with a little help in this new free world. The good news is that help is all around them. But they first need to identify where to go and whom to see for assistance.

Within each of these communities, you are likely to find a bewildering maze of federal, state, and local government agencies alongside donor- and government-supported nonprofit and faith-based organizations. Indeed, the **re-entry landscape** appears to be highly **fragmented and chaotic**. Nonetheless, the major players know through word of mouth the who, what, where, and when of the key players. They can give you good advice on what you need to do next as you make your way in this new re-entry world. Therefore, your number one job should be to quickly plug into this word of mouth re-entry advisory network.

> *Today's re-entry landscape appears to be highly fragmented and chaotic. Nonetheless, the major players know through word of mouth the who, what, where, and when of the key players.*

Most government agencies and nonprofit organizations specialize in assisting ex-offenders with one or two important elements of the re-entry process: documentation, food, clothing, transitional housing, employment, transportation, mental health, and substance abuse. Except for a few clearinghouse groups, no single agency or organization deals with all aspects of re-entry. Each ex-offender must take initiative to identify and coordinate this maze of programs and services to meet his or her needs. Remember, there is **no one source** you can go to get a comprehensive listing of all the players involved in the re-entry world. Your job is to research the cluttered re-entry landscape in your particular state and community, and pick and choose those services that best relate to your needs.

The first important lesson to learn about community-based re-entry services is the importance of "mapping" a community in order to understand how to best navigate its re-entry maze. For example, a **community** is more than just a place to live, work, and raise a family. It consists of many interacting and mutually dependent players – individuals, groups, organizations, and institutions – that cooperate and compete with one another. You can easily identify these players in the Yellow Pages of your local telephone book. Examples of such players include:

- Banks/financial organizations
- Schools/training groups
- Colleges and universities
- Retail/wholesale businesses
- Direct sales businesses
- Churches/temples/synagogues
- Nonprofit organizations
- Volunteer organizations
- Federal government agencies
- State government agencies
- Local government agencies
- Military bases/associations
- Professional associations
- Clubs/community groups
- Media groups
- Law firms/lawyers
- Law enforcement/security
- Hospitals/clinics
- Public health groups
- Doctors/health professionals
- Transportation firms
- Construction firms
- Temporary employment firms
- One-Stop Career Centers
- Staffing/placement firms
- Auto dealers/suppliers
- Real estate/property firms
- Shippers (UPS, FedEx)
- Communication firms
- Courts/judicial centers
- Substance abuse centers
- Mental health/wellness groups
- Contractors/consultants
- Restaurants/food outlets

These players should be viewed as opportunity structures for finding jobs through informal, word of mouth channels. They become important networks for locating job opportunities. The following figure illustrates the dynamic structure of communities and how the key players interrelate:

Community-Based Opportunity Network

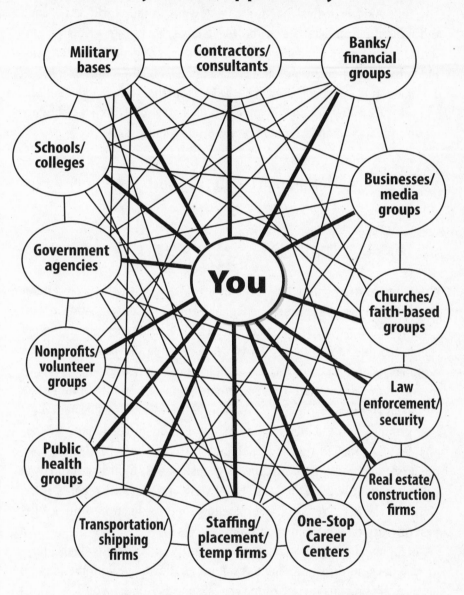

If you own this book, take a yellow highlighter and identify those community players (color the circle) you plan to contact and interact with during the next month as you conduct a community-based job search.

Gateway Programs and Services

The following websites function as gateways to the world of re-entry and rehabilitation services at the local level. Some are primarily designed for workforce development professionals engaged in developing and delivering re-entry services. Others are designed for end-users – individuals in need of such services. Taken together, these organizations and their well-developed websites expose newcomers to a whole new world of helping hands for achieving re-entry success.

National H.I.R.E. Network
www.hirenetwork.org

national **H·I·R·E** network

A terrific starting point on any journey to the world of ex-offender re-entry. It doesn't get much better than this interactive map to useful re-entry in your particular state. The H.I.R.E. Network appropriately stands for this mouthful of words: National Helping Individuals with criminal records Reenter through Employment Network. This is one of the most important state-by-state clearinghouses for identifying state and local re-entry resources. The resource-rich website is designed for four groups – individuals, employers, workforce professionals, and advocates. Established by the Legal Action Center in 2001 (lac.org) – a nonprofit law and policy organization designed to fight discrimination against people with addictions, HIV/AIDS, or criminal records – the National H.I.R.E. Network is a one-stop shop for locating some of the best re-entry resources in each state.

As an interested individual, you'll want to visit its "Individuals" page of resources, information, and assistance, as illustrated with the map on page 25. If you click on one of the states, such as Illinois, you'll get links to the following Illinois-based resources:

I. Illinois Department of Employment Security
    A. Federal Bonding Program
    B. Tax Credits
    C. Unemployment Insurance Office

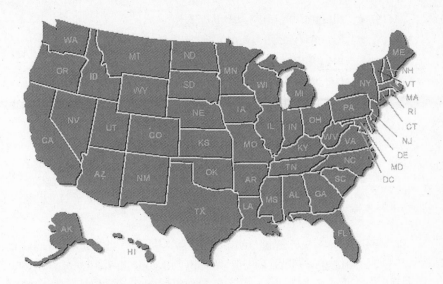

II. Criminal Record Repository

III. State Attorney General

IV. State Department of Corrections

V. Illinois Department of Corrections
 - Bureau of Field Operations

VI. Legal Assistance
 A. State Public Defender
 B. Legal Services
 C. State Bar Association

VII. Local Services Providers
 - Association House of Chicago
 - Career Advancement Network, Inc.
 - The Cara Program
 - Chicago Jobs Council
 - Community Assistance Programs
 - Heartland Alliance for Human Needs and Human Rights
 - Howard Area Community Center
 - Illinois Employment and Training Centers
 - Inspiration Corporation
 - North Lawndale Employment Network

- Phalanx Family Services
- Prison Action Committee/Community Re-Entry Program (CRP)
- Roosevelt's University's Life Skills Reentry Program in Chicago
- Safer Foundation
- St. Leonard's Ministries
- STRIVE Chicago Employment Service, Inc. - South
- STRIVE Chicago Employment Service, Inc. - West
- STRIVE Chicago Employment Service, Inc. - North
- Westside Health Authority

While the information/contact template is similar for other states, visit the H.I.R.E. site to get oriented toward re-entry in your particular state. Keep in mind that this information is just a starting point – it's by no means comprehensive and complete. It's often sketchy and out-of-date for some states. For example, there are thousands of additional organizations, especially faith-based organizations and other nonprofits with government training and service contracts occupying Illinois's re-entry space. Many of the organizations identified through H.I.R.E. may also serve as gateways to similar organizations in your community. For example, in the case of Illinois you may need to search for other re-entry websites for a more detailed directory to specific re-entry-friendly services at the state and county level. Start by exploring these three useful resources:

- www.reentryillinois.net
- www.exoffenders.net/reentry-programs-assistance/illinois
- http://lionheart.org/prison/state-by-state-listing-of-re-entry-programs-for-prisoners/

If you are a **workforce development professional** involved with ex-offender re-entry, you'll want to click on the "Workforce Professionals" section of the H.I.R.E. website, which goes to this page:

hirenetwork.org/workforce-professionals

It attempts to address the concerns of workforce development professionals, many of whom are new to working with ex-offender populations, such as how to answer this frequently asked question from ex-offenders:

Do you have a list of employers who hire
people with criminal histories?

The answer, of course, is "no." But there are things professionals can do to help the ex-offender put together his or her own list of ex-offender-friendly employers. You'll also find useful information here on accessing FBI and state rap sheets, federal occupational restrictions, and model re-entry practices. Access to some of these sections for professionals requires a paid annual or lifetime membership. For individuals, membership is free based on H.I.R.E.'s philosophy on helping people turn their lives around.

National Reentry Resource Center CSG Justice Center

https://csgjusticecenter.org/nrrc

The Council of State Governments Justice Center is a nonprofit organization tasked with providing policymakers at all government levels with advice and strategies for improving public safety and strengthening communities. Its evidence-based focus and data-driven approach are targeted on the criminal justice system, with re-entry, mental illness, and justice reinvestment taking center stage.

The Justice Center's re-entry clearinghouse provides some basic contact information on re-entry programs and services for both individuals and professionals as well as conducts useful webinars. The website has three major sections of interest to individuals and professionals:

- Justice Center   csgjusticecenter.org
- National Reentry Resource Center   csgjusticecenter.org/nrrc
- What Works in Reentry Clearinghouse   http://whatworkcsgjustice
                                                center.org

Individuals will be most interested in the **Reentry Services Directory**, which consists of a map to help ex-offenders and their families find local reentry services: '

csgjusticecenter.org/reentry/reentry-services-directory

Individual state listings are spotty at best – definitely a work in progress. For example, in the Illinois section, the directory only lists five nonprofit organizations for all of Illinois:

- Catholic Charities Diocese of Joliet (Lombard)
- Helping Hands of Springfield (Springfield)
- Men and Women in Prison Ministries (Chicago)
- Safer Foundation (Chicago)
- Springfield Community Federal (Springfield)

In reality, Illinois has hundreds of such organizations involved in re-entry along with many government agencies, which are included in this resource center.

Professionals involved with re-entry issues will find the **What Works in Reentry Clearinghouse** section especially useful:

http://whatworks.csgjusticecenter.org

This is billed as "a one-stop shop for research on the effectiveness of a wide variety of reentry programs and practices." Indeed, it's a goldmine section for reviewing effective re-entry programs in both the past and present. Under "Employment," this site features the following programs whose effectiveness has been variously evaluated for reducing recidivism and increasing employability:

- Affordable Homes Programs (AHP)
- Beaver County Work Release Program
- Center for Employment Opportunities (CEO)
- Correctional Industries Program: Class I Employment
- Federal Prison Industries, or UNICOR
- Florida Department of Corrections Vocational Training Programs
- Florida Work Release
- Kintock Group, Inc., Employment Resource Center
- Ohio Department of Rehabilitation and Correction Vocational Training Program
- Prison Industries

- Washington State Work Release
- Wichita Work Release Program

As it further develops, this section has the potential of providing very useful information to professionals involved in setting up and operating re-entry programs that show evidence of effectiveness in reducing recidivism, increasing employment, and tackling substance abuse.

The Justice Center section of this website (csgjusticecenter.org) includes a wealth of informative news and articles on re-entry as well as serves as a center for conducting useful webinars on a variety of correctional issues, from re-entry, mental health, substance abuse, and youth to corrections, courts, and law enforcement.

SAMHSA
(Substance Abuse and Mental Health Services Administration)
www.samhsa.gov

Wow! This is where taxpayers really get their money's worth, and where government can make a big difference in the lives of its citizens. Operated by the U.S. Department of Health and Human Services, this is one of the finest online resources available for finding help and treatment related to substance abuse and mental health services. If re-entry websites were modeled after this one, ex-offenders would have one of the most complete and comprehensive resources for locating useful re-entry services. But what we do have here is a gem well worth exploring and bookmarking for future reference. This website deals with two of the biggest re-entry issues affecting hundreds of thousands of ex-offenders – substance abuse/addiction/relapse and mental health/illness.

Indeed, since nearly 70 percent of all ex-offenders have addiction and substance abuse issues, and relapse after release from prison is a frequent reality (overdosing within the first two weeks after release frequently occurs), the SAMHSA website may well become a lifeline for many who regress in the not-so-free drug-filled world. Since mental illness issues are a reality for at least 25 percent of ex-offenders, and many of them experience dual disorders (substance abuse and mental illness), the SAMHSA website should prove very useful for this population that needs such professional help at part of their re-entry experience.

The SAMHSA website includes four useful search sections focused on different distress issues:

- Behavior Health Treatment Locator
- National Suicide Prevention Lifeline
- National Helpline
- Disaster Distress Helpline

The **Behavior Health Treatment Locator** (https://findtreatment.samhsa.gov) helps users quickly find treatment facilities and programs throughout the U.S. and its territories related to substance abuse/addiction and/or mental health problems. If you're connected to the Internet, go to the SAMHSA website, find the Behavioral Health Treatment Services Locator, enter your zip code location, and hit "Go." The site immediately generates a list of treatment facilities (address, telephone number, website, distance, and directions) along with a zoomable map for visually pinpointing specific facilities. It doesn't get much easier than that to find professional help! For example, when I put in my location in Northern Virginia, the search feature yields a list of 77 relevant facilities within a 20-mile radius of my home. That's even better than finding a Walmart or McDonald's online!

If you or anyone else contemplates suicide, be sure to check out SAMHSA's **National Suicide Prevention Lifeline** (www.suicidepreventionlifeline.org). You can either call 24/7 (1-800-273-8255) or initiate an online chat with a skilled, trained counselor. This section of the site also has a dedicated suicide prevention section for veterans, young adults, and those experiencing bullying.

SAMHSA's **National Helpline** (www.samhsa.gov/find-help/national-helpline) is a free, confidential, 24/7 treatment referral and information service for anyone experiencing mental health and/or substance use disorders. You can call (1-800-662-4357) or visit the online treatment locators for assistance. Each month this Helpline receives nearly 30,000 calls. Keep in mind that this service doesn't offer online or telephone counseling services – only referrals and information to assist you in finding appropriate treatments.

SAMHSA's **Disaster Distress Helpline** (www.samhsa.gov/find-help/disaster-distress-helpline) provides crisis counseling and support to those experiencing emotional distress related to natural or human-caused disasters, such as tornadoes, hurricanes, floods, wildfires, earthquakes, drought, and incidents of mass violence. Stress, anxiety, and other depression-like symptoms are common reactions to such disasters. Launched in 2012, this disaster distress hotline has provided counseling and support in response to such disasters as Hurricane Sandy, the Boston Marathon bombing, and the ebola outbreak. It provides toll-free, multilingual, and confidential crisis support services. Call **1-800-985-5990** or text **TalkWithUs to 66746** to connect to a trained crisis counselor.

Incarcerated Veterans Transition Program (IV-TP)
www.dol.gov/vets/Education%20and%20Outreach/Program%20
Brochures/Production%20PDFs/INCARCERATED%20WEB.pdf

Veterans constitute a significant number of inmates in prisons and jails throughout the United States – nearly 8% of all federal and state prisoners (175,000 inmates). Because many of them have special needs (mental health) and benefits (veterans), the federal government and several states have developed special programs for incarcerated veterans. Centered in the U.S. Department of Labor, Veterans' Employment and Training Service (VETS), the Incarcerated Veterans Transition Program (IV-TP) is designed to help ex-offender veterans who are at risk of homelessness to re-enter the workforce. The program provides direct services – through a case management approach – to link incarcerated veterans with appropriate employment and life skills support as they transition from a correctional facility into the community. The primary objectives of IV-TP are to:

- Provide services to assist in reintegrating incarcerated veterans into meaningful employment within the labor force.
- Stimulate the development of effective service delivery systems that will address the complex problems facing ex-offender veterans.

The employment services provided to incarcerated veterans may include:

- Job search activities/counseling
- Job preparatory training
- Classroom training
- Job placement and follow-up services

Exoffenders.Net
www.exoffenders.net

State-by-State Resources

This is a very noble and ambitious work in progress, a useful website operated by a few dedicated individuals who struggle to keep it up-to-date and relevant to ex-offenders in need of useful information and a variety of re-entry services. With nearly 9,000 members belonging to this online group (see exoffenders.net/contact-us to connect and subscribe for updates), exoffenders.net provides information and resources on all aspects of the ex-offender re-entry process. One of the most informative sections focuses on state-by-state re-entry resources for felons:

exoffenders.net/reentry-programs-assistance

The site offers useful sections with relevant articles, recommended resources, felon-friendly employers, local jobs, and voting rights. Since this is a work in progress operated by dedicated volunteers, don't expect to find everything you might want on re-entry and ex-offender employment. In fact, you might want to contribute to the development of this website by submitting comments and asking how you might help them further develop what could be one of the most useful re-entry websites for ex-offenders and professionals involved with re-entry. Kudos to those who are involved in trying to make a difference in the lives of ex-offenders through this dedicated website.

HelpForFelons
www.helpforfelons.org

HELP FOR FELONS

This website is designed to assist felons and ex-offenders in finding jobs and careers, achieve successful re-entry, find felon-friendly housing, and acquire loans and grants. Its "Jobs for Felons" section includes work-from-home jobs that don't require background checks and which can be started immediately. Most of these jobs are Internet-based and require a computer with a high speed Internet connection and a headset or microphone. Some are also freelance jobs. The site also includes a state-by-state directory to re-entry programs and services as well as information on housing, grants, loans, and felony expungement. It has a blog, message board, and bookstore links.

JobsForFelonsHub
jobsforfelonshub.com

This popular website (claims 10,000 visitors a day) is designed to assist ex-offenders with the re-entry process by emphasizing the importance of finding jobs, getting an education, and using numerous re-entry program resources. It includes a state-by-state directory of re-entry programs accessed through an interactive map. Its "Jobs for Felons" section includes useful links to online resume builders and examples of effective resumes. It also includes a free downloadable job search book for felons with tips on how to best conduct an effective job search despite red flags in one's background. The "Education" section includes numerous tips on how to get an affordable college education, including loans and grants for ex-offenders. The site's blog includes many useful articles relating to jobs for felons. Employers are encouraged to list jobs on the site's free job board.

Homeless Shelter Directory
www.homelessshelterdirectory.org

Competing with employment needs, housing ranks either number one or number two as the most pressing need for newly released ex-offenders. For ex-offenders who are destitute and living outside a safety net of welcoming family and friends, finding transitional housing can be extremely difficult and stressful for daily living. Newly released sex offenders in particular face numerous barriers to finding such housing because of special restrictions placed on them due to their criminal conviction.

The online Homeless Shelter Directory is one of the most useful gateway websites for locating homeless shelters throughout the United States. This is not a dedicated ex-offender re-entry website, because homeless shelters cater to a much larger population of individuals and families who find themselves homeless and in need of transitional housing: victims of domestic violence (battered women and children), homeless veterans, evicted renters and homeowners, and other people living on the streets (poor, disabled, and mentally ill).

One of the nice features of this website is the colorful interactive search map that enables users to locate homeless shelters and service organizations throughout all 50 states.

www.homelessshelterdirectory.org

Once you click on a relevant state, you can search for homeless shelters by city by entering the city name in a search box.

This site also addresses many of the larger service and transitional issues affecting the homeless and needy, such as food pantries, soup kitchens, monetary assistance, free clinics (medical and dental), outreach centers, relief organizations, and low-cost or free addiction and rehab treatment centers. Since many ex-offenders may find themselves in a homeless or transitional housing situation immediately upon release, which also multiplies into other difficult living issues (food, health, addiction treatment), this is an excellent gateway website that can help many ostensibly forgotten and invisible people who fall through the many expensive cracks in the American economy. The website also is a great resource for

individuals wishing to volunteer at most of these shelters.

This site's top homeless shelter searches are for these seven communities: Chicago, Michigan, California, Orlando, New York City, San Diego, and Los Angeles. Such searches may mirror the major centers for such transitional housing.

Transitional Housing
www.transitionalhousing.org

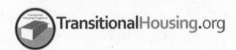

This site represents the Web's largest directory to transitional housing with a database of nearly 5,500 shelters nationwide. Most transitional housing is designed for people in crisis, such as the working homeless and victims of domestic violence. Transitional housing is normally for a limited period of time, usually from two weeks to 24 months.

This database is easy to use. Just enter your desired zip code in the search box and the site will generate a list of transitional housing contacts in your search area. From there you can contact the provider for detailed information on availability, qualifications, etc.

The site also offers related supportive services for those who need to live more independently, such as sober, detox, and drug treatment and addiction rehabilitation services. It advertises a toll-free number (800-334-8893) that connects with an alcohol or dug abuse counselor.

Housing Assistance Online
www.housingassistanceonline.com

This site is designed to assist anyone in finding emergency housing assistance, low-income housing assistance, elderly housing assistance, disabled housing assistance, and housing assistance for single parents with children. It includes a state search map as well as a search box that enables users to search for housing assistance by zip code. Once you locate the appropriate local resource, just call the telephone number for more information on housing assistance.

HUD Rental Assistance
portal.hud.gov/hudportal/HUD?src=/topics/rental_assistance

This is the federal government's (Department of Housing and Urban Development) official housing portal for finding subsidized housing, public housing, and using the Housing Choice Voucher Program (Section 8). It includes a HUD Resource Locator for contacting HUD offices and programs throughout the country, including rural areas. It also include useful information on variety of housing subjects such rental help in your state, housing counseling (call 1-800-569-4287), your housing rights and responsibilities, and buying versus renting.

Low Income Housing
www.LowIncomeHousing.us

This nationwide search site enables users, including seniors (62+ years old), to find affordable rentals and housing options for low-income families and individuals. Various sections focus on Section 8 housing programs, income-based/tax credits housing, low-income rentals, housing authorities, subsidized housing, and HUD, low-income, and income-based affordable apartments. Users can search for such housing by entering their state and/or zip code. The site includes published rental rates as well as useful phone numbers for calling the housing sources directly. This site also includes tips on how to play the low-income housing game, such as getting on as many apartment waiting lists as possible since the wait time can be extraordinarily long (years!).

Rental Assistance
www.rentalassistance.us

This site functions as an online directory to nearly 3,400 government, nonprofit, and charitable rent assistance programs throughout the United States relevant to single mothers, the elderly, and those considered to be low-income individuals and families with housing needs. You can locate such programs and services by using the site's interactive map of the U.S. as well as enter zip codes in its search box. Since each organization listed has its own eligibility rules and conditions, you'll need to complete their online registration forms or call them. Rent Assistance also tries to keep in touch with users through its Facebook page: www. facebook.com/Rent-Assistance274391785999/.

Food Pantries
www.foodpantries.org

This site includes a database of nearly 9,500 food pantries throughout the United States using an interactive U.S. map and state listings. New York State, for example, alone has 1,205 food pantries listed. The entries include descriptions and hours (usually limited) for food pantries. Some of the large food pantries, such as SERVE in Virginia, are also multifaceted public assistance groups that also provide emergency shelter for families and individuals; emergency assistance for utility, rent, water, and gas payments; access to free and reduced cost dental and specialty medical care; Early Head Start programs; and job skills and life skills training and support.

Soup Kitchens, Food Pantries, and Food Banks
www.homelessshelterdirectory.org/foodbanks

This online directory includes 12,250 emergency food programs variously referred to as soup kitchens, food pantries, and food banks. **Food banks** are actually distribution hubs that supply food to soup kitchens, food pantries, shelters, and other groups. As such, they do not distribute food directly to individuals in need. This site includes an interactive map of states for locating the program/services nearest you.

Free Public Assistance
www.freepublicassistance.com

FREEPUBLICASSISTANCE.COM

For this site, free public assistance comes in many different forms: food banks, food pantries, homeless shelters, transitional housing, clinics and low-cost affordable treatment, rental assistance, welfare offices, drug and alcohol treatment, job training, and vocational training. The site includes an interactive state map and state listings for identifying public assistance programs and services nearest you.

Free Treatment Centers
www.FreeRehabCenter.com

This site presents a directory of free, sliding-scale, discounted, low-cost, and Medicaid-sponsored treatment centers for individuals with substance abuse and addiction issues, especially drugs and alcohol but also gambling and other addictions. While the emphasis is on locating free treatment centers, the site also includes affordable treatment centers by state or zip code. The site also advertises a toll-free telephone number for speaking with an alcohol or drug abuse counselor: 1-800-607-2263.

Free Dental Care
www.FreeDentalCare.us

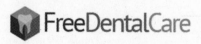

Are you facing dental care issues without insurance or independent financial means – cavities (tooth decay), gum disease, sensitive teeth, bad breath, toothache, grinding teeth, root canal pain, tooth replacement, new dentures, or oral cancer? Do you require routine care or occasional emergency care? Tooth pain can be one of the most excruciating and debilitating pains – it can literally immobilize you, lead to depression, and affect your whole outlook on life. It can also be very expensive, with root canals and caps running from $750 to $5,000 a tooth! Don't let dental issues get out of control.

If you can't afford dental care, this website can be of great help. Just click on the alphabetical list of states to find the clinics nearest you. Indeed, this is one of the best sites for locating dental clinic resources for people with little or no money. It includes free and sliding-scale dental resources based on income and/or discounted in other ways. It includes three sections: Free Dental Care, Obamacare Dental Care, and Sliding Scale Clinics (for emergencies). You can locate dental clinics and services by entering your state or zip code in the search box.

Free Medical Clinics/Camps
www.FreeMedicalClinics.org or www.freemedicalcamps.com

This site includes links to hundreds of free temporary and permanent medical and dental clinics throughout the United States that cater to people without insurance or who lack independent financial means. It also includes clinics that may charge a small supportive fee or ask for a small donation. Some are only for low-income people, the homeless, or local community residents. Some specifically focus on HIV treatment and other specialized medical issues. In addition to the free clinic sources identified on this website, you're also advised to consider contacting your local county Health Department, religious organizations, charities, and doctors' and nurses' organizations, and doing Internet searches.

Temporary Cash Assistance for Needy Families (TANF)
www.Tanf.us

Need cash to tide you over in a rough patch of your family's life? This government resource (Office of Family Assistance, U.S. Department of Health and Human Services) – an informational website that is not an official government website – provides cash assistance for pregnant women and families with one or more dependent children who need help in paying for food, shelter, utilities and expenses other than medical. As its name suggests – Temporary Cash Assistance for Needy Families (TANF) – this is a temporary program. It helps families become self- sufficient, offers preventative measures for out-of-wedlock pregnancies, encourages two-parent families, dispenses food stamps (SNAP benefits), and assists with job preparation. Rather than use payday loan services, which can charge up to 600% annual interest, families that participate in the TANF program can avoid such debilitating financial obligations. The site includes a TANF program state map for finding the TANF program nearest to your location. Families can receive up to 60 months of TANF benefits over their lifetime. To be eligible for this program, you must be a U.S. citizen, have a Social Security number, and meet certain income requirements.

STRIVE
striveinternational.org

Operating since 1984, this East Harlem-based employment and training program for poor people and disadvantaged groups now operates in 20 cities nationwide and in five cities overseas. It helps people with significant barriers to employment, including those with rap sheets, receive the necessary training and support they need to find jobs and achieve economic self-sufficiency. Look for their operations in Boston, New York City, Yonkers (NY), White Plains (NY), Mount Vernon (NY), Hartford

(CT), Bridgeport (CT), Philadelphia, Atlanta, Baltimore, Washington, DC, Greenville (NC), New Orleans, Flint (MI), Chicago, and San Diego. They also operate in London and four locations in Israel (Jerusalem, Tel Aviv, Beer Sheva, and Haifa).

Volunteers of America
Correctional Re-Entry Services
www.voa.org/correctional-re-entry-services

VOA has been a pioneer in offering re-entry services to ex-offenders ("the formerly incarcerated") for 119 years. Today, it remains a major player in the re-entry field. Indeed, it operates a variety of halfway houses, work-release programs, day reporting, diversion and pre-trial services, residential treatment, family supports, and dispute resolution and mediation services. Its website includes a useful search function for locating re-entry services across the country by entering zip codes.

Reentry Central
www.reentrycentral.org

This gateway site is especially useful for re-entry professionals who want to keep up on the latest news and developments on re-entry and related criminal justice issues. Functioning as an information clearinghouse, it includes many informative articles on re-entry. It also includes a library of archived articles, re-entry facts, videos, grants, upcoming events, and links. Annual subscriptions cost $35 for individuals and $100 for organizations.

Ex-Offender Re-Entry
www.exoffenderreentry.com

This is my gateway website to hundreds of ex-offender re-entry and related resources that we both publish and distribute. It's literally a one-stop shop for prison survival and ex-offender re-entry materials, with an emphasize on finding employment. The site pulls together the largest collection of books, pocket guides, DVDs, curriculum programs, assessment instruments, games, pamphlets, and workbooks relevant to ex-offenders and correctional administrators, which are available through Impact Publications – www.impactpublications.com. If you're looking for specific resources and we don't have them, give us a call and we'll most likely be able to locate what you need or at least advise you where to go: 1-800-361-1055. This site also includes links to other re-entry-related resources.

Prison Fellowship
www.prisonfellowship.org

PRISON FELLOWSHIP

Representing the world's largest faith-based outreach program for prisoners, ex-prisoners, and their families, the evangelical Prison Fellowship has been in operation for nearly 40 years. Founded by Chuck Colson, who was famous for his religious transformation while serving a seven-month prison sentence for obstruction of justice (he was President Nixon's "hatchet man") in the Watergate scandal of 1974, Prison Fellowship is a Bible-based program designed to change prisoners' mindsets, turn around their lives, strengthen their families, and save their souls. The focus of the program is on Bible study, prayer, church leadership training, and church-based preparation for re-entry (life-skills training, marriage and parenting classes, and other skills training). Prison Fellowship also conducts an InnerChange Freedom Initiative in Texas and

Minnesota, which focuses on values and life skills training for up to 18 months in prison and mentor and church support 12 months after release.

Each month over 25,000 prisoners in 380+ prisons participate in Prison Fellowship classes. A network of more than 11,000 Prison Fellowship volunteers ensures the operation of the programs. Individuals participating in the re-entry program benefit from the network of various mentors, churches, and organizations that assist former prisoners in several aspects of re-entry, especially in finding jobs.

This program, however, has not been without controversy, because it straddles a fine line between church and state and raises issues about the role of evangelical ministries in the U.S. prison system. In fact, Prison Fellowship has been the subject of lawsuits claiming that prisoners participating in their "born again" programs are sometimes put into special units called the "God Pod," where they receive preferential treatment within prisons – special visitation rights, more outdoor recreation time, more out-of-cell time, movie-watching privileges, access to computers, and access to early parole classes. Indeed, Jews, Muslims, and inmates of other religious persuasions are left out of these state-supported faith-based re-entry initiatives. You literally need to be in the "Bible loop" in order to benefit from such programs. But such controversy is not new, especially since the federal government long ago established faith-based offices within the departments of Labor and Justice as well as within the White House (for examples of current operations, see ojp.gov/fbnp/reentry.htm and www.whitehouse.gov/administration/eop/ofbnp). The justification for such programs is that they tend to reduce recidivism rates, they are cost-effective given their volunteer emphasis, and not many other groups have stepped up to the plate to take responsibility for prisoner transformation and re-entry. Putting re-entry on an evangelical Christian Bible route paved with belief, faith, and prayer rather than on a cognitive behavior therapy and life skills route of evidence-based science should keep heads turning for some time in the correctional field.

Catholic Charities
www.catholiccharitiesusa.org

Catholic Charities is all about caring for society's most vulnerable populations and communities. It's one of the nation's largest social service networks and outreach programs, the domestic missionary arm of the U.S. Catholic Church. Emphasizing safety, security, social justice, and caring for those in need, Catholic Charities consists of 164 member agencies serving 2,631 locations in the United States. It's devoted to helping individuals, families, and communities, from providing disaster relief to promoting poverty reduction through research and legislative reform. Emphasizing the importance of marriage and families, its mission is to help those in need – poor, homeless, disabled, distressed, children, teens, single mothers, ex-offenders, immigrants, seniors – with food, shelter, education, training, financial security, healthy lifestyles, counseling, and adoptions. In many communities Catholic Charities is very much involved in operating ex-offender re-entry programs as well as substance abuse, mental health, transitional housing, and restorative justice programs. They are involved with prison ministries, support chaplains, and are advocates for juvenile justice, prison reform, and abolishing capital punishment. Often working on the margins of society, these agencies operate child development centers, food pantries, refugee resettlement programs, housing projects, and senior centers.

Foundations, Institutes, and Nonprofits

Several key foundations and institutes play important roles in conducting research, advocating for correctional changes, and conducting hands-on re-entry programs. Many are funded by government contracts and grants whereas others are well endowed and designed to have their own donor streams for financing operations. Some of the most well respected such foundations, institutes, and nonprofits include the following.

Goodwill Industries International, Inc.
www.goodwill.org

Goodwill Industries is the nation's largest nonprofit provider of job training services with a network of 164 independent, community-based Goodwills and dozens of corporate and nonprofit partners, such as AT&T, Bank of America, Caterpillar, Microsoft, Sprint, Walmart, Annie E. Casey Foundation, Lumina Foundation for Education, and the Ford Foundation. Financed through a combination of donations, retail sales, and contracts and grants, Goodwill works with thousands of ex-offenders each year through its Second Chance Program (*2nd Chance @ Work*). A leader in the successful reintegration of ex-offenders into mainstream society, Goodwill operates several programs designed to help ex-offenders find and keep jobs, acquire safe and stable housing, and deal with substance abuse and health (both physical and mental) issues. To find a Goodwill location nearest you, visit their website and enter your zip code in its location search box.

Salvation Army
www.salvationarmyusa.org/usn/prison-ministries

The Salvation Army is very active in working with prison, probation, and parole officials through its prison ministries programs. In some areas, prisoners are paroled to the direct custody of The Salvation Army. Re-entry-related services include Bible correspondence courses, prerelease job training programs, and employment opportunities. Most of The Salvation Army's efforts are handled through its Adult Rehabilitation Centers and Harbor Light Centers, which function as halfway houses for ex-offenders who participate in work release programs. The **Adult Rehabilitation Centers** (ARCs) provide spiritual, social, and emotional assistance to men and women who have difficulty coping with personal problems and providing for themselves. The Centers offers residential housing, work, and group and individual therapy to prepare them for re-entry into society and return to gainful employment. A faith-based program, it's primarily supported by the sale of donated goods through The Salvation Army's popular thrift stores. **Harbor Light Centers** function as homeless shelters that also provide six-month treatment programs for individuals experiencing chemical dependency. Each center provides detoxification services, residential treatment, transitional housing, and outpatient treatment for men and women. Treatment includes group and individual counseling, education, skills for managing grief and anger, and training for independent living, meaningful employment, and money management.

Phoenix House Foundation
www.phoenixhouse.org

Phoenix House

Focusing on substance abuse and mental health issues affecting millions of Americans, including the majority of ex-offenders, Phoenix House offers a variety of outpatient and residential treatment options through its many assessment, counseling, and treatment centers around the country. With nearly 50 years of experience, it currently operates 130+ programs in 13 states: California, Connecticut, Florida, Maine, Maryland, Massachusetts, Metro DC, New Hampshire, New York, Rhode Island, Texas, Vermont, and Virginia. In addition to standard assessment and treatment services, Phoenix House also offers the following programs: medical and dental care; psychiatric assessment, treatment, monitoring, and referral; family services; high school education and GED prep; vocational assessment, referral, training, and job placement; housing services; recreation, fitness, meditation, and yoga; horticulture therapy; animal therapy; and performing and visual arts therapy. The Phoenix House Academy has been designated by the U.S. Department of Justice as a "model program" and listed in the Substance Abuse and Mental Health Services Administration's (SAMHSA) National Registry of Evidence-Based Programs and Practices (NREPP). Many of their clients are ex-offenders with nagging substance abuse issues who need treatment rather than jail. Call for information on eligibility: 1-888-671-9392.

The Safer Foundation
www.saferfoundation.org

Safer Foundation is truly a hands-on re-entry organization that has helped thousands of ex-offenders reclaim their lives by helping them find and keep jobs (the key to re-entry success) and adjust to life in the outside world. Primarily focusing on employment and re-employment of ex-offenders in northern Illinois (primarily Chicago) and the Quad Cities region of Iowa, the Safer Foundation is one of America's largest not-for-profit providers of such services. Its evidence-based programs address barriers to employment and include pioneering programs designed for youth and adults with criminal records. It also offers intensive case management and prevention education as well as promotes supportive services and other ancillary services. Each year it helps more than 4,000 ex-offenders find employment through its various programs. The Foundation's website includes useful re-entry and criminal justice resources, news, success stories, eligibility requirements, videos, and statistics.

Annie E. Casey Foundation
www.aecf.org

This foundation is very much focused on improving the lives of children, families, and communities across the United States. One of its important focuses is on reforming the juvenile justice system. It conducts studies and pilot projects aimed at developing effective models that can replicated across the country. It's especially noted for its Juvenile Detention Alternatives Initiative (JDAI) reform model that has been implemented in more than 250 U.S. counties as well as several intensive projects to help states and localities analyze and reorient their juvenile justice policies away from incarceration. Its ground-breaking study, *No Place for Kids: The Case for Reducing Reliance on Juvenile Incarceration*, has proven that the current system of youth incarceration is dangerous, ineffective, obsolete, wasteful, and unnecessary, with no net benefit to public safety.

The Vera Institute of Justice
www.vera.org

This is one of America's most respected institutes for criminal justice reform. Operating for more than 50 years, the Vera Institute of Justice has been an innovative nonpartisan, nonprofit center focused on improving the criminal justice system through research, demonstration projects, and technical assistance. Headquartered in New York City, it has offices in Washington, DC, New Orleans, and Los Angeles and operates throughout the United States and abroad. Its specialized centers and programs focus on the following: immigration and justice, sentencing and corrections, victimization and safety, youth justice, family justice, prosecution and racial justice, and substance use and mental health. It partners with foundations, government officials, and community organizations at the local, state, federal, and international levels to improve criminal justice and safety systems. Its numerous successful demonstration projects have been adopted by governments, with 17 being incorporated as independent nonprofit organizations. Its recent study of jail trends in the United States (trends.vera.org) has raised some troubling questions about the unexpected, and largely unexplained, growth of incarceration in rural areas.

Lionheart Foundation
www.lionheart.org

The Lionheart Foundation provides social emotional learning (literacy) programs and rehabilitative services for incarcerated adults, at-risk adolescents, and teen parents. Its director, Robin Casarjian, developed three widely used books and training programs that have been used by hundreds of correctional institutions and schools nationwide: *Houses of Healing, Power Source*, and *Power Source Parenting*. Lionheart's newly designed website includes information on these resources, including video clips, as well as a very useful state-by-state listing of re-entry programs for ex-offenders, a bookstore, and blog.

The Urban Institute
www.urban.org

Operating since 1968, The Urban Institute has been conducting policy research on America's criminal justice system for decades. Combining the rigor of academic research and analytical skills with the practical street-level operations of policymakers, community leaders, and practitioners, The Urban Institute serves as a research powerhouse focused on a variety of urban issues, including the criminal justice and re-entry systems. A leading policy development and think tank headquartered in Washington, DC, it conducts numerous studies relating to incarceration and re-entry, including program evaluations. It analyzes crime trends, evaluates prevention initiatives, examines emerging criminal justice technologies, and recommends solutions to criminal justice system issues facing neighborhoods, cities, states, and the federal government. The **Crime and Justice** section of the Institute's website includes information on its activities as well as synopses of its many relevant research reports. Among its 11 different policy centers, the Institute's **Justice Policy Center** focuses on developing strategies for combating crime and promoting public safety.

Prisoner Reentry Institute
John Jay College of Criminal Justice
johnjayresearch.org/pri/

This university-based institute, which is leader in educating criminal justice professionals, primarily focuses on conducting policy-relevant research focused on the criminal justice system and re-entry policies. Its defined mission relates to these types of projects and activities:

- Developing, Managing, and Evaluating Innovative Reentry Projects.
- Providing Practitioners and Policymakers with Cutting Edge Tools and Expertise.
- Promoting Education Opportunities for Currently and Formerly Incarcerated Individuals as a Vehicle for Successful Reentry and Reintegration.
- Identifying "Pulse Points" and Creating Synergy Across Fields and Disciplines.

The Institute also functions as an information source for many media outlets that cover criminal justice and re-entry issues in the United States. Its director, Ann Jacobs, is frequently quoted in the media as an expert on re-entry.

The Fortune Society
http://fortunesociety.org

Operating since 1967, The Fortune Society primary focuses on helping ex-offenders successfully re-enter society. Servicing approximately 4,500 men and women in three primary locations in New York City, it focuses on various re-entry services: housing, employment, education, family, mental health, substance abuse treatment, and health. Many of The Fortune Society's approaches to re-entry have become models for other programs nationwide. The Society produces several useful re-entry publications (*The Fortune News,* special reports, and toolkits) that can be downloaded from their website. A highly respected re-entry organization that also promotes criminal justice education and reform through a policy center dedicated to its founder – David Rothenberg Center for Public Policy (DRCPP) – which focuses on changing counterproductive laws and policies that create barriers to successful community re-entry.

The Center for Employment Opportunities
www.ceoworks.org

Operating transitional jobs programs for more than 30 years, the Center for Employment Opportunities annually offers life skills education, transitional employment, job placement, and post-placement services to more than 3,000 ex-offenders (disproportionately black and hispanic) returning to New York City as well as to others under community supervision. Its model work experience program – the Neighborhood Work Project (NWP) – provides participants with immediate, paid, and short-term employment while they take part in a program to develop skills for rejoining the workforce and restarting their lives. Much of CEO's focus is on the most at-risk populations, especially young adults ages 18-25, who have limited work experience and face strong barriers to entering the workforce. The program provides an intensive four-day job readiness workshop that deals with resume writing, job search skills, interview preparation, dress, and discussing one's conviction and incarceration. It also assesses individual needs for support services, such as housing, clothing, child care, transportation, and documentation. Participants undergo vocational assessment (reading, math, job-related skills), develop an employment plan, regularly meet with a job coach, and receive paid transitional employment (NWP) four days a week. Sixty percent of program participants are placed in permanent jobs within two to three months. The program closely supervises those placed as well as continues to offer participants post-placement, job coaching, and support services for an additional 12 months. CEO has offices in New York (New York City, Albany, Binghamton, Buffalo, Rochester), Pennsylvania (Philadelphia), California (Oakland, San Bernardino, San Diego), and Oklahoma (Oklahoma City and Tulsa).

Delancey Street Foundation
www.delanceystreetfoundation.org

DELANCEY STREET
FOUNDATION

Based in San Francisco, this is one of America's most respected and emulated residential self-help rehabilitation and vocational training programs/services for substance abusers, ex-offenders, the homeless, and others who have hit bottom. The average resident has been a hard-care drug addict for 16 years, abused alcohol and multiple drugs, dropped out of school at the 7th grade level, and been institutionalized many times. Many also have been former gang members with a history of poverty and violence. Delancey Street focuses on reintegrating its residents into society by requiring them to participate in a variety of businesses managed by its participants, especially restaurants, bookstores, cafes, and catering and moving companies. Most residents live at Delancey Street from two to four years during which time they receive a high school equivalency degree (GED), acquire training in three marketable skills, and develop important social and interpersonal skills for effectively functioning in society. For more than 40 years Delancey Street has developed a successful model of social entrepreneurship, education, rehabilitation, and change that has positively affected the lives of thousands of ex-offenders.

Gemeinschaft Home
www.gemeinschafthome.com

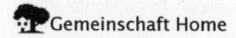

Gemeinschaft Home is a model therapeutic transitional facility for non-violent, non-sexual ex-offenders who have been released or diverted from incarceration in Virginia. In operation for more than 30 years and modeled after the Delancey Street program in San Francisco, it offers residential re-entry and therapy programs. Combining counseling and therapy services to help residents deal with substance abuse issues, the program focuses on relapse prevention, developing life skills, and participation in group and individual therapy.

Pioneer Human Services
pioneerhumanservices.org

Centered in Washington State (Seattle-Tacoma area), this large organization serves nearly 13,000 ex-offenders each year with a comprehensive program focused on housing, education, job training, employment, counseling and case management, substance abuse treatment, life skills, and social enterprise services. Its programs are designed to help people stay out of prison by participating in a variety of integrated programs and services: job training and placement, youth and family counseling, housing, and substance abuse treatment. The organization is especially noted for the large number of self-supporting social enterprises it operates that employ ex-offenders and thus provide them with core job training skills and employment opportunities.

3

Documentation:

IDs, Rap Sheets, and Online Reputations

Y OU HAVE A NAME and personal history, but most recently you've been known primarily by your prison number. You've also developed a recent incarceration history, which is probably not widely known outside the prison walls, unless you behaved badly. Without that number, you could easily get lost in the system. Even your family and closest friends would have difficulty locating you without knowing your number.

Whether you think it's fair or not, your recent incarceration experience is a big red flag for those on the outside who might otherwise be receptive to you. One of your major tasks is to overcome that red flag by assuring people that you are now a different person who is both responsible and trustworthy.

Now that you're released and ostensibly free, no one really wants to know your prison number, including yourself. Instead, many people and institutions want to know the following personal identifiers, which frequently pop up on applications and serve as security screening questions for verifying your identity:

- Who are you – your name?
- What's your Social Security number?
- Where were you born?
- How old are you?
- Are you a U.S. citizen?
- Are you a local resident?
- What's your address?
- What's your telephone number?
- What's your email address?
- What's your mother's maiden name?

In addition, they want more than simple identification information. They want to know something about the real you, especially your **pattern of behavior**. Who are you? What have you done? What are your strengths? What are your weaknesses? How well do you get along with others? Indeed, more and more people are answering these questions by quietly asking this **online reputation question**, which can be as deadly as a rap sheet:

Is there anything negative about you on the Internet?

Do you have a Facebook page, Twitter account, or any other social media presence? What are you saying about yourself both verbally and nonverbally? Better still, how do others portray you online? In today's fast-paced digital world, reputation is everything! Indeed, it can make or break you.

What You Need ASAP

Once you're released from prison, you'll need adequate documentation to function in the free world. This usually takes two forms:

- Personal ID or identification documents
- Criminal record or rap sheet

Unfortunately, much of your criminal record and rap sheet may have migrated to the Internet, which can be easily accessed by anyone who knows how to conduct basic Internet searches. You'll need to first find out how you are being profiled online and then consider cleaning up your online presence as well as developing a fire wall against any future negative online information about you.

You should also develop a **resume** for finding a job, but that should come only **after** you're taken care of these initial documentation issues. That resume will document who you are in terms of a work history. When you get to the resume production stage, check out ***Best Resumes and Letters for Ex-Offenders*** (Impact Publications) for tips on how to most effectively present your qualifications to employers.

Unfortunately, many ex-offenders lack these basic documents, which can jeopardize their re-entry success. Indeed, you will need one or more of the following personal identification documents in order to apply for other documents as well as qualify for and access most of the re-entry services identified throughout this directory. Circle "Yes," "No," or "Maybe" if you have the following forms of ID:

■ Social Security card	Yes	No	Maybe
■ Driver's license	Yes	No	Maybe
■ Birth certificate (certified)	Yes	No	Maybe
■ State ID card	Yes	No	Maybe
■ U.S. passport or passport card	Yes	No	Maybe
■ U.S. military ID	Yes	No	Maybe
■ Marriage certificate	Yes	No	Maybe
■ Court order or judgments	Yes	No	Maybe

If you're trying to verify your local residency, you also may be asked to present a copy of a bill with your current address from a bank, mortgage company, utility company, credit card company, doctor, or hospital. Some places may also ask for the following forms of identification: pay stub, W2 form, 1099 form, marriage certificate, divorce decree, and court documents establishing a legal name change.

A driver's license, passport, certified birth certificate, and valid credit card are the most acceptable forms of personal identification. You'll often need two forms of documentation in order to simply cash a check, acquire wire transfers, get a driver's license, apply for a job, access credit, qualify for a library card, apply for licenses and certifications, use public education services, gain admissions to secured areas, travel by air or rail, and acquire numerous other services that require identity verification and security screening. Even if you're living on the margins of society, you'll have difficulty gaining access to food pantries, soup kitchens, and clothing centers, as well as acquiring transitional housing and health care services, without presenting one or two acceptable forms of personal identification.

Unfortunately, many people living on the margins of society do not physically possess such documents – someone has them, but they are often at a loss as to where to go and whom to contact to get certified copies of essential documents establishing their legal identity. Indeed, most such people are "unbanked" (no credit card or bank accounts – savings or checking); don't own a car or drive (no driver's license); don't travel abroad (lack a passport); and haven't applied for a Social Security card by age 18, they lost or misplaced it, or they haven't memorized this essential ID number.

As most people soon discover – especially undocumented immigrants lacking a path to citizenship – personal identification is a big issue for functioning in American society. Without proper identification, they encounter many obstacles to getting ahead with daily living. Indeed, much of life is a "cash only" operation as they constantly duck government radar that requires basic documentation for acquiring all types of governmental and nongovernmental services as well as for ensuring that you are a good taxpaying citizen and resident. If you lack proper documentation and basically operate on a "cash only" basis, you're probably not paying taxes and thus you're a "free rider" when it comes to acquiring government services. If that is the case, it's time to come in from the cold underground cash economy, get yourself documented, and move beyond the margins of society.

Acquire Acceptable IDs

Getting proper documentation often involves a Catch 22 – if you don't have a permanent address, you can't complete application forms. The same is true with your Social Security number. If you don't have a Social Security number, you won't be able to get other forms of ID or properly complete a job application (most law-abiding employers need that number for 1099 filing requirements with the IRS).

Here's what you need to do in order to acquire basic personal identification documents to get up and running on the outside. First, understand who does what, where, when, and how. For example, the **federal government** only issues three forms of identification: Social Security card/number, passport, and military ID. All other forms of identification – from birth and marriage certificates to divorce decrees, driver's licenses, and state IDs – are the responsibilities of **state government** agencies. Second, don't waste your time looking through paper directories and phone books and then plan to physically visit the agency (other than the state DMV for a driver's license). The paper sources will most likely soon be outdated and frustrating to use, and most applications for identification can be completed by following online instructions. Simplify your life by **going online** to find accurate up-to-date information. Third, you may need original documents or certified copies that will require the seal and signature of a **notary public**. You can quickly find a notary public near your location by searching for them on these websites: www.123notary.com and www.notaryconnect.org. Banks, city halls, county courthouses, shipping offices (UPS and FedEx), and Postal Annexes usually offer such services for free.

If you have access to the Internet, in a couple of minutes you should be able to find the address, phone number, and details on how to acquire these official documents. If you don't have Internet access, find someone who does and ask for assistance. If you're at a loss as to whom to turn to for Internet assistance, just go to the information desk at your local library and ask for help. You should be able to use one of the library computers that's connected to the Internet. If that fails, ask the library personnel for the contact information you need for Vital Records offices. They will most likely look it up for you if you give them the following information.

Birth, Marriage, Divorce, Death Documents

You'll need to write or visit the **vital statistics office** in the state or community where you were born in order to get a copy of your birth certificate. The quickest way to find these offices is to visit the **Centers for Disease Control and Prevention** (CDC) gateway website, which lists the addresses, phone numbers, and costs of all state and territorial Vital Records offices, along with details on how to acquire birth, death, marriage, and divorce documents:

<u>www.cdc.gov/nchs/w2w.htm</u>

For example, in the case of Nebraska, this is the type of information you will get from the CDC vital records site:

Type of document: Birth Certificate

Cost of copy: $17.00 (personal check or money order made payable to Nebraska Vital Records)

Address: Nebraska Vital Records
P.O. Box 95065
Lincoln, NE 68509-5065

Telephone number: 402-471-2871 (recorded message to verify current fees)

Requirements: Photocopy of requestor's valid government-issued photo identification, i.e., valid driver's license, valid state ID card, valid passport or visa

If you need a copy of your marriage certificate or divorce decree, you'll also get that information from the same Nebraska Vital Records office.

The only difference for requesting these documents will be the cost per copy, which you should always verify by calling their phone number:

Marriage Certificate:	$16.00
Divorce Decree:	$16.00
Death Certificate:	$16.00

Once you're on this gateway CDC website, just click onto any other state or territory to access the same information as outlined in the example for Nebraska. In the end, accessing this documentation information is relatively easy if you know what you're doing by going to this website.

If this website address should change sometime after publication of this directory, the easiest way to locate state vital records offices is to go online and search for "state vital records offices." Any of the major search engines (Google, Bing, Yahoo, Ask, WebCrawler, DuckDuckGo, Dogpile) will generate the latest links to this information.

Social Security Card/Number

When anyone turns 18, they need a Social Security number in order to get a job, acquire government services, and collect Social Security benefits. Once you get a Social Security card, be sure to put it in a secure place and memorize (especially the last four digits) and/or write down the number somewhere for easy access. Do not carry it with you. And be careful who you give that number to since many scam operations focus on stealing Social Security numbers in order to access your financial data, assuming you are a "banked" person (have a bank account).

If you've not applied for a Social Security number, or if you need your Social Security card replaced, here's what you need to do. First, you once again need Internet access. Second, go to the Social Security Administration's website for information on applying for a new Social Security card or replacing a lost card:

www.ssa.gov/ssnumber/cards.htm

This site has all the information you need, including details on three types of Social Security cards, which pertain to different types of non-citizens who may or may not be permitted to work in the United States. While on this website, you may want to create your own Social Security account which is called "*my* Social Security." By so doing, you'll gain quick access to information about your Social Security future, including earned benefits:

www.ssa.gov/myaccount

This account allows you to apply for a replacement card online if you are a U.S. citizen age 18 or older with a U.S. mailing address, are not requesting any changes on your card, such as a name change, and have a valid driver's license or a state-issued identification card from one of the following: District of Columbia (driver's license only), Michigan, Nebraska, Washington, or Wisconsin (driver's license only).

If you are applying for a new, replacement, or corrected card, you will need to follow a three-step process outlined at www.ssa.gov/ssnumber: (1) acquiring a certified copy of a document showing a birth, marriage, or divorce that took place in the United States; (2) completing an online application and printing it out; and (3) mailing the information to a Social Security Administration office nearest your zip code (you can quickly look it up on this website or call 1-800-772-1213). This office also gives this "free" advice about anyone using Social Security services:

> "Some businesses offer Social Security name changes or cards for a fee. Social Security provides those services and more for free. Do not pay for something we will give you free. Social Security is the best place to get information about Social Security."

Driver's License

A driver's license is one of the best forms of picture identification, often the first form of ID requested by those who wish to establish your legal identity. If you don't have a driver's license or if your license has expired, you'll need to contact your nearest state DMV (Division of Motor Vehicles) office. You should initially go online to get application details, including a copy of the application (see the example of Virginia's form on the next page). You'll still need to visit the DMV office to apply for the license in person or renew your license. Several state DMVs also issue state identification (ID) cards.

When you fill out a driver's license and/or state ID application, you will need additional information: address, Social Security number, and daytime phone number. If you don't have these, you most likely will not be able to get or renew a driver's license. To find the office nearest you, use one of the Internet search engines (Google, Yahoo, Ask) to locate the address, look in the blue pages of the telephone book, or ask someone at the information desk at your local library.

www.dmv.state.va.us/webdoc/pdf/dl1p.pdf

Completion of this section is requested but not required to apply for a driver's license or ID Card. (Virginia Code §2.2-3806)
INFORMATION FOR THE DEPARTMENT OF ELECTIONS

Are you a citizen of the United States of America?		Do you want to apply to register to vote or change your voter registration address?	
YES (INITIAL BOX)	**NO** (INITIAL BOX)	**YES** (INITIAL BOX)	**NO** (INITIAL BOX)

INFORMATION FOR THE VIRGINIA TRANSPLANT COUNCIL
☐ Yes, I would like to remain or become an organ, eye and tissue donor.

dmv www.dmvNow.com
Virginia Department of Motor Vehicles
Post Office Box 27412
Richmond, Virginia 23269-0001

DRIVER'S LICENSE AND IDENTIFICATION CARD APPLICATION

DL 1P (07/01/2015)

LOG #

Purpose: Use this form to apply for a Virginia Driver's License or Identification Card.

Instructions: Complete the front and back of this application. Note: A $5 service fee applies to each license or ID card renewal conducted in a CSC if the transaction is eligible to be performed by Internet, automated telephone or mail, unless the renewal is conducted with another transaction that must be completed in person at a CSC.

Note: Va. Code §§46.2-323 and 46.2-342 require that you provide DMV with the information on this form (including your social security number). It is not necessary to provide a social security number for an identification card. This social security number is for record keeping purposes and may be disseminated only in accordance with Va. Code §§46.2-208 and 46.2-209. Persons convicted of certain sexual offenses (as listed in Va. Code §9.1-902) must register or re-register with the Virginia Department of State Police as provided in Va. Code §§9.1-901, 9.1-903, and 9.1-904. If you provide a non-Virginia residence/home address or non-Virginia mailing address, your application for a driver's license or identification (ID) card may be denied.

APPLICATION TYPE (Check one)

1. ☐ Driver's License
2. ☐ Learner's Permit and Driver's License
3. ☐ Motorcycle Learner's Permit (classification not applicable)
4. ☐ Driver's License with School Bus Endorsement (to carry less than 16 passengers)
5. ☐ Driver's License Testing for Foreign Diplomats
6. ☐ Commercial Learner's Permit or License
7. ☐ Identification (ID) Card
8. ☐ Hearing Impaired ID Card
9. ☐ Emancipated Minor ID Card

10. Motorcycle ☐ Renew Virginia Motorcycle Class ☐ New/Upgrade/Transfer Motorcycle Class* ☐ Motorcycle Only License*

*Check one if New/Upgrade/Transfer or Motorcycle Only ---▶ ☐ M 2 (2 wheels) ☐ M 3 (3 wheels) ☐ M (both 2 wheels and 3 wheels)

11. Replacement license or identification card (check one of the following): ☐ I am surrendering my current license or ID card.
☐ I certify I cannot surrender my current license or ID card because it is: ☐ Lost ☐ Stolen ☐ Destroyed or Mutilated

Do you currently have or have you ever held a driver's license, commercial driver's license or learner's permit from Virginia, another state, U.S. territory or foreign country? ☐ No ☐ Yes – provide the following:

LICENSE NUMBER	ISSUE DATE (mm/dd/yyyy)	EXPIRATION DATE (mm/dd/yyyy)	STATE/COUNTRY

APPLICANT INFORMATION
NOTE: YOUR ADDRESS BELOW MUST BE CURRENT. THE U.S. POSTAL SERVICE WILL NOT FORWARD.

FULL LEGAL NAME (last, first, middle, suffix)		SOCIAL SECURITY NUMBER	BIRTHDATE (mm/dd/yyyy)

DAYTIME TELEPHONE NUMBER	GENDER (check one) ☐ MALE ☐ FEMALE	WEIGHT LBS.	HEIGHT FT. IN.	EYE COLOR	HAIR COLOR

STREET ADDRESS	APT NO.	CITY	STATE ZIP CODE

IF YOUR NAME HAS CHANGED, PRINT YOUR FORMER NAME HERE	NAME OF CITY OR COUNTY OF RESIDENCE ☐ CITY ☐ COUNTY OF

MAILING ADDRESS (if different from above - this address will show on your license/ID card)	APT NO.	CITY	STATE ZIP CODE

1. Do you wear glasses or contact lenses? ☐ YES ☐ NO
2. Do you have a physical or mental condition which requires that you take medication? ☐ YES ☐ NO
3. Have you ever had a seizure, blackout, or loss of consciousness? ☐ YES ☐ NO
4. Do you have a physical condition which requires you to use special equipment in order to drive? ☐ YES ☐ NO
5. Have you been convicted within the past ten years in this state or elsewhere of any offense resulting from your operation of, or involving, a motor vehicle? (Do not include parking tickets.) ☐ YES ☐ NO
6. Has your license or privilege to drive ever been suspended, revoked, or disqualified in this state or elsewhere, or is it currently suspended, revoked or disqualified? ☐ YES ☐ NO

SPECIAL INDICATOR REQUEST
Please show the following indicator(s) on my license or ID card:
☐ Insulin-dependent diabetic
☐ Speech impairment
☐ Hearing impairment (license only)
☐ Intellectual disability (IntD)
☐ Autism spectrum disorder (ASD)
Must submit required physician statement

If you answered YES to any of the above provide an explanation here.

FOR DMV USE ONLY — DO NOT WRITE BELOW THIS LINE

REQUIRED TESTS	PASS	FAIL	CUSTOMER NUMBER	TRANSACTION TYPE	FEE
VISION				☐ ORIGINAL ☐ REISSUE ☐ DUPLICATE ☐ RENEWAL	
DL ROAD SIGNS EXAM					
DL KNOWLEDGE EXAM			PROOF OF ID (primary)	PROOF OF ID (secondary)	
DL SKILLS					
MOTORCYCLE KNOWLEDGE			PROOF OF SOCIAL SECURITY (specify)	PROOF OF RESIDENCY	
MOTORCYCLE SKILLS M2					
MOTORCYCLE SKILLS M3			PROOF OF LEGAL PRESENCE (specify)		

REMARKS/PAID STAMP	Document Type	Document Number	Expiration Date (mm/dd/yyyy)
	Document Type	Document Number	Expiration Date (mm/dd/yyyy)
	Document Type	Document Number	Expiration Date (mm/dd/yyyy)
	CSR SIGNATURE AND LOGONID	DOCUMENT VERIFIER SIGNATURE AND LOGONID	

Valid Passport

It doesn't get much better for establishing your identity than a valid U.S. passport. This document is one of the most trusted IDs since it requires a more thorough vetting process than other forms of identification. However, people who do not travel outside the U.S. do not need a passport. In addition, individuals convicted of a felony are prohibited from entering many countries. The United States also puts restrictions on issuing passports to convicted felons. While convicted felons can apply for a passport, their application may be denied based on these disqualifiers: convicted international drug traffickers, individuals with outstanding federal arrest warrants, unpaid loans while in prison abroad, court order forbidding travel outside the United States, participation in a release program for felony drug charges, owe more than $5,000 in child support, or have unpaid loans for assistance with repatriation. Based on these restrictions, you need to consider whether or not it's worth going to the expense ($110.00) and trouble (up to six weeks) of applying for a U.S. passport.

Know Your Rap Sheets

Your rap sheet is officially known as your **Record of Arrests and Prosecutions** – it's your history of encounters with the criminal justice system. What appears on your rap sheet is a record of your arrests and the disposition of each case, regardless of whether you were found guilty or not guilt, or if the case was dismissed. Each state compiles and distributes rap sheets on individuals who are arrested and fingerprinted. While they also may note that you have an out-of-state record, they will not keep details of such arrests and convictions. But the FBI does. It collects criminal record information it receives from the states and includes it with any federal arrests and convictions. Therefore, you may need to contact both state agencies and the FBI for copies of your rap sheets.

Since potential employers, landlords, and other key re-entry players can easily do **background checks** on you, make sure you know what information is given about you in public records. Be prepared to address any red flags that might be in the public records. Remember, in today's highly digitized world, there is no place to hide. Just assume others will find out about your criminal history as well as any civil judicial proceedings by using such inexpensive instant background check websites as CheckPeople, BackgroundChecks, FindOutTheTruth, BeenVerified, and CriminalWatchDog. In fact, you might want to search for yourself on these sites to see what information is available about your criminal background and any court proceedings or judgments. You may be shocked to find out how much negative information is so easily available (takes less than 60 seconds) on you by just searching your name and location. Unfortunately, your next rejection may be just a "Google search" away!

One of the first things you need to do is to get a copy of your rap sheets and review them for any errors. At the state level, you can get a copy of your rap sheet by contacting your state's **criminal record repository**. To identify the appropriate repository agency in each state, visit the "Resource and Assistance" section of the National H.I.R.E. Network website – www.hirenetwork.org – and look for a subsection called "Criminal Record Repository" for each state. They include the mailing address and phone number of the repository. Be sure to ask that agency who else can legally access your record.

The FBI also keeps rap sheets (they refer to it as an "Identity History Summary") on individuals with state and federal criminal records who were fingerprinted in connection with an arrest. You can get a copy of your FBI rap sheet by contacting the FBI's Criminal Justice Information Services (CJIS) division: FBI CJIS Division, Record Request, 1000 Custer Hollow Rd., Clarksburg, WV 26306. For more information on how this process works with the FBI, visit their relevant web page:

www.fbi.gov/about-us/cjis/identify-history-summary-checks

Despite its relatively new (2014) IT system, the FBI is slow in processing such requests – anticipate 12-14 weeks plus mail delivery time.

For a good summary of issues relating to a rap sheet – what it is, where to get them, who sees them, possible errors, how to correct errors, model request and correction letters – see the useful booklet produced by the Legal Action Center (www.lac.org) on rap sheets for the State of New York:

lac.org/wp-content/uploads/2014/12/Your_New_
York_State_Rap_Sheet_2013.pdf.

Consider Online Reputation and Repair Strategies

Especially as an ex-offender, you should do a "Google search" of your name to see how easily you can be found on the Internet and how you, or someone with a similar name (hopefully not a sex offender), may be portrayed in this public arena. Is your "crime story" on the Internet? After all, this is one of the first things employers, landlords, and licensing groups will do in screening your name – search for you on the Internet.

So what's being said about you on the Internet? Do strangers see red flags waving around your name? Some companies now specialize in cleaning up your online presence and reputation. If you search for "clean up online reputation," you'll find several large firms, such as Brand Yourself and Reputation.com, that claim they can help you, but it will cost you, and there's no guarantee they can deliver on their promises. Some of these services are free, but others can cost up to $1,000 a month!

One of the best things you can do, and it's free, is to set up a Google Alert page (www.google.com/alerts#) to regularly monitor your online presence. If completed properly, Google Alerts will send you emails when something appears on the Internet about you. Also, be sure to create key social media accounts, such as LinkedIn and Twitter, as well as your own personal website, and include detailed positive content about yourself. Several websites provide useful free advice on how to best repair your online reputation. Just search for "online reputation repair" for such sources.

4

Release and Re-Entry Programs

THE FEDERAL GOVERNMENT, along with most states and many counties and communities, promote different types of re-entry programs in their prisons and jails as well as within communities, churches, and nonprofit organizations. Most of these programs focus on finding and keeping jobs, with many closely tied to local workforce development programs. Others are more concerned with religious and spiritual transformation while, at the same time, dealing with such critical re-entry issues as housing, addiction, anger management, and mental health.

To varying degrees, all of these state- and nonprofit-run programs are concerned with strengthening public safety, transforming lives, reducing recidivism, and empowering low-income groups. They also share one other commonality – they work with one of the most challenging groups of individuals who are in desperate need of help. Indeed, many seasoned professionals would rather work with more highly skilled, educated, and entrepreneurial groups that have few red flags in their backgrounds and who are more responsive to evidence-based approaches to behavioral change.

In fact, it's not unusual for local government workforce development programs to assign re-entering ex-offenders, who may constitute 20 percent of their clientele, to the most recently hired and inexperienced professionals. Anticipating difficulties in showing effectiveness in working with such groups, they face a very challenging situation. Other groups, especially nonprofits such as Delancey Street Foundation, have for decades taken on the struggle of transforming the lives of America's most difficult population through social entrepreneurship, education, and rehabilitation with some remarkable successes.

Welcome to the re-entry world of extraordinary human challenges. Nothing is simple or comes easy in this complex world of individuals, groups, and communities struggling to transform lives and lower the costs of recidivism.

The Recidivism Issue and Argument

Re-entry programs are receiving increasing attention and support in efforts to significantly reduce the shockingly high recidivism rates (60-70 percent) that plague communities and thus largely characterize the U.S. criminal justice system as fundamentally flawed and systematically dysfunctional, depending on how you look at it.

But the 60-70 percent recidivism statistic may not be as shocking as it initially appears, especially when you understand how this term is defined by government. Recidivism normally refers to a re-arrest and perhaps a return to jail or prison. In fact, however, most ex-offenders who come into contact with the criminal justice system again do so because of **technical violations** to the terms of their release, such as failing to show up for a meeting with their parole officer or not paying child support in a timely manner. Over 9,000 people are in prison today for failing to quickly find a job – a violation of their terms of release. Such technical violations are relatively easy to commit given the limited resources and inconvenient lifestyles of many ex-offenders who lack jobs, housing, and transportation. The number of ex-offenders who are arrested for committing **new crimes** – which many argue should be the true test of recidivism – is less than 25 percent. In fact, very few individuals who serve long prison sentences commit **new crimes**. Like crime in general, recidivism tends to be disproportionately a problem for young offenders who lack strong employability, organizational, and life skills.

What Works in America's Many Re-Entry Laboratories

Indicative of re-entry changes taking place is the CSG Justice Center's **What Works in Reentry Clearinghouse** (http://whatworks.csgjustice center.org). The Clearinghouse is an effort to share evidence-based best practices among organizations and institutions involved with re-entry.

An emerging consensus now points to **what doesn't work**, which are essentially America's past "catch and release" jail and prison programs that are costly organization and management nightmares. At the same time, some successes, centered around cognitive behavioral therapy (changing mindsets), smart decision-making, treatment programs (drug and alcohol), vocational and job search training, housing assistance, and mentoring are increasingly taking center stage in arguing for investing in more effective re-entry programs. Indeed, a recent (2015) Congressional Research Service report (see page 72) concluded the following:

> Researchers in the offender reentry field have suggested that the best programs begin during incarceration and extend throughout the release and reintegration process. Despite the relative lack of highly rigorous research on the effectiveness of some reentry programs, an emerging "what works" literature suggests that programs focusing on work training and placement, drug and mental health treatment, and housing assistance have proven to be effective.

But what really works in re-entry programs for lowering recidivism rates remains a mystery. Indeed, recidivism seems to be an intractable problem for communities. Criminal thinking, illegal patterns of behavior, bad decision-making, and lifestyles filled with obstacles are very difficult to change, especially among young offenders who disproportionately occupy America's prisons and jails. We do know that recidivism, along with crime in general, tends to decline with age.

The good news is that America's states and communities function as huge **experimental laboratories** for operating a variety of re-entry programs and services. The state of Ohio, for example, has a reputation for managing a smart and innovative re-entry program which, in turn, has been adopted by the state of Connecticut as part of its new Second Chance Society Initiative. Recidivism rates in both states have declined substantially during the past few years – indicators of program successes – which increasingly transform ex-offenders into taxpayers rather than tax burdens.

At the same time, eligibility changes in the federal government's Medicaid program has become a big game-changer for the criminal justice system and ex-offenders who are likely to re-offend. With access to Medicaid, many vulnerable and struggling ex-offenders, who leave prisons and are mainstreamed into communities with chronic substance abuse and mental health problems, can now get access to treatment on the outside and thus avoid many barriers that often lead them down a well trodden recidivism path relating to untreated health issues.

Today's Re-Entry Landscape

Today's re-entry landscape includes what may initially appear to be a bewildering array of traditional, experimental, and innovative release and reintegration programs, services, and practices. The truth is that most re-entry efforts are very difficult to evaluate and compare. But with a little effort, you'll discover many exciting initiatives, emerging trends, and noteworthy gems for emulation, including several free off-the-shelf re-entry training programs and manuals, which are the subject of Chapter 5.

Eager to claim effectiveness, many re-entry providers boast short-term anecdotal success stories and positive testimonials from participants and clients. Indeed, there's no such thing as a "re-entry science" or "proof of performance" – just a large assortment of "wishful thinking," "good hunches," "best practices," and "testimonials." As many seasoned re-entry specialists soon discover, changing patterns of human behavior and eliminating barriers to success are difficult to do even under the best of circumstances. Like an orchestra without a director, all this re-entry activity and related programs produce a great deal of noise, but it also has shifted more attention to rethinking past approaches to crime and punishment. Why, for example, do some communities build more prisons and jails than schools? Is there something wrong with a system that produces high recidivism rates? Maybe this system needs to be re-invented and restructured rather than tweaked with do-gooder reforms?

Some re-entry programs are conducted within prisons as **transition courses** in preparation for release into the community. These pre-release programs focus on a typical menu of re-entry **issues and activities** that participants need to deal with as part of their pre-release orientation:

- Documentation
- Housing
- Employment
- Transportation
- Food

- Clothing
- Health and wellness
- Mental health
- Substance abuse

- Education
- Parenting
- Personal finance
- Tattoo removal

Being classroom-based discussion and activity programs, with a strong cognitive behavioral therapy theme, these efforts primarily focus on **changing mindsets** and **making smart re-entry decisions**.

Other re-entry programs and services are offered within communities by nonprofit groups, especially faith-based organizations (Prison

Fellowship, pages 43-44) and addiction treatment groups (Phoenix House, pages 47-48), that have contracts and grants to conduct re-entry training. Some of these groups focus on one or two major re-entry issues, such as employment and substance abuse. Others try to deal with a full menu of re-entry issues, including parenting and personal finance. These hands-on groups focus on reducing recidivism rates by making sure participants are fully engaged in the day-to-day details of transitioning to the community and that they receive the necessary supports (helping hands) that supposedly ensure re-entry success.

On the other hand, faith-based groups with an evangelical Christian theme operate on the church/state edge by proselytizing to inmates on the inside and to ex-offenders on the outside as they go about their business of establishing "God pods," and engaging in "Church Plantings." Pre-release faith-based re-entry operations are often funded through churches and private donations rather than through government budgets, which makes them especially attractive (free training) to correctional personnel who manage lean budgets and limited staff. These faith-based programs also have the added advantage of involving many **volunteers** who also serve as **mentors** in helping program participants in their post-release phase find housing, jobs, and community services through their network of members – one of the most effective re-entry approaches. The mentor and his religious support network play essential roles in helping the ex-offender transition to the free world by providing them with a critical lifeline.

Federal Re-Entry Programs and Activities

The U.S. Department of Justice's Federal Bureau of Prisons (BOP) is responsible for managing 122 institutions, 6 regional offices, a headquarters office, 2 staff training centers, and 26 residential re-entry offices. It also administers contracts with private prison corporations (mainly The GEO Group, Inc., www.geogroup.com, and the Corrections Corporation of America, www.cca.com) that operate 14 additional correctional institutions. As of 2015, BOP's 39,951 employees were responsible for the custody and care of 195,893 inmates. Altogether, BOP's reach involves a diverse mix of correctional facilities:

- Residential Reentry Management Offices (RRMs)   26
- Private Correctional Centers (CI)   14
- Federal Correctional Complexes (FCC)   15

- Federal Correctional Institutions (FCI)   75
- Federal Detention Centers (FDC)   5
- Federal Prison Camps (FPC)   6
- Federal Medical Centers (FMC)   5
- Federal Transfer Centers (FTC)   1
- Metropolitan Correctional Centers (MCC)   3
- Medical Center for Federal Prisoners (MCFP)   1
- Metropolitan Detention Centers (MDC)   3
- U.S. Penitentiaries (USP)   22

BOP's rehabilitation and reentry efforts encompass a variety of skills-building and vocational programs through its Federal Prison Industries (www.unicor.gov), vocational training opportunities, and other occupational education courses. Within 18 months of release, inmates participate in a **Release Preparation Program**, which includes classes on resume writing, job search, and job retention and re-entry presentations provided by community groups.

BOP also contracts with **Residential Reentry Centers** (RRCs), better known as **halfway houses**, to assist inmates with their final transition to the community. The RRCs are supposed to provide a safe, structured, and supervised environment focused on transitional housing, employment counseling, job placement, financial management, and other programs and services. The primary emphasis of these programs is on gradually rebuilding ties to communities through activities that are closely monitored and supervised, from sign-in procedures, on-site visits, and random drug and alcohol testing. Participants are expected to be employed for 40-hour workweeks and within 15 days after arriving at their RRC. They also are required to pay a subsistence fee to help defray the cost of their confinement (25 percent of their gross income). The contractor helps them find suitable housing (if necessary) to which they can released from the RRC. For more information on this re-entry program, visit this section of BOP's website:

www.bop.gov/about/facilities/residential_
reentry_management_centers.jsp

The Bureau of Prisons is not the only federal government agency operating re-entry programs. Other federal government agencies also are involved with offender re-entry programs:

- U.S. Department of Labor (DOL)
- U.S. Department of Education (DOE)
- U.S. Department of Housing and Urban Development (HUD)
- U.S. Department of Health and Human Services (HHS)

For a summary of these other federal re-entry programs, including coordination between federal agencies, see the 2015 Congressional Research Service report on federal re-entry programs by Nathan James:

Offender Reentry: Correctional Statistics, Reintegration into the Community, and Recidivism

fas.org/sgp/crs/misc/RL34287.pdf

State and Local Re-Entry Initiatives

States serve as huge laboratories for experimenting with all kinds of re-entry programs. According to 2013 data from the Bureau of Justice Statistics, the 10 states with the largest number of inmates are Texas (221,800), California (218,800), Florida (154,500), Georgia (91,600), Pennsylvania (85,500), New York (81,400), Ohio (69,800), Illinois (69,300), Virginia (59,800), and North Carolina (55,300). The 20 states with the most pressing re-entry needs are the ones with the highest percentage of incarcerated citizens and thus the highest per capita criminal justice tax burdens:

State	Incarceration rate per 100,000 adults	Total incarcerated citizens
Louisiana	1,420	50,100
Oklahoma	1,300	37,900
Mississippi	1,270	28,800
Alabama	1,230	46,000
Georgia	1,220	91,600
Texas	1,130	221,800
Arizona	1,090	55,200
Arkansas	1,010	22,800
Florida	990	154,500
New Mexico	980	15,500
Missouri	950	44,500
Kentucky	950	32,100
Nevada	930	19,900
Virginia	910	58,800

Indiana	910	45,400
Pennsylvania	850	85,500
Michigan	790	60,200
Ohio	780	69,800
California	750	218,800
North Carolina	730	55,300

Approximately 25-30 percent of these inmates are released into communities each year, with most inmates serving less than three years in prison.

ALABAMA

"In Alabama, women released from prison are given $10, a white shirt, and a one-way bus ticket back to the same county of their conviction. By and large, there is no meaningful transitional program that helps women exiting the justice system re-entry society."

– Lovelady Center assessment of issues they face

- **Alabama Department of Economic and Community Affairs (ADECA)**
  401 Adams Ave., Montgomery, AL 36104, Tel. 334-242-5100
  www.adeca.alabama.gov

- **Aid to Inmate Mothers**
  660 Morgan Ave., Montgomery, AL 36104, Tel. 334-262-2245
  www.inmatemoms.org

- **Alabama Christian Veterans Center of America**
  Find presence on www.facebook.com

- **Alabama Department of Corrections**
  www.doc.state.al.us/ReentryOverview.aspx

- **Alabama Non-Violent Offenders Organization**
  701 Andrew Jackson Way, Suite 118, Huntsville, AL 35801,
  Tel. 256-288-3175, www.anvoo.org

- **Ark Dothan, Inc.**
  475 West Main St., Dothan, AL 36301, Tel. 334-794-7223
  www.thearkdothan.org

- **Career Center – Bay Minette**
  201 Faulkner Dr., Bay Minette, AL 36507, Tel. 251-937-4161
  http://joblink.alabama.gov

- **Career Center – Brewton**
  1023 Douglas Ave., Suite 314, Brewton, AL 36426,
  Tel. 251-867-4376, http://joblink.alabama.gov

- **Career Center – Foley**
  200 West Michigan Ave., Foley, AL 36535, Tel. 251-943-1575
  http://joblink.alabama.gov

- **Career Center – Jackson**
  3090 Highway 43, Jackson, AL 36545, Tel. 251-246-2453
  http://joblink.alabama.gov

- **Career Center – Monroeville**
  33 Outlet Dr., Monroeville, AL 36460, Tel. 251-575-3894
  http://joblink.alabama.gov

- **Catholic Social Services**
  4455 Narrow Lane Rd., Montgomery, AL 36116,
  Tel. 334-288-8890, www.cssalabama.org

- **A Day of New Beginnings** (for women)
  114 Brown Ave., Suite #B, Rainbow City, AL 35906,
  Tel. 256-399-6908

- **First Baptist Church Community Ministries**
  213 Broadway St., Montgomery, AL 36110, Tel. 334-263-6663
  www.montgomeryfbc.org.

- **The Foundry Ministries/The Re-Entry Ministries** (for men)
  P.O. Box 824, 1800 4th Ave. North, Bessemer, AL 35020,
  Tel. 205-424-HOPE(4673), www.foundryministries.com

- **Foundry Rescue Mission and Recovery Center**
  1804 6th Ave. North, Bessemer, AL 35020, Tel. 205-426-9000
  www.thefoundryonline.org

- **Fountain House** (for women)
  116 N. McDonough St., Montgomery, AL 36104,
  Tel. 334-391-7508, www.thefountainhouse.net

- **Independent Reading/Counseling Service, Inc.**
  3104 Walnut Ave., Anniston, AL 36201, Tel. 256-770-7226

- **LifeSource, Inc.**
  1103 5th Ave., SW, Decatur, AL 35601, Tel. 256-476-2975
  www.lifesourcedecatur.com

- **The Lovelady Center** (for women)
  7916 2nd Ave., S, Birmingham, AL 36206, Tel. 205-836-3121
  www.loveladycenter.org

- **Madison County Government, Project Focus**
  100 Northside Sq., Huntsville, AL 35801, Tel. 256-532-3300
  www.madisoncountyga.us

- **The Ordinary People Society (TOPS)**
  403 West Powell St., Dothan, AL 36303, Tel. 334-671-2882
  www.wearetops.org

- **Renascence, Inc.**
  215 Clayton St., Montgomery, AL 36104, Tel. 334-832-1402
  https://halfway-home.net/

- **Shepherd's Fold**
  404 12th St., SW, Birmingham, AL 35211, Tel. 205-780-6211

- **State of Alabama Department of Corrections, Birmingham Community Based Facility**
  1216 25th Street North, Birmingham, AL 36234. Tel. 205-252-2994

- **United Way – 2-1-1 Connects Alabama**
  www.211connectsalabama.org

- **Winners, Inc. (Women in Need of Nurturing, Education and Recovery Services)**
  8800 Three Mile Rd., Irvington, AL 36544, Tel. 251-824-1585

ALASKA

- **Alaska Correctional Ministries**
  6901 DeBarr Rd., Suite 204, Anchorage, AK 99504,
  Tel. 907-339-0432
  godinprison.org (alaskacorrectionalministries.org)

- **Alaska Department of Corrections: Reentry**
  www.correct.state.ak.us/rehabilitation-reentry

- **Alaska Family Services**
  1825 S. Chugach St., Palmer, AK 99645, 1-800-746-4080 or
  907-746-4080, www.akafs.org

- **Alaska Legal Services Corporation**
  www.alsc-law.org

- **Alaska Mental Health Trust Authority**
  3745 Community Park Loop, Suite 200, Anchorage, AK 99508,
  Tel. 907-269-7960, www.mhtrust.org

- **Alaska Native Justice Center**
  3600 San Jeronimo Dr., Suite 264, Anchorage, AK 99508,
  Tel. 907-793-3550, www.anjc.org/?page_id=869

- **Alaska Public Assistance**
  dhss.alaska.gov/dpa/Pages/default.aspx

- **Catholic Social Services**
  3710 E. 20th Ave., Anchorage, AK 99508, Tel. 907-222-7300
  www.cssalaska.org

- **Food Bank of Alaska**
  2121 Spar Ave., Anchorage, AK 99501, Tel. 907-272-3663
  www.foodbankofalaska.org

- **New Life Development**
  3016 E. 9th Ave., Anchorage, AK 99508, Tel. 907-646-2200
  www.newlifeak.org

- **No Limits Inc. - South Side Reentry Center**
  253 Romans Way, Fairbanks, AK 99701, Tel. 907-451-9650
  www.nolimitinc.org

- **Partners for Progress/Partners Reentry Center**
  417 Barrow St., Anchorage, AK 99501, Tel. 907-258-1192
  www.partnersforprogressak.org/focus-on-re-entry

- **Southcentral Foundation**
  4501 Diplomacy Dr., Anchorage, AK 99508, Tel. 800-478-3343
  www.southcentralfoundation.com

- **United Way – Alaska 2-1-1**
  701 W. 8th Ave., Suite 230, Anchorage, AK 99501
  www.alaska211.org

ARIZONA

- **Arizona 2-1-1**
  www.211arizona.org/reentry
- **Arizona Justice Center**
  5534 W. Palamaire Ave., Glendale, AZ 85301,
  Tel. 623-847-2772, www.azjusticecenter.org
- **Arizona Women's Education and Employment (AWEE) – Central Phoenix**
  640 N. 1st Ave., Phoenix, AZ 85003-1515, Tel. 602-223-4333
  www.awee.org
- **Arizona Women's Education and Employment (AWEE) – North Central**
  914 W. Hatcher Rd., Phoenix, AZ 85021-3139,
  Tel. 602-371-1216, www.awee.org
- **Arizona Women's Education and Employment (AWEE) – Prescott**
  805 Whipple St., Suite C, Prescott, AZ 86301-1617,
  Tel. 928-778-3010, www.awee.org
- **Arouet Foundation** (for women)
  4636 E. University Dr., Suite 150, Phoenix, AZ 85034-7498,
  Tel. 480-303-7089, www.arouetfoundation.org
- **AZ Common Ground**
  2406 S. 24th St., Suite E-114, Phoenix, AZ 85034-6822,
  Tel. 602-914-9000, www.azcommonground.org
- **Buckeye Outreach for Social Services (B.O.S.S.) Ex-Offender Services**
  501 E. Mahoney Ave., Buckeye, AZ 85326-3223,
  Tel. 623-386-6365, www.bosssite.org
- **Central Arizona Shelter Services (CASS)**
  230 S. 12th Ave., Phoenix, AZ 85007, Tel. 602-256-6945
  ext. 1100, www.cassaz.org

- **Catholic Charities**
  4747 North 7th Ave., Phoenix, AZ 85013, Tel. 602-285-1999
  www.catholiccharitiesaz.org

- **Center for Life Skills Development, LLC** (sexual offenses)
  2001 W. Orange Grove Rd., Suite 604, Tucson, AZ 85704-1141,
  Tel. 520-229-6220, www.lifeskillstucson.com

- **Behavioral Health Services Court-Ordered Programs (CPES)**
  (sexual offenses)
  4825 N. Sabino Canyon Rd., Tucson, AZ 85750, Tel. 520-884-7954
  www.cpes.com

- **Goodwill Industries of Northern Arizona Fresh Start**
  4308 E. Route 66, Flagstaff, AZ 86004, Tel. 928-526-9188
  www.goodwillna.org

- **Family Service Agency Community Re-Integration Program**
  2400 N. Central Ave., Suite 101, Phoenix, AZ 85004-1315, Tel.
  602-264-9891, http://fsaphoenix.org

- **Father Matters Reentry Program**
  P.O. Box 13575, Tempe, AZ 85284, Tel. 602-774-3298
  www.fathermatters.org

- **Health Care for Re-Entry Veterans Program**
  355 E. Germann Rd., Suite 201, Gilbert, AZ 85297,
  Tel. 480-397-2700, www.benefits.va.gov/persona/veteran-
  incarcerated.asp

- **Hope's Crossing, Inc.** (for women)
  830 N. 1st Ave., Suite 212, Phoenix, AZ 85003-1402,
  Tel. 602-795-8098, www.hopescrossing.org

- **Old Pueblo Community Series**
  4501 E. 5th St., Tucson, AZ 85711, Tel. 530-546-0122
  www.helptucson.org

- **The Potters House Substance Abuse Center**
  4220 North 20th Ave., Suite 100, Phoenix, AZ 85015,
  Tel. 602-254-9701, www.thepottershousesacenter.org

- **SISTER Connection**
  400 E. University Blvd., Tucson, AZ 85705-7851, Tel. 520-271-2226
  www.sister-connection.org

- **SISTER Ministries, Inc.**
  8802 N. 19th Ave., Phoenix, AZ 85021-4205, Tel. 602-684-3458
  www.sisterministries.org

- **Traditions**
  2420 W. Vista Ave., Phoenix, AZ 85021, Tel. 602-535-5958
  www.traditionsrecovery.com

- **VIVRE**
  2719 W. Maryland Ave., Phoenix, AZ 85017, Tel. 602-421-8066
  www.vivrehousing.org

ARKANSAS

- **Arkansas Community Correction**
  Two Union National Plaza, 105 W. Capitol Ave., Little Rock,
  AR 72201, Tel. 501-682-9510, www.dcc.arkansas.gov/reentry

- **Arkansas Department of Correction**
  adc.arkansas.gov/reentry/Pages/default.aspx

- **Central Arkansas Legal Services**
  303 W. Capitol Ave., Little Rock, AR 72201,
  Tel. 501-376-3423, lawyers.justia,com/legalservice/central-
  arkansas-legal-services-9030 w

- **Central Arkansas Reentry (CARE) Coalition**
  Willie E. Horton Center, 3805 W. 12th St., Little Rock, AR 72204
  (monthly meeting place – first Wednesday – and re-entry service
  directory), Tel. 501-444-2273, www.arkansasreentry.com

- **Center for Women in Transition**
  1116 Garland St., Little Rock, AR 72201, Tel. 501-372-5522
  www.cwitlr.org

■ **City of Little Rock Re-Entry Services**
500 W. Markham St., Little Rock, AR 72201, Tel. 501-371-4510
www.littlerock.org/citydepartments/commu nityprograms/
re-entry.aspx

■ **Goodwill Industries of Arkansas**
1110 W. 7th St., Little Rock, AR 72201, Tel. 501-372-5151
www.goodwillar.org/career_training/reentry-services.html

■ **Gyst House**
8101 Frenchmans Lane, Little Rock, AR 72209, Tel. 501-568-1682
www.gysthouseinc.com

■ **Our House, Inc.**
302 E. Roosevelt Rd., Little Rock, AR 72206, Tel. 501-374-7383
ourhouseshelter.org

■ **Pathway to Freedom, Inc.** (for men)
P.O. Box 1010, 22522 Asher Rd., Wrightsville, AR 72183,
Tel. 501-897-0764, www.ptfprison.org

■ **River City Ministry**
P.O. Box 2179, 1021 E. Washington, North Little Rock, AR 72115,
Tel. 501-376-6694, www.rivercityministry.org

CALIFORNIA

■ **211 San Diego**
P.O. Box 420039, San Diego, CA 92142, Tel. 858-300-1211
www.211sandiego.org/Re-entry

■ **Alameda County Joint Reentry One Table**
calreentry.com/alameda-county-reentry-network/

■ **Amity (Amity Foundation)**
2202 S. Figueroa St., Suite 717, Los Angeles, CA 90007, Tel.
213-743-9075, www.amityfdn.org/California/

■ **Anti-Recidivism Coalition**
448 South Hill St., Suite 908, Los Angeles, CA 90013
www.antirecidivism.org

- **Arriba Juntos** (3 satellite offices)
  1850 Mission St., San Francisco, CA 94103, Tel. 415-487-3240
  www.arribajuntos.org

- **California Reentry Hubs**
  California Department of Corrections and Rehabilitation
  www.cdcr.ca.gov/rehabilitation/reentry-hubs.html

- **California EDD**
  California Employment Development Department
  Sacramento, CA 94280, www.edd.ca.gov

- **California Reentry Institute**
  P.O. Box 51, Clayton, CA 94517, Tel. 925-549-1416
  californiareentryinstitute.org

- **California Reentry Program**
  San Quentin State Prison (Tuesday and Thursday evenings)
  ca-reentry.org

- **California (Re-Entry) Resource Guides**
  1730 Franklin St., Suite 300, Oakland, CA 94612-3417
  www.rootandrebound.org/california-resource-guides/

- **State of California Prison Industry Authority (CALPIA)**
  560 E. Natoma St., Folsom, CA 95630
  pia.ca.gov

- **Center Force**
  P.O. Box 415, San Quentin, CA 94964, Tel. 415-456-9980
  centerforce1.org/programs/

- **Christian Help Center**
  2166 Sacramento St., Vallejo, CA 94590, Tel. 707-553-8192
  www.christianhelpcenter.org

- **Community Connection Resource Center**
  4080 Centre St., Suite 202, San Diego, CA 92103,
  Tel. 619-543-8500, www.community-connection.org

- **Community Resources Directory**
  www.cdcr.ca.gov/Community_Partnerships/resource_
  directory.aspx

- **California Reentry Council Network (CRCN)**
  calreentry.com

- **Delancey Street Foundation**
  600 Embarcadero, San Francisco, CA 94107, Tel. 415-512-5104
  www.delanceystreetfoundation.org

- **Fighting Back Partnership**
  505 Santa Clara St., Third Floor, Vallejo, CA 94590,
  Tel. 707-648-5230, fight-back.org

- **The Homeboy Hotline (Root and Rebound Re-Entry Program)**
  1730 Franklin St., Suite 300, Oakland, CA 94612,
  Tel. 510-279-4662 or 415-685-1653, www.homeboyhotline.org

- **Inmate Family Council CSP Solano**
  2100 Peabody Rd., Vacaville, CA 95687
  www.ifc-solano.org/reentry

- **KickStart Reentry Employment Services**
  730 La Guardia St., Room 102, Salinas, CA 93905,
  Tel. 800-870-4750, www.kickstart-employment.com

- **Los Angeles Regional Reentry Partnership (LARP)**
  2202 S. Figueroa, #717, Los Angeles, CA 90007,
  info@lareentry.org, www.lareentry.org

- **Men of Valor Academy**
  6118 International Blvd., Oakland, CA 94621, Tel. 510-567-1308
  www.menofvaloracademy.org

- **Merced Jail Reentry Program**
  702 J St., Los Banos, CA 93635, Tel. 209-385-7576
  www.georeentry.com/locations

- **Metro United Methodist Urban Ministry**
  6154 Mission Gorge, Suite 104, San Diego, CA 92116,
  Tel. 619-285-5556, www.metrosandiego.org/aboutus.html

- **Northern California Service League**
  Center on Juvenile and Criminal Justice, 40 Broadman Pl., San
  Francisco, CA 94103, Tel. 415-621-5661
  www.cjcj.org/about/northern-california-service-league.html

- **Orange County Re-Entry Partnership**
  ocreentry.com

- **Parolee Service Network (PSN)**
  www.dhcs.ca.gov/provgovpart/Pages/Parolee
  ServiceNetwork%20(PSN).aspx

- **Partnership for Re-entry Program (PREP)**
  Sister Mary Sean Hodges, O.P.
  P.O. Box 77850, Los Angeles, CA 90007, Tel. 213-438-4820, ext. 23
  www.la-archdiocese.org/org/orj/Pages/ministries-prep.aspx

- **Oakland Private Industry Council, Inc.**
  1212 Broadway, Suite 100, Oakland, CA 94612, Tel. 510-768-4400
  www.oaklandpic.org

- **Playa Vista Job Opportunities and Business Services (PVJOBS)**
  4112 South Main St., Los Angeles, CA 90037, Tel. 323-432-3955
  www.pvjobs.org

- **Project 180**
  470 E. 3rd St., Suite C, Los Angeles, CA 90013, Tel. 213-620-5712
  www.project180la.com

- **Rubicon Programs, Inc., Reentry Success Center**
  2500 Bissell Ave., Richmond, CA 94804, Tel. 510-235-1516
  www.rubiconprograms.org

- **Santa Clara County Reentry Services**
  151 W. Mission St., San Jose, CA 95110, Tel. 408-535-4280
  www.sccgov.org/sites/reentry/resourcecenter/
  Pages/Resource-Center.aspx

- **Second Chance/STRIVE**
  6145 Imperial Ave., San Diego, CA 92114, Tel. 619-234-8888
  www.secondchanceprogram.org

- **Time for Change Foundation**
  P.O. Box 25040, San Bernardino, CA 92406, Tel. 909-886-2994
  www.timeforchangefoundation.org

- **VOA Bay Area Reentry (Volunteers of America Northern California and Northern Nevada)**
  3434 Marconi Ave., Sacramento, CA 95821, Tel. 916-265-3400
  www.voa-ncnn.org/community-re-entry-bay-area

- **VOA Greater Los Angeles (Volunteers of America Greater Los Angeles, Reintegration of Ex-Offenders J.O.B.S. Program)**
  543 Crocker St., Los Angeles, CA 90013, Tel. 213-228-1911
  www.voala.org

- **Welcome Home Ministries**
  1701 Mission Ave., Oceanside, CA 92054, Tel. 760-439-1136
  www.welcomehomeint.org

- **Weingart Center for the Homeless**
  566 South San Pedro St., Los Angeles, CA 90013,
  Tel. 213-627-5302, weingart.org/index.php

- **The WorkPlace CA**
  Tel. 714-392-4231, www.theworkplaceca.com

COLORADO

- **72 Hour Fund**
  2015 Glenarm Place, Denver, CO 80205, Tel. 303-292-2304
  www.doinghistime.org

- **Center for Spirituality at Work**
  P.O. Box 102168, Denver, CO 80250-2168, Tel. 303-383-1610
  www.cfsaw.org

- **Charity House Ministries**
  3022 Welton St., Denver, CO 80205, Tel. 303-291-0275
  www.charityhouseministries.org

- **Colorado Community Re-Entry**
  888 Garden of the Gods, Colorado Springs, CA,
  Tel. 719-633-1469, Ext. 16332325

  Denver Community Re-Entry Center,
  940 Broadway, Denver, CO, Tel. 303-763-2481

  3642 S. Galapago St., Englewood, CO, Tel. 303-761-2670,
  Ext. 3001

2516 Foresight Circle, Suite 9, Grand Junction, CO, Tel. 970-255-9126, Ext. 4151

800 8th Ave., Jerome Building, Suite 140, Greeley, CO, Tel. 970-356-0839, Ext. 3013

3000 S. College Ave., Suite 100, Fort Collins, CO, Tel. 970-223-2232, Ext. 3015

310 East Abriendo, Suite D, Pueblo, CO, Tel. 719-546-0009, Ext. 3021

8800 Sheridan Blvd., Westminster, CO, Tel. 303-426-6198, Ext. 4143
www.doc.state.co.us/sites/default/files/CRE%20Brochure%20 August%202013.pdf

- **Colorado Correctional Industries**
2862 S. Circle Dr., Colorado Springs, CO 80906, Tel. 719-226-4208, www.coloradoci.com

- **Colorado Criminal Justice Reform Coalition**
5855 Wadsworth Bypass, Unit A, Arvada, CO 80003, Tel. 720-898-5900, www.coloradogives.org/CCJRC/programs, www.communityfirstfoundation.org, and www.ccjrc.org/pdf/ReEntry_Guide-Cover_and_TOC.pdf

- **e-Colorado Reentry Services (Colorado Department of Labor and Employment)**
633 17th St., Suite 700, Denver, CO 80202-3660, Tel. 303-318-8822, e-colorado.coworkforce.com/File.aspx ?ID=24271

- **Community Re-Entry Project**
391 Delaware St., Denver, CO 80204, Tel. 720-865-2330 www.communityreentryproject.org

- **Denver Inner City Parish**
1212 Mariposa St., #1, Denver, CO 80204, Tel. 303-629-0636 dicp.org

- **Empowerment Program** (for women)
1600 York St., Denver, CO 80206, Tel. 303-320-1989 www.empowermentprogram.org

- **FOCUS Reentry**
  4705 Baseline Rd., Boulder, CO 80303, Tel. 720-304-6446
  focusreentry.org

- **Redeemed Ones Jail and Prison Ministry, Inc.**
  P.O. Box 31105, Aurora, CO 80041, Tel. 720-290-0721
  www.redeemedonesoutreachministries.org

- **The Road Called STRATE**
  1532 Galena St., Suite 395, Aurora, CO 80010, Tel. 303-520-5118
  www.theroadcalledstrate.com

- **St. Francis Center Employment Services**
  1630 E. 14th Ave., Denver, CO 80218, Tel. 303-813-0005
  www.turnaboutprogram.org

CONNECTICUT

- **American Job Center (Connecticut Department of Labor)**
  200 Folly Brook Blvd., Wethersfield, CT 06109
  www.ctdol.state.ct.us/ajc/FactSheets.htm

- **Career Resources ReEntry Works**
  350 Fairfield Ave., Bridgeport, CT 06604, Tel. 203-334-5627
  careerresources.org/services/program-director/

- **The Council of Churches of Greater Bridgeport, Inc. (CCGB)**
  1100 Boston Ave., Bldg. 5A, Bridgeport, CT 06610,
  Tel. 203-334-1121, www.ccgb.org/CCGB/?g=LCM-AdultServ

- **City of New Haven Project Fresh Start**
  Office of the Mayor, 165 Church St., New Haven, CT 06510,
  Tel. 203-946-6721
  www.cityofnewhaven.com/mayor/prisonreentry.asp

- **Columbus House, Inc.**
  P.O. Box 7093, New Haven, CT 06519, Tel. 203-401-4400
  www.columbushouse.org

- **Community Partners in Action**
  110 Bartholomew Ave., Suite 3010, Hartford, CT 06106,
  Tel. 860-566-2030, www.cpa-ct.org

- **Community Renewal Team – Re-Entry Recovery Services**
  330 Market Street, Hartford, CT 06120-2901, Tel. 860-761-7900
  www.crtct.org/en.need-help/m-health/re-entry-recovery-services

- **Community Solutions, Inc.**
  340 West Newberry Rd., Bloomfield, CT 06002, Tel. 860-683-7100
  255 Islandbrook Ave., Bridgeport, CT 06606, Tel. 203-696-1323
  41 East Main St., Torrington, CT 06790, Tel. 860-496-0111
  555 Bank St., New London, CT 06320, Tel. 860-443-2168
  www.csi-online.org/adult_services/locations.html

- **Community Re-entry Services (CRS)**
  95 Hamilton St., New Haven, CT 06511, email: contactus@esginh.org
  386 Main St., 2nd Fl., Middletown, CT 06457,
  email: contactus@esginh.org.
  eastersealsgoodwill.org/crs-community-re-entry-services/

- **Connecticut Coalition to End Homelessness/Re-Entry**
  257 Lawrence St., Hartford, CT 06106, Tel. 860-721-7876
  www.cceh.org/data/re-entry

- **Connecticut Works Centers**
  Connecticut Department of Labor, 200 Folly Brook Blvd.,
  Wethersfield, CT 06109, Tel. 860-263-6000
  www.ctdol.state.ct.us

- **Family ReEntry (FRE)**
  9 Mott Ave., Suite 104, Norwalk, CT 06850, Tel. 203-838-0496
  www.familyreentry.org/reentry.jsp

- **New Opportunities**
  232 North Elm St., Waterbury, CT 06702, Tel. 203-575-9799
  www.newoppinc.org

- **STRIDE Program (Quinebaug Valley Community College, Administrative Services Division)**
  742 Upper Maple St., Danielson, CT 06239, Tel. 860-932-4000
  www.qvcc.edu/stride/

- **Wheeler Clinic**
  91 Northwest Dr., Plainville, CT 06062, Tel. 888-793-3500
  www.wheelerclinic.org/community-justice

DELAWARE

- **Center for Relational Living, Second Chances Program**
  100 W. 10th St., Suite 614, Wilmington, DE 19801,
  Tel. 302-428-3850, www.relationalliving.org

- **Delaware Center for Justice, Community Reentry Services**
  100 West 10th St., Suite 905, Wilmington, DE 19801,
  Tel. 302-658-7174, www.dcjustice.org

- **New Beginnings – New Step** (support group)
  Tel. 302-299-5600, http://newbeginnings-nextstep.org

- **One Stop Career Centers (Division of Employment and Training Services, Delaware Department of Labor)**
  4425 North Market St., Wilmington, DE 19802,
  Tel. 302-761-8085, https://joblink.delaware.gov/ada/

- **Professional Staffing Associates, Inc. (PSA) (New Start Reentry Program/Project New Start, Inc)**
  3301 Green St., Claymont, DE 19703, Tel. 302-798-3520
  www.professionalstaffinginc.com

- **The Way Home, Inc.**
  P.O. Box 1103, Georgetown, DE 19947, Tel. 302-856-9870
  thewayhomeprogram.wordpress.com

DISTRICT OF COLUMBIA

- **Catholic Charities – Welcome Home Reentry Program**
  924 G St., NW, Washington, DC 2001, Tel. 202-772-4300,
  ext. 040, www.catholiccharitiesdc.org

- **Court Services and Offender Supervision Agency for the District of Columbia (CSOSA)**
  633 Indiana Ave., NW, Washington, DC 20004-2902,
  Tel. 202-220-5300, www.csosa.gov/reentry/resources.aspx

- **D.C. Central Kitchen**
  425 2nd St., NW, Washington, DC 20001, Tel. 202-234-0707
  www.dccentralkitchen.org

- **Office of Returning Citizen Affairs (ORCA)**
  2100 Martin Luther King Jr. Ave., SE, Suite 301, Washington, DC 20020, Tel. 202-715-7670, Washington, DC 20020
  http://orca.dc.gov

- **The Reentry Network for Returning Citizens**
  4322 Sheriff Road, NE, Washington, DC 20019, Tel. 202-450-1401
  thereentrynetworkdc.wordpress.com

- **VisionQuest**
  www.vq.com/washington-dc

- **Voices for a Second Chance**
  1422 Massachusetts Avenue, SE, Washington, DC 20003,
  Tel. 202-544-2131, www.vscdc.org

FLORIDA

- **2nd Chance Mental Health Center**
  1541 SE Port St. Lucie Blvd., Suite F, Port St. Lucie, FL 34952,
  Tel. 772-335-0166, www.2ndchancemhc.com

- **Bridges of America**
  2001 Mercy Dr., Orlando, FL 32808, Tel. 407-291-1500
  www.bridgesofamerica.com

- **The Center for Women and Men at Deltona Campus**
  1200 W. International Speedway Blvd., Daytona Beach, FL 32114, Tel. 386-506-3000

  Fresh Start Program,
  Deltona and Flagler/Palm Coast Campus, Tel. 386-506-3059
  www.daytonastate.edu/centerforwomenandmen/freshstart.html

- **Community Legal Services of Mid-Florida**
  128 Orange Ave., Suite 300, Daytona Beach, FL 32114,
  Tel. 386-255-6573, www.clsmf.org

- **ConnectCity, Inc.: Northland Life Connections** (women)
  530 Dog Track Rd., Longwood, FL 32750, Tel. 407-949-4007
  www.connectcity.org

- **Dismas Charities, Inc.**
  6860 Edgewater Dr., Orlando, FL 32810, Tel. 407-285-1989
  www.dismas.com

- **Faith Re-Entry Enterprise**
  4851 South Apopka-Vineland Rd., Orlando, FL 32819,
  Tel. 407-876-4991, ext. 298, www.freelifelines.org

- **FDOC Reentry Resources Directory** (major gateway to dozens
  of reentry programs and services, organized and searchable by
  Florida county, city, and zip code)
  www.dc.state.fl.us/resourceDirectory/Search.aspx

- **Florida Institutional Legal Services, Inc.**
  Location directory: floridalawhelp.org/find-legal-help/directory
  www.floridalawhelp.org

- **Gulfstream Goodwill Industries**
  1715 Tiffany Dr. East, West Palm Beach, FL 33407,
  Tel. 561-848-7200, www.gulfstreamgoodwill.com

- **His Healing Hand Ministries and Final Freedom Aftercare**
  Goodwill Job Center, 3911 E. Colonial Dr., Orlando, FL 32803
  Goodwill Job Center, 3200 W. Colonial Dr., Orlando, FL 32808
  www.hishealinghand.com

- **House of Hope**
  29 SE 21st St., Gainesville, FL 32641, Tel. 352-672-5082
  www.houseofhopegnv.org

- **Operation New Hope**
  1830 North Main St., Jacksonville, FL 32206, Tel. 904-354-4673
  operationnewhope.org

- **Operation New Hope: Ready4Work**
  1830 North Main St., Jacksonville, FL 32206, Tel. 904-354-4673
  www.operationnewhope.com/ready4work

- **Pinellas Ex-Offender Re-Entry Coalition**
  6160 Ulmerton Rd., Unit 10, Clearwater, FL 33760,
  Tel. 855-505-7372
  1601 16th Street South, St. Petersburg, FL 33705, Tel. 727-954-3993
  1200 S. Pinellas Ave., Suite 8, Tarpon Springs, FL 34689,
  Tel. 855-505-7372, www.exoffender.org

- **Project 180: Reentry**
  P.O. Box 25684, Sarasota, FL 34277-2684, Tel. 941-677-2281
  www.project180reentry.org

- **Re-Entry Center of Ocala/Time for Freedom, Inc.**
  2006 N.E. 8th Road, Ocala, FL 34470, Tel. 352-351-1280
  www.reentrycenterofocala.com/time-for-freedom.php

- **Re-Entry Portals**
  Hillsborough County Portal, 1201 Orient Rd., Tampa, FL 33619,
  Tel. 813-247-8333

  Jacksonville Re-Entry Center, 1024 Superior St., Jacksonville,
  FL 32254, Tel. 904-301-2406

  Pinellas Safe Harbor, 14840 49th Street North, Clearwater, FL
  33760, Tel. 727-464-8058

  Xtreme Solutions, P.O. Box 5487, Ocala, FL 34478,
  Tel. 352-694-4888, www.dc.state.fl.us/orginfo/reentry/portals.html

- **Remar USA**
  1871 NW 62nd St., Miami, FL 33147, Tel. 305-757-2480
  818 S. Tennessee Ave., Lakeland, FL 33801, Tel. 863-682-1728
  www.remarusa.org

- **Restoration Ministries**
  1732 NW 2nd Ave., Ocala, FL 34478, Tel. 352-369-6364
  Find presence on www.facebook.com

- **Restoration Ministries for Women, Inc.**
  302 Buchanon Ave., Orlando, FL 32809, Tel. 407-438-0943
  www.rmwchanginglives.org

- **Spirit of Life Recovery Center**
  4816 North Orange Blossom Trail, Mount Dora, FL 32757,
  Tel. 352-735-2001, www.solrc.com

- **Tampa Crossroads, Inc.**
  5109 North Nebraska Ave., Tampa, FL 33603, Tel. 813-238-8557
  tampacrossroads.com

- **The Tree of Life Ministries**
  10 N. Hiawassee Rd., Orlando, FL 32835, Tel. 407-704-6923
  www.thetreeoflifeministries.org

- **The Weaver Foundation** (for women)
  5904 Lemos Ct., Orlando, FL 32808, Tel. 407-325-8225
  www.weaverforwomen.com

- **WorkForce Central Florida** (links to 9 state centers)
  Tel. 800-757-4598, careersourcecentralflorida.com

GEORGIA

- **Atlanta Center for Self Sufficiency**
  100 Edgewood Ave., NE, Suite 700, Atlanta, GA 30303,
  Tel. 404-874-8001, www.atlantacss.org

- **Georgia CALLS**
  1705 Enterprise Dr., Suite B, Buford, GA 30518,
  Tel. 678-251-4225, www.gacalls.org

- **Georgia Center for Opportunity** (think tank)
  333 Research Ct., Suite 210, Norcross, GA 30092,
  Tel. 770-242-0001
  georgiaopportunity.org/initiatives/prisoner-reentry/

- **Georgia Correctional and Re-Entry Programs**
  (reports/recommendations)
  www.ustimes.com/SupportiveHousing/2015busterevans.pdf
  gov.georgia.gov/sites/gov.georgia.gov/files/related_files/
  document/GA%20Criminal%20Justice%20Reform%20
  Council%20Report.pdf

- **Georgia Prisoner Reentry Initiative (Department of Community Supervision)**
  Governor's Office of Transition, Support and Reentry
  2 Martin Luther King Jr. Dr., SE, Suite 458, East Tower,
  Atlanta, GA 30334–4909, Tel. 404-656-9770
  des.georgia.gov/georgia-prisoner-reentry-initiative

- **Georgia Reentry Partnership Housing (RPH)**
  Governor's Office of Transition, Support and Reentry
  270 Washington St., Suite 1198, Atlanta, GA 30334,
  Tel. 770-639-8517
  www.dca.state.ga.us/housing/specialneeds/programs/rph.asp

- **Goodwill of North Georgia**
  235 Peachtree St., North Tower, Suite 2300, Atlanta, GA 30303,
  Tel. 404-420-9900, www.ging.org

- **Goodwill Industries of the Coastal Empire, Inc.**
  7220 Sallie Mood Dr., Savannah, GA 31406-3921,
  Tel. 912-354-6611

- **Gwinnett Reentry Intervention Program (GRIP)**
  United Way of Greater Atlanta, Tel. 404-527-3511
  (edanley@unitedwayatlanta.org)
  www.unitedwayatlanta.org/the-challenge/homelessness/grip/

- **Integrity Transformations Community Development Corporation**
  692 Lindsey St., Atlanta, GA 30314, Tel. 404-853-1780
  www.integritycdc.com

- **Post-Release Transitional Program**
  Georgia Department of Corrections, 2 Martin Luther King Jr. Dr.,
  SE, Twin Towers East, Room 756, Atlanta, GA 30334,
  Tel. 404-656-4593, www.dcor.state.ga.us

- **Re-Entry Coalition, Inc.**
  135 West Center St., Carrollton, GA 30117, Tel. 770-834-6093
  www.cfwg.net/re-entry-coalition-inc/

- **The Re-Entry Program, DeKalb Workforce Development**
  774 Jordan Lane, Building #4, Decatur, GA 30033,
  Tel. 404-687-3400, workdev.dekalbcountyga.gov

- **Reentry Project, Inc.**
  reentryproject.org

- **Reentry Handbooks**
  State Board of Pardons and Paroles
  pap.georgia.gov/reentry-handbooks

- **Savannah Impact Program**
  1700 Drayton St., Savannah, GA 31401, Tel. 912-651-4350
  scmpd.org/savannah-impact-program

- **Transitional Housing for Offender Reentry Directory**
  pap.georgia.gov/transitional-housing-offender-reentry

- **United Way Atlanta**
  100 Edgewood Ave., NE, Atlanta, GA 30303, Tel. 404-527-7200
  www.unitedwayatlanta.org/get-help2-1-1/

HAWAII

- **Big Island Substance Abuse Council**
  135 W. Kawaili St., Hilo, HI 96720, Tel. 808-935-1902
  www.bisac.org

- **Community Assistance Center, John Howard Association**
  200 North Vineyard Blvd., Suite 330, Honolulu, HI 96817,
  Tel. 808-537-2917, www.cachawaii.org

- **Going Home Hawaii** (consortium)
  296 Kilauea Ave., Hilo, HI 96720, Tel. 808-935-3050
  goinghomehawaii.org

- **Good News Jail and Prison Ministry Hawaii**
  P.O. Box 31006, Honolulu, HI 96820, Tel. 808-677-6665
  www.goodnewshawaii.org

- **Goodwill Industries of Hawaii, Inc.**
  2610 Kilihau St., Honolulu, HI 96819-2020, Tel. 808-836-0313
  www.higoodwill.org

- **Hawaii Department of Public Safety Reentry Guides**
  dps.hawaii.gov/about/divisions/corrections/about-corrections/

- **Hawaii Friends of Restorative Justice**
  P.O. Box 489, Waialua, HI 96791, Tel. 808-218-3712
  hawaiifriends.org

- **Honolulu County Re-Entry Programs** (portal)
  honolulucounty.hi.networkofcare.org/mh/services/subcategory.
  aspx?tax=ff-1900

- **HOPE Services**
  296 Kilauea Ave., Hilo, HI 96720, Tel. 808-935-3050
  hopeserviceshawaii.org

- **Ka Hale Ho'ala Hou No Na Wahine** (for women)
  T.J. Mahoney & Associates, 524 Kaaahi St., Honolulu, HI 96817,
  Tel. 808-748-4300, www.reawakeningforwomen.org

- **Makana O Ke Akua, Inc. (MOKA)**
  488 Kamokila Blvd., #0SS17, Kapolei, HI 96707, Tel. 808-778-7652
  makanaokeakua.org

- **Network Enterprises, Inc.**
  680 Iwilei Rd., Suite 695, Honolulu, HI 96817, Tel. 808-521-7774
  www.facebook.com/NEIHawaii

- **New Hope Prison Ministry**
  290 Sand Island Access Rd., Honolulu, HI 96819,
  Tel. 808-842-4242, Ext. 417
  www.enewhope.org/ministries/mini.php?id=45

- **Salvation Army Adult Rehabilitation Center**
  322 Sumner St., Honolulu, HI 96817, Tel. 808-522-8400
  www.hawaii.salvationarmy.org/hawaii/arc

- **WorkHawaii Prisoner Reentry Program**
  City and County of Honolulu Department of Community Services, Oahu WorkLinks, 1505 Dillingham Blvd., Suite 110,
  Honolulu, HI 96817, Tel. 808-768-5600
  www.honolulu.gov/dcs/workforce.html

- **WorkNet, Inc.: Restoring Lives, Strengthening Communities**
  The Nimitz Business Center, 1130 N. Nimitz Hwy., Suite B-224,
  Honolulu, HI 96817, Tel. 808-521-7770
  www.worknetinc.org

- **YWCA of Oahu**
  1040 Richards St., Honolulu, HI 96813, Tel. 808-538-7061
  www.ywca.org/site/pp.asp?c=9fLGJSOyHpE&b=279455

IDAHO

- **Easter Seals Goodwill Reentry Center**
  8620 W. Emerald St., Suite 100, Boise, ID 83704,
  Tel. 208-672-2900, www.esgw.org

- **Good Samaritan Rehabilitation**
  901 E. Best Ave., Coeur d'Alene, ID 83814, Tel. 208-664-1453
  www.goodsamrehabilitation.org/facilities.html

- **H&H Treatment Program**
  1005 E. Franklin Rd., Meridian, ID 83642,Tel. 208-855-9301

923 16th Ave., S., Nampa, ID 83651, Tel. 208-461-1884

163 2nd Ave., W., Twin Falls, ID 83301, Tel. 208-733-7600

Burley, ID, Tel. 208-733-7600, http://hhtreatmentidaho.com

- **Idaho 2-1-1 CareLine (United Way)**
  211 Idaho CareLine, P.O. Box 83720, Boise, ID 83720-0026,
  Tel. 2-1-1 or 1-800-926-2588, www.idahocareline.org

- **Idaho Reentry Services**
  1299 N. Orchard St., Suite 110, Boise, ID 83706
  www.idoc.idaho.gov/content/probation_and_
  parole/reentry_services

- **Offender Resources Idaho**
  www.offenderresourcesidaho.org

- **Reentry and Community Transition Guide**
  www.idoc.idaho.gov/content/document/pre_release_manual

- **Roman Catholic Diocese of Boise Prison Ministry**
  1501 S. Federal Way, Suite 400, Boise, ID 83705,
  Tel. 208-342-1311, www.catholicidaho.org/222

- **Wellbriety for Prisons, Inc.** (Tribal communities)
  912 12th Ave., S., Suite 204, Nampa, ID 83686,
  Tel. 208-484-0231, http://wellbrietyforprisons.wordpress.com

ILLINOIS

- **7-70 Re-entry Services, Inc.**
  9146 Lincoln Ave., Brookfield, IL 60513, Tel. 708-680-7075
  ilreentryresources.com

- **Association House of Chicago**
  1116 N. Kedzie Ave., Chicago, IL 60651, Tel. 773-772-7170
  www.associationhouse.org

- **Chicago Heights (GEO) Reentry Services Center**
  1010 Dixie Highway, Lower Level, Chicago Heights, IL 60411,
  Tel. 708-754-6980, www.georeentry.com/locations

- **Chatham (GEO) Reentry Services Center**
  8007 S. Cottage Grove Ave., Suite A, Chicago, IL 60619,
  Tel. 773-846-6260, www.georeentry.com

- **City of Chicago Ex-Offender Re-entry Inititatives**
  Office of the Mayor, 121 N. LaSalle St., Chicago, IL 60602,
  Tel. 312-744-5500, www.cityofchicago.org/city/en/depts/mayor/
  supp_info/ex-offender_re-entryinitiatives.html

- **Decatur (GEO) Reeentry Services Center**
  876 W. Grand Ave., East Side, Decatur, IL 62522,
  Tel. 217-428-5043, www.georeentry.com/locations

- **East St. Louis Reentry Services Center**
  10 Collinsville Ave., Suite 201, East St., Louis, IL 62201-3005,
  Tel. 618-482-5608, www.georeentry.com/locations

- **Illinois Voices for Reform, Inc.**
  P.O. Box 95114, Hoffman Estates, IL 60195, info@ilvoices.com
  ilvoices.com/reentry.html

- **Incarcerated Veterans: Illinois Guidebook**
  www.va.gov/HOMELESS/docs/Reentry/09_il.pdf

- **Inner-City Muslim Action Network (IMAN): Green ReEntry**
  2744 W. 63rd St., Chicago, IL 60629, Tel. 773-434-4626
  www.imancentral.org/project-green-reentry/

- **Lutheran Social Services of Illinois (LSSI)**
  Prisoner and Family Ministry, 1001 E. Touhy Ave., Suite 50,
  Des Plaines, IL 60018, Tel. 847-635-4600, www.lssi.org

- **MPOWR**
  303 N. Main St., Rockford, IL 61101, Tel. 815-997-1660
  www.mpower.com/public-safety

- **OAI, Inc.**
  180 N. Wabash Ave., Suite 750, Chicago, IL 60601,
  Tel. 312-528-3500, oaiinc.org

- **Re-Entry Illinois** (gateway)
  Corporation for Supportive Housing, 205 W. Randolph,
  Chicago, IL, 60606, Tel. 312-332-6690, ext. 21
  www.reentryillinois.net

- **Rockford Reentry Services Center**
  119 N. Church St., Suite 213, Rockford, IL 61101,
  Tel. 815-961-0281, www.georeentry.com/locations

- **Safer Foundation**
  571 West Jackson, Chicago, IL 60661, Tel. 312-922-2200
  www.saferfoundation.org

- **St. Leonard's Ministries**
  2100 W. Warren Blvd., Chicago, IL 60612, Tel. 312-738-1414
  slministries.org

- **Teamwork Englewood**
  815 W. 63rd St., Chicago, IL 60621, Tel. 773-488-6600
  www.teamworkenglewood.org

- **Thresholds** (mental illness)
  4101 N. Ravenswood Ave., Chicago, IL 60613,
  Tel. 773-572-5500, www.thresholds.org

- **Treatment Alternatives for Safe Communities (TASC)**
  700 S. Clinton St., Chicago, IL 60607, Tel. 1-855-827-2444
  www2.tasc.org

- **West Fulton Reentry Services Center**
  2650 West Fulton, Suite 5, Chicago, IL 60612, Tel. 773-638-5702
  www.georeentry.com/locations

INDIANA

- **Aftercare for Indiana Through Mentoring (AIM)**
  4155 Boulevard Place, Indianapolis, IN 46208
  Tel. 318-874-8470, www.aimmentoring.org

- **Bibleway Community Development**
  Bibleway Church of Gods Word, 220 East 49th Ave., Gary,
  IN 46409, Tel. 219-884-8730, www.bwcministries.org

- **Blue Jacket**
  2826 South Calhoun St., Fort Wayne, IN 46807,
  Tel. 260-744-1900, www.bluejacketinc.org

- **Brother's Keeper – A Prison Ministry of Tri-State Men's
  Center, Inc.**
  P.O. Box 6164, Evansville, IN 47719, Tel. 812-453-1747
  www.tristatemenscenter.org

- **Churches Embracing Offenders (CEO)**
  119 N. Morton Ave., #200C, Evansville, IN 47711,
  Tel. 812-422-2226, www.ceoevv.org

- **Community Action of Great Indianapolis**
  3266 N. Meridian St., Indianapolis, IN 46208,
  Tel. 317-396-1800, www.cagi-in.org

- **Community Outreach Network Services, Inc. (CONS)**
  2105 North Meridian St., Suite 102, Indianapolis, IN 46202
  www.consindy.org

- **Dismas House of South Bend**
  521 South Saint Joseph St., South Bend, IN 46601,
  Tel. 574-233-8522, www.dismas.org/about/south-bend

- **The Gilead House**
  406 East Sycamore St., Kokomo, IN 46901, Tel. 765-865-9427
  www.gileadhousekokomo.org

- **Gomer Inc./Women With Opulence**
  P.O. Box 891, Crown Point, IN 46308-0891, Tel. 773-827-1518
  www.gomerinc.com

- **Guidance Ministries**
  216 N. 2nd St., Elkhart, IN 46516, Tel. 574-296-7192
  www.guidanceministries.com

- **Kairos Prison Ministry of Indiana**
  P.O. Box 681515, Indianapolis, IN 46268-1515
  www.kairosofindiana.org

- **Keys to Work Staffing**
  1125 Brookside Ave., Suite 200, Indianapolis, IN 46202,
  Tel. 317-974-1500, www.keystowork.com

- **New Leaf-New Life**
  1010 S. Walnut St., Suite H, Bloomington, IN 47401,
  Tel. 812-355-6842, www.newleafnewlife.org

- **Planted Seed Ministries, Inc.**
  P.O. Box 11454, Merrillville, IN 46411, Tel. 877-300-8839, ext. 101
  www.plantedseed.org

- **Public Advocates in Community Re-Entry (PACE)**
  2855 North Keystone Ave., Suite 170, Indianapolis, IN 46218,
  Tel. 317-612-6800, www.paceindy.org

- **RecycleForce**
  1125 Brookside Ave., Suite D12, Indianapolis, IN 46202,
  Tel. 317-532-1367, www.recycleforce.org

- **SPA Women's Ministry Homes**
  512½ South Main, Elkhart, IN 46516, Tel. 574-333-3150
  www.spaministryhomes.org

- **Through the Gates**
  P.O. Box 6, Linden, IN 47955, Tel. 765-339-7300
  www.throughthegate.org

- **Use What You've Got Prison Ministry**
  3535 Kessler Blvd., North Dr., Suite 122, Indianapolis, IN 46222,
  Tel. 317-924-4124, www.usewhatyouvegotministry.org

- **VOA Indiana**
  Administrative Office: 927 N. Pennsylvania St., Indianapolis, IN
  46204, Tel. 317-686-5800

  Behavioral Health Clinic: 927 N. Pennsylvania St., Suite 1B,
  Indianapolis, IN 46204, Tel. 317- 686-9860

  Veteran Transitional Housing/Male Residential Community
  Correction Programs: 611 North Capitol Ave., Indianapolis, IN
  46204-1205, Tel. 317-686-9841

  Fresh Start Recovery Center: 927 N. Pennsylvania St., Indianapolis, IN 46204, Tel. 317-686-5800, ext. 1040

  STRIVE Indy: 1795 N. Meridian St., Indianapolis, IN 46202,
  Tel. 317-200-3632

  Second Chance Mentor Program: 1795 N. Meridian St.,
  Indianapolis, IN 46202, Tel. 317-200-5808

  Hope Hall: 811 E. Franklin St., Evansville, IN 47711-5623,
  Tel. 812-423-1949

  Homeless Veterans Reintegration Program: 333 E. Washington
  Blvd., Suite F, Fort Wayne, IN 46802, Tel. 260-498-2248
  www.voain.org/corrections

- **The Way of Rockport Indiana**
  317 Main St., Rockport, IN 47635, Tel. 812-649-2480
  718 Center St., Rockport, IN 47635 (men's transition center)
  http://thewayofrockport.org

- **WorkOne Centers** (dozens of centers in 12 regions throughout
  state) (Indiana Development of Workforce Development
  www.in.gov/dwd

- **YWCA of Muncie**
  310 East Charles St., Muncie, IN 46305, Tel. 765-284-3345
  www.muncieywca.org

IOWA

- **Beacon of Life**
  1717 Woodland Ave., Des Moines, IA 50309, Tel. 515-244-4713
  www.beaconoflifedm.org

- **Bridges of Iowa**
  1211 Vine St., Suite 1110, West Des Moines, IA 50265,
  Tel. 515-222-0910, www.bridgesofiowa.org

- **Catholic Charities**
  1229 Mt. Loretta Ave., Dubuque, IA 52003, Tel. 563-588-0558
  www.catholiccharitiesdubuque.org

- **Catholic Charities**
  Sister Mary Lawrence Community Center, 420 Sixth St. SE,
  Suite 200, Cedar Rapids, IA 52401, Tel. 319-364-7121
  www.catholiccharitiesdubuque.org

- **Catholic Charities**
  Kimball Ridge Center Building, 2101 Kimball Ave., Suite 138,
  Waterloo, IA 50702, Tel. 319-272-2080
  www.catholiccharitiesdubuque.org

- **Central Iowa Works**
  1111 9th St., Suite 260, Des Moines, IA 50314,
  Tel. 515-243-2130, centraliowaworks.org

- **Clare Guest House**
  1918 Douglas St., Sioux City, IA 51104, Tel. 712-255-1916
  www.clareguesthouse.org

- **Creative Visions Ex-Offender & Family Reunification Program**
  1343 13th St., Des Moines, IA 50314, Tel. 515-244-4003, ext. 16, http://creativevisionsia.org

- **Eyerly Ball Jail Division Program**
  945 19th St., Des Moines, IA 50314
  http://eyerlyball.org

- **Iowa Workforce Development**
  1000 East Grand Ave., Des Moines, IA 50319,
  Tel. 515-281-4748, www.iowaworkforce.org

- **Reentry AfterCare**
  P.O. Box 562, Altoona, IA 50009, Tel. 515-230-8815
  www.reentryaftercare.org

- **Reentry Reintegration Ministry of "The Inmates' Congregation"**
  The Church of the Damascus Road, 239 N. 11th St., Fort Dodge, IA 50501, Tel. 515-955-3579
  www.frontiernet.net/~codr/index.html

- **Safer Foundation - Iowa**
  1411 Brady St., Davenport, IA 52803, Tel. 563-322-7002
  www.saferfoundation.org

KANSAS

- **Brothers in Blue Re-Entry, Inc.**
  301 E. Kansas Ave., P.O. Box 2, Lansing, KS 66043,
  Tel. 913-727-3235
  brothersinbluereentry.org

- **Douglas County Sheriff's Office Reentry Program**
  Douglas County Correctional Facility, 3601 E. 25th St., Lawrence, KS 66046, Tel. 785-830-1000, www.dgso.org

- **Gracious Promise Foundation: Adult Re-Entry Mentoring**
  P.O. Box 642, Shawnee Mission, KS 66202, Tel. 913-342-1707
  www.graciouspromise.org

- **Kansas Offender Risk Reduction and Reentry (KOR3P)**
  714 SW Jackson, Suite 300, Topeka, KS 66603,
  Tel. 785-296-3317, www.doc.ks.gov/reentry

- **Kansas Legal Services**
  712 South Kansas Ave., Suite 200, Topeka, KS 66603,
  Tel. 785-233-2068, www.kansaslegalservices.org

- **One-Stop Career Center System**
  Community and Field Services Kansas DOC, 900 SW Jackson
  St., 4th Fl., Topeka, KS 66612, Tel. 785-296-3317
  www.dc.state.ks.us

- **Oxford House Kansas Re-Entry Program**
  (multiple locations)
  www.oxfordhousekansas.org/HOUSE-LISTING.html

- **Second Chance Risk Reduction Center**
  2700 East 18th St., Suite 150, Kansas City, MO 64127,
  Tel. 816-231-0450, www.secondchancekc.org

- **Sedgwick County Juvenile and Adult Field Services Divisions**
  Sedgwick County Department of Corrections,
  700 S. Hydraulic St., Wichita, KS 67211, Tel. 316-660-9750
  www.sedgwickcounty.org/corrections/

- **Shawnee County Reentry Program**
  Shawnee County Department of Corrections, 501 SE Ave.,
  Topeka, KS 66607, Tel. 785-291-5000
  www.snco.us/doc/programs_work_release.asp

- **Substance Abuse Center of Kansas's Re-Entry Program**
  731 North Water, Suite 2, Wichita, KS 67203, Tel. 316-267-3825
  www.saack.org/re-entry-program.php

KENTUCKY

- **Central Kentucky Career Center Re-Entry**
  Bluegrass Area Development District, 699 Perimeter Dr.,
  Lexington, KY 40517, Tel. 859-269-8021, www.bgadd.org

- **Family and Loved Ones**
  www.kentuckyreentry.org/family-loved-ones/

- **Goodwill Industries of Kentucky**
  909 E. Broadway, Louisville, KY 40204, Tel. 502-584-5221,
  www.goodwillky.org/programs/reentry-by-design/

- **The Healing Place**
  1020 W. Market St., Louisville, KY 40202, Tel. 502-585-4848
  www.thehealingplace.org

- **Jail and Prison Ministry at the Catholic Charities
  Diocese of Covington**
  3629 Church St., Covington, KY 41015, Tel. 859-581-8975, ext.
  117, www.covingtoncharities.org

- **Kentuckiana Works Reentry By Design**
  410 West Chestnut St., Suite 200, Louisville, KY 40202,
  Tel. 502-574-2500, www.kentuckianaworks.org

- **Kentucky Reentry Council** (10 regional locations)
  www.kentuckyreentry.org/links-resources

- **Louisville Metro Re-entry Task Force**
  St. Stephen Family Life Center, 1508 West Kentucky St.,
  Louisville, KY 40210, www.louisvillereentry.org

- **Mental Health America of Northern Kentucky and
  Southwest Ohio Offender Re-entry**
  912 Scott St., Covington, KY 41011, Tel. 859-431-1077
  www.mhankyswoh.org

- **Mountain Comprehensive Care Center:
  Offender Reentry Program**
  104 S. Front Ave., Prestonsburg, KY 41653, Tel. 806-886-8572
  www.mtcomp.org

- **New Beginnings Transition Homes**
  P.O. Box 1736, Murray, KY 42071, Tel. 270-753-0156
  www.nbth.org

- **Office of Employment and Training**
  http://kentuckycareercenter.ky.gov/Office/Locations.aspx

- **Prodigal Ministries, Inc.**
  P.O. Box 1484, Crestwood, KY 40014, Tel. 502-749-9194
  www.prodigalky.org

- **Seven Counties Services Inc.**
  101 West Muhammad Ali Blvd., Louisville, KY 40202
  www.sevencounties.org

LOUISIANA

- **Capital Area ReEntry**
  4829 Winbourne Ave., Baton Rouge, LA 70805,
  Tel. 225-771-8715
  www.caparadmin.org/louisiana-resources.html

- **Catholic Charities Archdiocese of New Orleans**
  1000 Howard Ave., Suite 1200, New Orleans, LA 70113, Tel.
  504-523-3755, ext. 2223, www.ccano.org

- **Enhanced Job Skills Program Parish Correctional Center**
  Lafayette Parish Correctional Center, P.O. Box 3508, Lafayette,
  LA 70502, Tel. 337-236-5494, www.lafayettesheriff.com

- **Food Bank of Northeast Louisiana**
  4600 Central Ave., Monroe, LA 71203, Tel. 318-322-3567
  www.fbnela.org/1822.html

- **Goodwill Industries Acadiana, Inc.**
  2435 W. Congress St., Lafayette, LA 70506,
  Tel. 337-261-5811, www.lagoodwill.com

- **Baton Rouge Goodwill Industries Workforce Training Center**
  647 Main St., Baton Rouge, LA 70801, Tel. 225-308-0220
  www.goodwillno.org

- **Job Centers**
  www.ldol.state.la.us

- **Louisiana Center for Children's Rights**
  1100-B Milton St., New Orleans, LA 70122, Tel. 504-658-6860
  www.laccr.org

- **Louisiana Department of Public Safety** (9 regional locations)
  www.doc.la.gov/pages/reentry-initiatives/community-resource-map/

- **Louisiana Re-Entry Initiative (LRI)**
  1515 Poydras St., Suite 1200, New Orleans, LA 70112,
  Tel. 504-301-9800, http://lphi.org

- **North Louisiana Goodwill Industries Rehabilitation Center, inc.**
  800 West 70th St., Shreveport, LA 71106, Tel. 318-869-2575,
  ext. 2223, www.goodwillnla.org

- **Re-Entry Benefiting Families**
  Refined by Fire Ministries, Inc., 5635 Main St., Suite A,
  Zachary, LA 70791, Tel. 225-963-2074, www.rbf.la/

- **Re-Entry Solutions**
  1617 Branch St., Suite 500, Alexandria, LA 71301,
  Tel. 318-443-0189, re-entrysolutions4la.com

- **Total Community Action. Inc.**
  1420 South Jefferson Davis Pkwy., New Orleans, LA 70125,
  Tel. 504-827-0334, www.tca-nola.org

- **Volunteers of America – Greater New Orleans Residential Reentry Program**
  4152 Canal St., New Orleans, LA 70119, Tel. 504-482-2130
  www.voagno.org

MAINE

- **Community Concepts, Inc.**
  17 Market Square, South Paris, ME 04281, Tel. 800-866-5588
  www.community-concepts.org

- **Cumberland County Community Corrections Work Release Program**
  Cumberland County Jail, 50 County Way, Portland, ME 04102,
  Tel. 207-774-5939, ext. 2131
  www.cumberlandso.org/31/Corrections-Division

- **Esther Residence**
  27 Thornton Ave., Saco, ME 04072, Tel. 207-283-0323
  http://goodshepherdparish.us/esther-residence

- **Kennebec Regional Re-Entry Program (KeRRP)**
  Maine Pretail Services-Kennebec County, 9 Green St., Suite 3-A,
  Augusta, ME 04330, Tel. 207-623-9677
  www.mainepretrail.org/locations.asp
  http://mainepretrial.org/resources/kerrp-handbook.pdf (handbook)

- **My Sister's Keeper**
  Cape Elizabeth United Methodist Church, 280 Ocean House Rd.,
  Cape Elizabeth, ME 04107, Tel. 207-799-8396, www.ceumc.org

- **Northern Maine Regional Reentry Center**
  Volunteers of America Northern New England, 14 Maine St.,
  Suite 301, Brunswick, ME 04011, Tel. 207-373-1140
  www.voanne.org

- **One-Stop Career Centers**
  Bureau of Employment Services, Maine Department of Labor,
  55 State House Station, Augusta, ME 04333, Tel. 207-624-6390
  www.mainecareercenter.com

- **Portland Recovery Community Center (PRCC)**
  Re-Entry Group
  468 Forest Ave., Portland, ME 04101, Tel. 207-553-2575
  www.portlandrecovery.org

- **Restorative Justice Institute of Maine**
  14 Maine St., Box 24, Brunswick, ME 04011,
  Tel. 207-619-3630, http://rjimaine.org

- **Southern Maine Re-entry Center** (for women)
  2 Layman Way, Alfred, ME 04002, Tel. 207-490-5205
  www.maine.gov/corrections/facilities/wrc/index.htm

- **Success With the Court's Help (SWITCH)**
  U.S. Probation and Pretrial Services - District of Maine,
  400 Congress St., 5th Fl., Portland, ME 04101, Tel. 207-780-3358,
  ext. 3621, www.mep.uscourts.gov/switch-success-court's-help

- **Volunteers for Hancock Jail Residents**
  272 Turkey Farm Rd., Blue Hill, ME 04614, Tel. 207-374-3608
  www.jailvolunteers.org

MARYLAND

- **Baltimore City Employment Development**
  Mayor's Office of Employment Development, Tel. 410-396-1910
  or 410-396-3009, www.oedworks.com/whatsnew

- **Catholic Charities Welcome Home Program**
  Reentry Coordinator, Montgomery County Pre-Release Center,
  11651 Nebel St., Rockville MD 20852, Tel. 240-773-4211

  Reentry Coordinator, Prince George's County Department of
  Corrections, 13400 Dille Dr., Upper Marlboro, MD 20773,
  Tel. 301-952-7119

  Correctional Support Specialist, 22-A Irongate Dr., Waldorf, MD
  20602, Tel. 301-367-0599
  www.catholiccharitiesdc.org/WelcomeHome

- **DHCDC Reentry**
  Druid Heights Community Development Corporation,
  2140 McCulloh St., Baltimore, MD 21217, Tel. 410-523-1350,
  ext. 230, druidheights.com

- **F.A.C.E. - Freedom Advocates Celebrating Ex-Offenders**
  1564 Sheffield Rd., Baltimore, MD 21218, Tel. 410-522-3223
  http://facebaltimore.org

- **Helping Up Mission**
  1029 East Baltimore St., Baltimore, MD 21202, Tel. 410-675-7500
  www.helpingupmission.org

- **Jericho Reentry Program**
  901 N. Milton Ave., Baltimore, MD 21213, Tel. 410-522-3293
  www.ecsm.org

- **Job Opportunities Taskforce**
  217 East Redwood St., Suite 1500, Baltimore, MD 21202, Tel.
  410-234-8046, www.jotf.org

- **Maryland Department of Public Safety and Correctional Services, The Reentry Program**
  Patuxent Institution, 7555 Waterloo Rd., Jessup, MD 20794,
  Tel. 410-799-3400
  www.dpscs.state.md.us/rehabservs/patx/reentry.shtml

- **Maryland Job Service** (25 one-stop centers throughout state)
  Division of Employment and Training, Maryland Department of
  Labor, Licensing, and Regulation, 110 North Eutaw Street, Baltimore, MD 21201, Tel. 866-247-6034
  www.dllr.state.md.us/ce

- **The Men's Center Re-Entry Program**
  2222 Jefferson St., Baltimore, MD 21205, Tel. 410-614-5353
  www.menandfamiliescenter.org

- **Montgomery County Reentry Resources**
  Montgomery County Correctional Facility, 22880 Whelan Lane,
  Boyds, MD 20841, Tel. 240-773-9982
  www.montgomerycountymd.gov/cor/reentry/reentry_services.html

- **National Women's Prison Project, Inc.**
  1701 Madison Ave., Suite #505, Baltimore, MD 21217,
  Tel. 410-233-3385, www.nwpp-inc.com

- **Opening Doors**
  Women Accepting Responsibility, Inc., 2200 Garrison Blvd.,
  2nd Fl., Baltimore, MD 21216, Tel. 410-878-0357
  www.womenacceptingresponsibility.org

- **Power Inside: Re-Entry and Aftercare**
  P.O. Box 4796, Baltimore, MD 21211, Tel. 410-889-8333
  http://powerinside.org

- **Reducing Barriers to Housing and Employment Imposed by Criminal Records**
  Homeless Persons Representation Project, Inc.,
  201 N. Charles St., Suite 1104, Baltimore, MD 21201,
  Tel. 410-685-6589, www.hprplaw.org

- **The Re-entry Center @ Northwest One-Stop Career Center**
  Mondawmin Mall, 2401 Liberty Heights Ave., Suite 302,
  Baltimore, MD 21215,Tel. 410-396-7873
  www.oedworks.com/whatsnew

- **Supporting Ex-Offenders in Employment, Training, and Transitional Services (SEETTS)**
  Goodwill Industries of the Chesapeake, Inc., 222 East Redwood
  St., Baltimore, MD 21201, Tel. 410-837-1800
  www.goodwillches.org

- **St. Vincent de Paul of Baltimore**
  2305 N. Charles St., Suite 300, Baltimore, MD 21218,
  Tel. 410-662-0500, www.vincentbaltimore.org

- **VOA Chesapeake's Residential Reentry Center**
  5000 East Monument St., Baltimore, MD 21205, Tel. 410-276-5880
  www.voachesapeake.org/rrc

- **Witness House of Hope**
  P.O. Box 2797, Salisbury, MD 21802, Tel. 410-749-1343
  www.witnessinternational.org

MASSACHUSETTS

- **After Incarceration Support Systems (AISS)**
  WW Johnson Life Center, 736 State St., Springfield, MA 01160,
  Tel. 413-781-2050, ext. 8328, www.hcsdmass.org/aiss.htm

- **The Bridge House Program - New England Aftercare Ministries**
  18 Summit St., Suite 20, Framingham, MA 01702,
  Tel. 508-872-6194, ext. 114
  http://newenglandaftercareministries.wordpress.com

- **Boston Worker's Alliance**
  411 Blue Hill Ave., Dorchester, MA 02121, Tel. 617-606-3580
  www.bostonworkersalliance.org

- **Bridge to Hope**
  P.O. Box 758, 320 Main St., Hyannis, MA 02601,
  Tel. 508-775-5073, www.bridgetohopecapecod.org

- **Catholic Charities South**
  169 Court St., Brockton, MA 02302, Tel. 508-587-0815
  www.ccab.org/?q=location-south-boston
- **Coming Home Directory** (annual directory to hundreds of re-entry organizations and services in the Greater Boston area)
  www.cominghomedirectory.org
- **Dismas House**
  P.O. Box 30125, Worcester, MA 01603, Tel. 508-882-0000
  dismashouse.org/programs/dismashouse
- **Ex-Prisoners and Prisoners Organizing for Community Advancement**
  EPOCA, 4 King St., Worcester, MA 01610, Tel. 774-420-2722
  www.exprisoners.org
- **Franklin Hampshire Career Center – Ex-Offender Services**
  One Arch Place, Greenfield, MA 01301, Tel. 413-774-4361
  (Greenfield) or 413-586-6506 (Northampton)
  http://fhcc-onestop.com/jobseekers/ex-offender-services
- **Friends of Boston's Homeless**
  12 Wise St., Boston, MA 02130, Tel. 617-942-8671
  www.fobh.org
- **Friends of Prisoners/Guindon House**
  84 Bearses Way, Hyannis, MA 02601, Tel. 508-790-8004
  www.friendsofprisoners.org
- **Moving Ahead Program - St. Francis House**
  P.O. Box 120499, Boston, MA 02112, Tel. 617-542-4211
  www.stfrancishouse.org
- **Span, Inc.**
  105 Chauncy St., 6th Fl., Boston, MA 02111, Tel. 617-423-0750
  http://spaninc.org
- **Straight Ahead Ministries**
  791 Main St., Worcester, MA 01610, Tel. 508-753-8700

  1 Munroe St., 3rd Floor, Lynn, MA 01901, Tel. 781-592-6070
  www.straightahead.org

- **STRIVE Boston Employment Service Program for Ex-Offenders**
  Boston Strive, 651 Washington St., Boston, MA 02124, Tel. 617-825-1800, www.bostonstrive.org/index.htm

MICHIGAN

- **Advocacy, Reentry, Resources, Outreach (A.R.R.O.) – North West Initiative**
  510 W. Ottawa St., 2nd Floor, Lansing, MI 48933, Tel. 517-999-2894, http://nwlansing.org/programs/a-r-r-o/

- **Community Re-Entry Services, Detroit Central City Community Mental Health**
  10 Peterboro St., Detroit, MI 48201, Tel. 313-831-3160 www.dcccmh.org/page_id-319

- **CORRECTIONS - Prisoner Re-entry**
  Michigan Department of Corrections, P.O. Box 30003, Lansing MI 48909, www.michigan.gov/corrections

- **Detroit Recovery (DRP) - Doing It Together**
  1121 E. McNichols Rd., Detroit, MI 48203, Tel. 313-365-3100 http://recovery4detroit.com

- **Gateway to Glory Ministries, Inc.**
  14000 Metropolitan Pkwy., P.O. Box 863, Sterling Heights, MI 48312, Tel. 586-833-3392, www.thegatewaytoglory.org

- **Goodwill Industries of Greater Detroit**
  Work Readiness Program, 3111 Grand River Ave., Detroit, MI 48208, Tel. 313-964-3900, ext. 406 www.goodwilldetroit.org

- **Goodwill of West Michigan, Career Center** (Ex-offenders in Transition Program and Prisoner Reentry Program)
  271 East Apple Ave., Muskegon, MI 49442, Tel. 231-722-7871 www.goodwillwm.org/program-a-services/

- **Jewish Vocational Services (JVS)**
  29699 Southfield Rd., Southfield, MI 48076-2063 Tel. 248-559-5000, www.jvsdet.org

- **Michigan's Prisoner Re-Entry Initiative (MCCD)**
  Michigan Council on Crime and Delinquency,
  1000 West St. Joseph, Suite 400, Lansing, MI 48915,
  Tel. 517-482-4161, www.miccd.org/index.php

- **Michigan Works!** (Operates 120 One-Stop Centers throughout state's 25 regions)
  2500 Kerry St., Suite 210, Lansing, MI 48912, Tel. 517-371-1100
  www.michiganworks.org

- **Oak County LESP (Life Employment and Skills Program for Felons)**
  1201 N. Telegraph Rd., Bldg. 10E, Pontiac, MI 48341,
  Tel. 248-858-5093, www.oakgov.com/commcorr/Pages/program_service/lesp_felony.aspx

- **Oakland County Re-Entry Program - Crossroads for Youth**
  930 East Drahner, P.O. Box 9, Oxford, MI 48371, Tel. 248-628-2561
  www.crossroadsforyouth.org/index.html

- **Returning Citizens - Detroit Employment Solutions Corporation**
  440 E. Congress St., Detroit, MI 48226, Tel. 313-876-0674
  www.descmiworks.com/jobseekers/intensive-programs/returning-citizens/

- **Transition of Prisoners, Inc. (TOP)**
  P.O. Box 02938, Detroit, MI 48244, Tel. 313-875-3883

- **Urban League of Detroit**
  208 Mack Ave., Detroit, MI 48201, Tel. 313-832-4600
  www.detroiturbanleague.org

- **United Way of Southeastern Michigan** (300+ program sites in Greater Detroit area)
  600 Woodward Ave., Suite 300, Detroit, MI 48226,
  Tel. 313-226-9200, www.liveunitedsem.org

MINNESOTA

- **180 Degrees - Sonic Program**
  236 Clifton Ave. South, Minneapolis, MN 55403,
  Tel. 612-813-5000, www.180degrees.org/adult-accountability.php

- **AccessAbility, Inc.**
  360 Hoover St., NE, Minneapolis, MN 55413, Tel. 612-331-5958
  www.accessability.org

- **Alpha Human Services** (sex offenders)
  2712 Fremont Ave., S., Minneapolis, MN 55408, Tel. 612-872-8218
  http://alphaservices.org

- **Amicus – The RECONNECT Program**
  3041 4th Ave. S., Minneapolis, MN 55408, Tel. 612-877-4250
  www.amicususa.org

- **Better Futures Minnesota**
  2620 Minnehaha Ave. S., Minneapolis, MN 55406,
  Tel. 612-455-6133, http://betterfuturesenterprises.com

- **Breaking Free**
  P.O. Box 4366, St. Paul, MN 55104, Tel. 651-645-6557
  www.breakingfree.net

- **Central Minnesota Re-Entry Project (CMNRP)**
  1121 Lincoln Ave., Sauk Rapids, MN 56379, Tel. 320-656-9004
  http://cmnrp.org

- **Damascus Way Re-Entry Center**
  1449 4th Ave., SE, Rochester, MN 55904, Tel. 507-292-1700
  5730 Olson Memorial Highway, Golden Valley, MN 55422,
  Tel. 763-545-6558

- **Freedom Works**
  3559 Penn Ave. N., Minneapolis, MN 55412, Tel. 612-522-9007
  myfreedomworks.com

- **Goodwill/Easter Seals Reentry Services – Prisoner ReEntry Initiative (PRI)**
  Minnesota St. Paul Campus, 553 Fairview Ave., N., St. Paul,
  MN 55104, Tel. 651-379-5867, www.goodwilleasterseals.org/
  site/PageServer?pagename=serv_other_reentry

- **The Minnesota Second Chance Coalition (MSCC)**
  (Coalition of 50 organizations focused on criminal justice.)
  www.mnsecondchancecoalition.org

- **Momentum**
  1179 15th Ave., SE, Minneapolis, MN 55414, Tel. 612-555-1234
  www.momentummn.com

- **Portland House**
  514 11th Ave., SE, Minneapolis, MN 55414, Tel. 612 -331-1087
  www.lssmn.org/portlandhouse/

- **Re-Armor Homes**
  515 Farrington St., St. Paul, MN 55103, Tel. 651-888-0912
  rearmorhomes.com

- **Reentry Ashland – ES EDEN**
  532 Ashland Ave., St. Paul, MN 55102, Tel. 651-292-1466
  www.rseden.org

- **Reentry Metro – ES EDEN**
  444 West Lynnhurst Ave., St. Paul, MN 55104, Tel. 651-644-1951
  www.rseden.org

- **Reentry West – RS EDEN**
  855 West 7th St., St. Paul, MN 55102, Tel. 651-227-6291
  www.rseden.org

- **Second Chance Ranch Group Home**
  25167 Highway 248, Minnesota City, MN 55959, Tel. 507-410-2080
  www.secondchanceranch.info

- **St. Stephen's Ex-Offenders Housing Services**
  2211 Clinton Ave. South, Minneapolis, MN 55404,
  Tel. 612-874-0311, www.endhomelessness.org

- **Step Ahead: Career Planning for People With Criminal Convictions** (online workbook)
  ReEntry Services Unit, Minnesota Department of Corrections,
  Tel. 651-361-7200, www.iseek.org/exoffenders/index.html

- **Winona County CARE Program**
  Winona County Criminal Justice Coordinating Council (CJCC),
  202 W. 3rd St., Winona, MN 55987, Tel. 507-474-2687
  www.co.winona.mn.us/page/3080

MISSISSIPPI

- **Buried Treasures Home** (for women)
  P.O. Box 720672, Byram, MS 39272, Tel. 601-371-9835
  www.buriedtreasureshome.com

- **Daylight Ministries Home – Our Program** (for women)
  P.O. Box 325, Tougaloo, MS 39174, Tel. 601-454-3843
  www.daylightministrieshome.org

- **The Dismas Difference: Education, Employment, and Support**
  Dismas Charities, Inc., 5209 Hwy. 42 Bypass, Hattiesburg, MS 39401, Tel. 601-582-0843, www.dismascharities.org

- **Goodwill Industries of Mississippi, Inc.**
  104 E. State St., Ridgeland, MS 39157, Tel. 601-853-8110
  www.goodwillsms.org

- **Goodwill Industries of South Mississippi, Inc.**
  2411 31st St., Gulfport, SM 39501, Tel. 228-863-2323
  www.goodwillsms.org

- **Metro Counseling Center, Inc.**
  P.O. Box 706, Jackson, MS 39205, Tel. 601-353-0502
  www.metrocounselingcenter.org

- **Mississippi Department of Rehabilitative Services**
  1281 Highway 51, Madison, MS 39110, Tel. 800-443-1000
  www.mdrs.ms.gov/Pages/default.aspx

- **Mississippi Reentry Guide** (essential guide to county programs/services)
  Foundation for the Mid South (www.fndmidsouth.org)
  www.msreentryguide.com

- **New Way Mississippi Inc.**
  1896 N. Frontage Rd., Clinton, MS 39056, Tel. 601-924-3807
  http://newwayms.webs.com

- **Sue's Home for Women and Children**
  Community Care Network, 7400 Fountainbleau Rd., Ocean Springs, MS 39564, Tel. 228-215-2662, www.ccnms.org

MISSOURI

- **Catholic Charities Kansas City - St. Joseph**
  850 Main St., Kansas City, MO 64105, Tel. 816-221-4377

  902 Edmond St., St. Joseph, MO 64501, Tel. 816-232-2885

  123 East Gay St., Warrensburg, MO 64093, Tel. 816-344-3699
  www.catholiccharities-kcsj.org

- **Center for Women in Transition, Inc.**
  7525 South Broadway, St. Louis, MO 63111, Tel. 314-771-5207
  www.cwitstl.org

- **Corizone: Missouri Reentry**
  missouri.corizonreentry.com

- **Criminal Justice Ministry – Saint Louis**
  P.O. Box 15160, St. Louis, MO 63110, Tel. 314-652-8062
  www.cjmstlouis.org

- **Criminal Justice Ministry (CJM) of St. Vincent de Paul**
  Society of St. Vincent de Paul of St. Louis, 1310 Papin St.,
  Suite 104, St. Louis, MO 63105-3132, Tel. 314-881-6000
  www.svdpstlouis.org

- **Employment Connection of St. Louis**
  2838 Market St., St. Louis, MO 63103, Tel. 314-333-5627
  www.employmentstl.org

- **Fresh Start**
  Powerhouse Community Development Corporation,
  1445 West College St., Marshall, MO 65340, Tel. 660-886-8860
  www.pwrhousecdc.org

- **Job Point Reentry Services**
  2116 Nelwood Dr., Suite 200, Columbia, MO 65202,
  Tel. 573-474-8560, www.jobpointmo.org

- **Love INC of Columbia, MO**
  1516 Business Loop 70 West, Columbia, MO 65202,
  Tel. 573-256-7662, www.columbialoveinc.org/reentry

- **Mission Gate Ministry After Care Program**
  P.O. Box 6644, Chesterfield, MO 63006, Tel. 636-391-8560
  www.missiongateministry.org

- **Missouri Department of Corrections: Reentry**
  2729 Plaza Dr., P.O. Box 236, Jefferson City, MO 65102,
  Tel. 573-751-2389, doc.mo.gov/OD/DO/MRP.php

- **Next Steps Home**
  1120 S. 6th St., Suite 120, St. Louis, MO 63104, Tel. 314-772-7720
  http://humanitri.org

- **North County Community Development Corporation (NCCD)**
  6614 West Florissant Ave., St. Louis, MO 63136, Tel. 314-867-9160
  www.northcountycdc.org

- **Power House Community Development Corporation**
  263 W. Morgan, Marshall, MO 65340, Tel. 660-886-8860
  www.pwrhousecdc.org

- **Project COPE**
  3529 Marcus Ave., St. Louis, MO 53115, Tel. 314-389-4804
  www.projectcope.org

- **Project REACH**
  St. Patrick Center, 800 N. Tucker Blvd., St. Louis, MO 63101,
  Tel. 314-802-0700, www.stpatrickcenter.org

- **STAR (St. Louis Alliance for Reentry)**
  539 North Grand Blvd., 6th Fl., St. Louis, MO 63103,
  Tel. 314-534-0022, www.stlreentry.org

- **Start Here: St. Louis Area Re-Entry Resource Directory**
  (free online and paper)
  Inside Dharma, P.O. Box 220721, St. Louis, MO 63122,
  Tel. 314-726-2982, www.startherestl.org

- **STL Alliance for Reentry** (38 organizations)
  www.stlreentry.org

MONTANA

- **Family Matters Program**
  The Center for Children and Families, 3021 3rd Ave., N., Billings,
  MT 59101, Tel. 406-294-5090, www.forfamilies.org

- **Gallatin County Work Release & Re-entry Program**
  675 S. 16th Ave., Bozeman, MT 59715, Tel. 406-994-0300
  www.cccscorp.com/programs/gcrp/

- **Great Falls Weed & Seed Transition Coalition**
  NeighborWorks Great Falls, 509 1st Ave., S., Great Falls, MT
  59401, Tel. 406-761-5861, www.gfweedandseed.org

- **Helena's Prerelease Center**
  Boyd Andrew Community Services, 805 Colleen St., Helena, MT
  59601. Tel. 406-443-2343, www.boydandrew.com/services/
  helena-pre-release-center/

- **Hope for Men**
  Great Falls Rescue Mission, 311 2nd Ave., S., Great Falls, MT
  59403, Tel. 406-761-2653, http://gfrm.org/

- **Montana Correctional Enterprises**
  Montana Department of Corrections, 350 Conley Lake Rd.,
  Deer Lodge, MT 59722, Tel. 406-846-1320
  https://cor.mt.gov/Adult/MCE

- **Montana Reentry Initiative**
  Montana Department of Corrections, 5 South Last Chance Gulch,
  Helena, MT 59620-1301, Tel. 406-444-0340, cor.mt.gov/reentry

- **Montana Women's Prison and Passages** (Pre-Release)
  701 S. 27th St., Billings, MT 59101, Tel. 406-247-5160
  montana.networkofcare.org

- **Opening Doors**
  P.O. Box 1868, Great Falls, MT 59404, Tel. 406-205-4657
  http://openingdoorsmt.org

- **The Parenting Place: Support for Families**
  Touched by Incarceration
  1644 S. 8th St., W., Missoula, MT 59801, Tel. 406-728-5437
  www.parentingplace.net

- **Programs for the Next Step (Rescue, Recover, Restore)**
  Montana Rescue Mission, 2902 Minnesota Ave., Billings, MT
  59101, Tel. 406-259-3800, http://montanarescuemission.org

- **Teach, Encourage, Assist, and Model (T.E.A.M.) Mentoring**
  P.O. Box 30642, Billings, MT 59107, Tel. 406-656-8326
  http://teammentoring.org

- **Veterans Re-Entry Program**
  3678 Veterans Dr., Ft. Harrison, MT 56636, Tel. 406-442-6410
  www.va.gov/homeless/reentry.asp

NEBRASKA

- **Bridges to Hope**
  3107 S. 6th St., Suite 107, Lincoln, NE 68502, Tel. 402-420-5696
  bridgestohopene.org

- **Center for People in Need**
  3901 N. 27th St., Unit 1, Lincoln, NE 68521, Tel. 402-476-4358
  http://centerforpeopleinneed.org

- **Central Nebraska Goodwill Industries, Inc.**
  1804 S. Eddy St., Grand Island, NE 68802, Tel. 308-384-7896
  www.goodwill.org/state/ne/grand_island.htm

- **Compassion in Action, Inc.**
  2001 North 35th St., Omaha, NE 68111, Tel. 402-502-9890
  www.compassioninactioninc.com

- **CrossOver Prison Ministries**
  18616 Anne St., Omaha, NE 68135, Tel. 402-871-7904
  www.facebook.com/CrossOver-Prison-Ministries-62649475309/

- **Crossroads Connection**
  851 N. 74th St., Omaha, NE 68114, Tel. 402-516-2403
  www.crossroadsconnectionne.org

- **Department of Correctional Services: Reentry**
  P.O. Box 94661, Lincoln, NE 68509-4661, Tel. 402-471-2654
  www.corrections.nebraska.gov/reentry.html

- **Destination...Dad**
  Nebraska Christian Heritage Children's Home,
  14880 Old Cheney Rd., Walton, NE 68461, Tel. 402-421-5437
  www.chne.org

- **Freedom Road 3/4 House**
  825 N. 48th St., Omaha, NE 68132, Tel. 402-991-8044
  www.freedomroadhouse.com

- **Friends & Family of Inmate - NEPEN**
  P.O. Box 84424, Lincoln, NE 68501, Tel. 402-477-8568
  http://nebraskapen.org/Family/FFI.htm

- **GoldStar Institute**
  GoldStar Global, P.O. Box 6147, Omaha, NE 68106,
  Tel. 402-312-0121, www.goldstarinstitute.org

- **Good News Jail and Prison Ministry**
  702 S. 17th St., Omaha, NE 68102, Tel. 402-599-2293
  http://local.goodnewsjail.org/omaha

- **Goodwill Industries Serving Eastern Nebraska and Southwest Iowa**
  4805 N. 72nd St., Omaha, NE 68134, Tel. 402-341-4609
  www.goodwillomaha.com

- **Goodwill Industries Serving Southeast Nebraska, Inc.**
  2100 Judson St., Lincoln, NE 68521, Tel. 402-438-2002
  www.lincolngoodwill.org

- **Heartland Workforce Solutions**
  American Job Center, 5752 Ames Ave., Omaha, NE 68104,
  Tel. 402-444-4700 or 402-218-1166, www.hws-ne-org

- **Nebraska Aftercare in Action (NAIA)**
  P.O. Box 6757, Lincoln, NE 68506, Tel. 308-991-2310
  www.aftercareinaction.com

- **Nebraska Fathers**
  nebraskafathers.org

- **Nebraska Workforce Development Career Centers**
  550 S. 16th St., Lincoln, NE 68509, Tel. 402-471-9948
  dol.nebraska.gov

- **New Hope Life Center for Women**
  3507 Harney St., Omaha, NE 68131, Tel. 402-345-4673

- **Opening Doors to Success**
  Eastern Nebraska Community Action Partnership (ENCAP),
  2406 Fawler Ave., Omaha, NE 68111, Tel. 402-453-5656,
  ext. 202, http://encapomaha.org

- **People's City Mission**
  110 Q St., Lincoln, NE 68508, Tel. 402-475-1303
  http://peoplescitymission.org, http://www.reentryhaftercare.org

- **Reentry Alliance of Nebraska (RAN)**
  Calvery United Methodist, 1610 S. 11th St., Lincoln, NE 68502,
  Tel. 402-476-7353, www.re-entrynebraska.org

- **Released and Restored**
  P.O. Box 22962, Lincoln, NE 68542, Tel. 402-806-0565
  http://releasedandrestored.org

- **St. Vincent de Paul Omaha**
  P.O. Box 241201, Omaha, NE 68124, Tel. 402-346-5445
  www.svdpomaha.com

NEVADA

- **Broken Chains Outreach Ministry of Las Vegas**
  Broken Chains Missionary Church, 2550 E. Desert Inn Rd.,
  Suite 585, Las Vegas, NV 89121, Tel. 844-772-5623
  http://brokenchainsoutreach.com

- **Friends and Family of Incarcerated Persons**
  P.O. Box 27708, Las Vegas, NV 89126, Tel. 702-870-5577
  ffipnv.org

- **Hope for Prisoners**
  3430 E. Flamingo Rd., Suite 350, Las Vegas, NV 89121,
  Tel. 702-586-1371, https://hopeforprisoners.org

- **Las Vegas Rescue Mission Recovery Program**
  480 West Bonanza Rd., Las Vegas, NV 89106, Tel. 702-382-1766
  www.vegasrescue.org

- **Nevada JobConnect**
  www.nevadajobconnect.com

- **Re-Entry Initiatives Supporting Ex-Offenders (RISE) Program**
  Las Vegas Urban League, 3575 W. Cheyenne Ave., Suite 101,
  North Las Vegas, NV 89032, Tel. 702-636-3949
  http://lvul.org/re-entry-initiatives-supporting-ex-offenders

- **RExO Champs**
  Las Vegas Urban League Re-Entry of Ex-Offenders, 1024 West
  Owens Ave., Las Vegas, NV 89106, Tel. 702-483-4200
  www.allegrawebsites.net/urbanleague3/rexo.html

- **Ridge House**
  900 West 1st St., Suite 200, Reno, NV 89503, Tel. 775-322-8941
  www.ridgehouse.org

- **Southern Nevada Prison Ministries**
  Tel. 702-277-9315, http://prisonministry.net/snvpm

- **Transitional Living Communities**
  210 N. 10th St., Las Vegas, NV 89101, Tel. 702-387-3131

- **Walter Hoving Home, Inc.** (women)
  3353 Red Rock St., Las Vegas, NV 89146, Tel. 702-386-1965
  www.walterhovinghome.com

- **WestCare Foundation**
  1711 Whitney Mesa Dr., Henderson, NV 89014,
  Tel. 702-385-2090, www.westcare.com

- **WestCare Nevada Re-Entry Programs of Las Vegas**
  Community Involvement Center - Las Vegas Campus, 401 S.
  Martin Luther King Blvd., Las Vegas, NV 89106, Tel. 702-385-3330
  www.westcare.com/page/where-we-serve_NV

- **The Wellness, Redemption, and Rehabilitation**
  Program (WRRP, Inc.)
  1555 E. Flamingo Rd., Suite 158, Las Vegas, NV 89119,
  Tel. 702-385-9097, www.wrrp.org

NEW HAMPSHIRE

- **Access-To-Recovery (ATR)**
  Headrest, Inc., 14 Church St., Lebanon, NH 03766,
  Tel. 603-448-4872, www.headrest.org/home

- **Alternative Solutions Associates, Inc.**
  5 Red Bridge Lane, South Hadley, MA 01075, Tel. 413-533-1517
  www.alternativesolutionsassociations.com

- **Assertive Community Treatment (ACT)**
  Center for Life Management, 10 Tsienneto Rd., Derry,
  NH 03038, Tel. 603-434-1577, www.centerforlifemanagement.org

- **Christian Aftercare Ministries**
  50 Lowell St., Manchester, NH 03101, Tel. 603-669-5090
  www.christianaftercare.com

- **CRJ Hampshire House**
  1490-1492 Elm St., Manchester, NH 03101, Tel. 603-518-5128
  www.crj.org/sjs

- **Keystone Hall**
  615 Amherst St., Nashua, NH 03060, Tel. 603-881-4848
  www.keystonehall.org

- **New Hampshire Works**
  Office of Workforce Opportunity, 172 Pembroke Rd., Concord,
  NH 03301, Tel. 603-271-7275, www.nhworks.org

- **Rise Again Outreach**
  34 Staniels Rd., Suite 5, Loudon, NH 03307, Tel. 800-266-5017
  www.riseagainoutreach.org

NEW JERSEY

- **City of Newark: Office of Reentry**
  1008 Broad St., Newark, NJ 07102, Tel. 973-733-3747
  www.ci.newark.nj.us/government/departments/
  economic-and-housing-development/office-of-reentry

- **Community Education Centers, Inc. (CEC)**
  35 Fairfield Place, West Caldwell, NJ 07006, Tel. 973-226-2900
  www.cecintl.com/index.html

- **GEO Reentry**
  Atlantic City Community Reentry Center: 26 S. Pennsylvania Ave., 4th Fl., Atlantic City, NJ 08401, Tel. 609-344-6785

  Elizabeth Community Reentry Center: 208 Commerce Place, 2nd Fl., Elizabeth, NJ 07201-2320, Tel. 908-282-1001

  Neptune Community Reentry Center: 2040 6th Ave., Suite A, Neptune City, NJ 07753, Tel. 732-774-0777

  Perth Amboy Community Reentry Center: 207 New Brunswick Ave., Perth Amboy, NJ 08861, Tel. 732-826-4200

  Vineland Community Reentry Center: 1338 N. Delsea Dr., Suite 4, Vineland, NJ 08360, Tel. 856-696-4579
  www.georeentry.com/locations

- **Guidebook for Reentry Veterans in New Jersey**
  www.va.gov/HOMELESS/docs/Reentry/09_nj.pdf

- **Jersey City Employment and Training Program (JCETP) : Re-Entry Program**
  Martin's Place, 398 Martin Luther King Jr. Dr., Jersey City, NJ 07305, Tel. 551-222-4323, jcetp.org

- **New Jersey Association on Correction**
  986 South Broad St., Trenton, NJ 08611, Tel. 609-396-8900
  www.njaconline.org/index.html

- **Offender Aid and Restoration of Essex County**
  1064 Clinton Ave., Suite 170, Irvington, NJ 07111,
  Tel. 973-373-0100

- **One-Stop Career Centers** (21 centers)
  lwd.state.nj.us/WorkForceDirectory/index.jsp?displayID=
  5&printacrossID=1

- **Redeem-Her**
  101 3rd Ave., Neptune City, NJ 07753, Tel. 732-966-3788
  www.redeem-her.org, http://www.georeentry.com/locations

- **Reentry Coalition of New Jersey**
  986 S. Broad St., Trenton, NJ 08611, Tel. 609-396-8900
  reentrycoalitionofnj.org

- **Seeds of Hope Ministries**
  1700 S. Broadway, Camden, NJ 08104, Tel. 856-963-0312
  www.seedsofhopeministries.org

- **STEP: Stages to Enhance Parolee Success**
  New Jersey State Parole Board, Division of Community
  Programs, P.O. Box 862, Trenton, NJ 08625, Tel. 609-292-4257,
  ext. 5, www.state.nj.us/parole/comm_progs.html@program_4

- **VoA Delaware Valley**
  Volunteers of America Delaware Valley's
  Re-Entry Services Division
  235 White Horse Pike, Collingswood, NJ 08107,
  Tel. 856-854-4660 (headquarters)

  Hope Hall (male), 676 Fairview St., Camden, NJ,
  Tel. 856-963-6166

  Fletcher House (male), 517 Penn St., Camden, NJ,
  Tel. 856-964-5100

  Garrett House (female), 509 Cooper St., Camden, NJ,
  Tel. 856-964-6966

  PROMISE (mental illness), 1812 Federal St., Camden, NJ,
  Tel. 856-671-6199

  Face Forward 2, 1812 Federal St., Camden, NJ, Tel. 856-583-1404
  (vocational education)

  Community Resource Center, 17th and Mickle Streets,
  Camden, NJ, Tel. 856-963-7972,
  www.voa.org/correctional-r-eentry-services

NEW MEXICO

- **Albuquerque Salvation Army Substance Abuse Recovery Program**
  4301 Bryn Mawr Dr., NE, Albuquerque, NM 87107,
  Tel. 505-881-4292, www.salvationarmyalbuquerque.com/#!adult-rehabilitation-program/c11ge

- **Celebrate Recovery Inside**
  www.cr-inside.org

- **Crossroads for Women**
  805 Tijeras Ave., NW, Albuquerque, NM 87102, Tel. 505-242-1010
  www.crossroadsabq.org

- **Dismas House New Mexico**
  St. Martin's Hospitality Center, P.O. Box 27258, Albuquerque,
  NM 87125, Tel. 505-343-0746
  www.smhc-nm.org/what-we-do/programs/dismas/

- **FPM Access to Recovery**
  Footprints Ministry Inc., P.O. Box 65092, Albuquerque, NM
  87193, Tel. 505-508-4605, www.footprintsministry.org

- **Joy Junction**
  4500 2nd Street SW, Albuquerque, NM 87105,
  Tel. 505-877-6967, www.joyjunction.org

- **Kairos Outside of New Mexico**
  Kairos Prison Ministry, P.O. Box 4226, Roswell, NM 88201,
  Tel. 505-304-5578 (Albuquerque) and 505-730-6741 (Bernalillo)
  www.kairosoutsideofnm.org

- **La Entrada Offender Reentry Program**
  Amity Foundation, 609 Gold Ave., SW, Albuquerque, NM 87102,
  Tel. 505-246-9300, www.amityfdn.org/newmexico

- **Learn, Earn and Develop Success** (Ages 16-21)
  Families and Youth, Inc., 1320 S. Solano, Las Cruces,
  NM 88001, Tel. 575-522-4004, www.fyinm.org

- **Metropolitan Detention Center's Community Custody Program (CCP)**
  100 Deputy Dean Miera Dr., SW, Albuquerque, NM 87151, Tel. 505-839-8700, www.bernco.gov/metropolitan-detention-center

- **NewLife Homes**
  6101 Central Ave., NE, Albuquerque, NM 87108, Tel. 505-266-7000 www.newlifehomesnm.com

- **New Mexico - CURE (Citizens United for the Rehabilitation of Errants)**
  P.O. Box 543, Deming, NM 88031, Tel. 575-546-9003 www.curenational.org

- **New Mexico Women's Justice Project (NMWJP)**
  P.O. Box 25501, Albuquerque, NM 87125, Tel. 505-999-1935 http://nmwip.org

- **New Mexico's Men's Recovery Academy (NMMRA)**
  1000 W. Main St., Bldg. 23, P.O. Box 1890, Los Lunas, NM 87031, Tel. 505-866-0590, http://cd.nm.gov/ppd/ppd.html

- **New Mexico's Women's Recovery Academy (NMWRA)**
  6000 Isleta Blvd., SW, Albuquerque, NM 87105, Tel. 505-873-2761 www.cecintl.com/facilities_rr_nm_002.html

- **Offender Re-Entry Resource Manual for Barnalillo County**
  cd.nm.gov/apd/rr/resource_manual.pdf (downloadable 232-page resource guide)

- **Oxford House, Inc.**
  www.oxfordhouse.org/directory_listing.php

- **A Peaceful Habitation: Post Prison and Aftercare Ministry**
  P.O. Box 53516, Albuquerque, NM 87153, Tel. 505-440-5937 www.apeacefulhabitation.org

- **St. Martin's Hospitality Center: The Albuquerque Heading Home Program**
  Shelter & Behavioral Health, 1201 3rd St., NW, Albuquerque, NM 87102, Tel. 505-764-8231
  www.smhc.nm.org/project-end-homelessness

- **Therapeutic Living Services**
  5601 Domingo Rd., NE, Albuquerque, NM 87108,
  Tel. 505-268-5295, www.tls-nm.org/

- **The Women's Housing Coalition**
  3005 San Pedro, NE, Albuquerque, NM 87110, Tel. 505-884-8856
  www.womenshousingcoalition.org

- **Workforce Development One-Stop Career Centers**
  (list of locations) www.servicelocator/org/search/etasearchoffice.
  asp?state=NM

NEW YORK

- **America Works, Inc. – Criminal Justice Program**
  (5 locations) www.americaworks.com/locations/newyork

- **Argus Community Re-Entry Initiative (ACRI)**
  760 East 160th St., Bronx, NY 10456, Tel. 718-401-5726
  www.arguscommunity.org/argus-programs/acri/

- **The Bronx Defenders**
  360 East 161st St., Bronx, NY 10451, Tel. 718-838-7878
  www.bronxdefenders.org

- **Bronx Justice Corps**
  Phipps Neighborhoods, 1409 Fulton Ave., Bronx, NY 10456,
  Tel. 347-329-4004, ext. 5050
  www.nycjusticecorps.org/justice-corp/the-bronx

- **Center for Alternative Sentencing and Employment
  Services (CASES)**
  www.cases.org/contactus/ (headquarters + 19 locations)

- **Center for Community Alternatives (CCA)**
  115 E. Jefferson St., Suite 300, Syracuse, NY 13202,
  Tel. 315-422-5638, www.communityalternatives.org/index.html

- **Center for Court Innovations: Reentry**
  520 8th Ave., 18th Fl., New York, NY 10018, Tel. 646-386-3100

  One Park Place, 300 South State St., Syracuse, NY 13202,
  Tel. 315-266-4330, www.courtinnovation.org/topic/reentry

- **Center for Employment Opportunities**
  50 Broadway, Suite 1604, New York, NY 10004, Tel. 212-422-4430
  www.ceoworks.org

- **Center for Urban Community Services**
  198 East 121st St., New York, NY 10035, Tel. 212-801-3300
  www.cucs.org

- **College and Community Fellowship (CCF)**
  475 Riverside Dr., Suite 1626, New York, NY 10115,
  Tel. 646-380-7777, www.collegeandcommunity.org

- **College Initiative**
  Tel. 646-781-5113, www.collegeinitiative.org

- **Community Service Society of New York**
  633 Third Ave., 10th Floor, New York, NY 10017,
  Tel. 212-254-8900, www.cssny.org

- **DCJS County Re-Entry Take Force Initiative**
  www.criminaljustice.ny.gov/crimnet/ojsa/initiatives/offender_
  reentry.htm

- **Developing Justice Project**
  Fifth Avenue Committee, 141 Fifth Ave., Brooklyn, NY 11217,
  Tel. 718-237-2017, www.fifthave.org

- **Exodus Transitional Community** (3 locations)
  www.etcny.org/contact

- **Fathers Count and Re-Entry Plus**
  Family Services of Westchester, 20 South Broadway,
  Yonkers, NY 10701, Tel. 914-964-6767, ext. 126, www.fsw.org

- **Fifth Avenue Committee**
  621 DeGraw St., Brooklyn, NY 11217, Tel. 718-237-2017
  www.fifthave.org

- **The Fortune Society**
  (3 locations) www.fortunesociety.org

- **Given the Chance (GTC) @ AIDS Council of
  Northeastern New York**
  927 Broadway, Albany, NY 12207, Tel. 718-433-4724
  www.allianceforpositivehealth.org/contact-us/

- **Good Help Program**
  Brooklyn Chamber of Commerce, 25 Elm Place, Suite 200,
  Brooklyn, NY 11201, Tel. 718-875-1000
  www.ibrooklyn.com/site/chamberdirect/goodhelp

- **Getting Out and Staying Out (GOSO) Partner Network**
  75 East 116th St., New York, NY 10029, Tel. 212-831-5020
  http://gosonyc.org

- **Greenhope Services for Women Greenhope**
  Greenhope Housing Development Fund, Inc., 435 East 119th St.,
  7th Fl., New York, NY 10035, Tel. 212-996-8633
  www.greenhope.org

- **Harlem Community Justice Center**
  170 E. 121st St., New York, NY 10035, Tel. 212-360-4131
  Resource Guide: www.realcostofprisons.org/materials/
  welcome-home.pdf
  www.courtinnovation.org/project/harlem-community-justice-center

- **Harlem Justice Corps**
  Center for Court Innovation, 127 W. 127th St., New York, NY
  10027, Tel. 646-593-8520
  www.nycjusticecorps.org/justice-corp/harlem-corp

- **Here's Life Inner City NYC**
  The Inner City Ministry of Cru, 9-11 44th Dr., Long Island City,
  NY 11101, Tel. 718-391-4500, www.hlicnyc.org

- **Hour Children, Inc.**
  36-11A 12th St., Long Island City, NY 11385, Tel. 718-433-4724
  www.hourchildren.org

- **Legal Action Center**
  225 Varick St., New York, NY 10014, Tel. 212-243-1313
  www.lac.org

- **NYS Prisoner JuNetwork**
  New York State Prisoner Justice Coalition, 33 Central Ave.,
  Albany, NY 12210, Tel. 518-434-4037
  www.nysprisonerjustice.org

- **The Osborne Association**
  809 Westchester Ave., Bronx, NY 10455, Tel. 718-707-2600

  175 Remsen St., Suite 800, Brooklyn, NY 11201, Tel. 718-637-6560

  388 Ann St., Newburgh, NY 12550, Tel. 845-345-9845
  www.osborneny.org

- **The Prisoner Reentry Institute**
  John Jay College of Criminal Justice, 524 W. 59th St.,
  Rm. 609B-BMW, New York, NY 10019, Tel. 646-558-4532
  http://johnjayresearch.org/pri

- **Providence House**
  703 Lexington Ave., Brooklyn, NY 11221, Tel. 718-455-0197
  www.providencehouse.org

- **Queens Justice Corps**
  Center for Alternative Sentencing and Employment Services,
  Inc., 89-31 - 161st St., Jamaica, NY 11432, Tel. 347-474-1896
  www.nycjusticecorps.org/justice-corpqueens/

- **Reentry Resource Center: New York**
  www.reentry.net/ny

- **Re-thinking Reentry**
  http://rethinkingreentry.blogspot.com

- **Second Chance Reentry**
  Tel. 516-587-0526, www.secondchancereentry.org

- **SMART – Safer Monroe Area Reentry**
  215 Alexander St., Rochester, NY 14607, Tel. 585-325-7746
  www.smartny.org

- **Supportive Housing Network of New York: Re-Entry**
  247 W. 37th St., 18th Fl., New York, NY 10018,
  Tel. 646-619-9640

  146 Washington Ave., Albany, NY 12210, Tel. 518-465-3233
  shnny.org/research-reports/research/reentry/

- **Think Outside the Cell Foundation**
  511 Avenue of the Americas, Suite 525, New York, NY 10011,
  Tel. 877-267-2303, www.thinkoutsidethecell.org

- **Urban Pathways, Inc.**
  575 8th Ave., 16th Fl., New York, NY 10018, Tel. 212-736-7385, ext. 29, www.urbanpathways.org

- **Vera Institute of Justice**
  233 Broadway, 12th Fl., New York, NY 10279, Tel. 212-334-1300
  www.vera.org

- **VoA – Greater New York**
  340 West 85th St., New York, NY 10024, Tel. 212-873-2600
  www.voa-gny.org

- **Walter Hoving Home: New York Branch**
  40 Walter Hoving Rd., Garrison, NY 10524, Tel. 845-424-3674
  http://walterhovinghome.org/new-york-branch

- **Wildcat Service Corporation**
  2 Washington Street, 3rd Fl., New York, NY 10004,
  Tel. 212-209-6000, www.wildcatnyc.org

- **Women's Prison Association (WPA)**
  110 2nd Ave., New York, NY 10003, Tel. 646-292-7742
  www.wpaonline.org

- **Youth Advocate Programs** (14 county locations)
  www.yapinc.org/newyork

NORTH CAROLINA

- **Barnabas House of Northeastern North Carolina, Inc.**
  P.O. Box 1205, Elizabeth City, NC 27906,
  info@barnabashousenc.org, barnabashousenc.org

- **Benevolence Farm**
  P.O. Box 1313, Graham, NC 27253, Tel. 336-545-9339
  http://benevolencefarm.org

- **Coastal Horizons Center, Inc.**
  Willie Stargell Office Park, 615 Shipyard Blvd., Wilmington,
  NC 28412, Tel. 800-672-2903, www.coastalhorizons.org

- **Center for Community Transitions**
  P.O. Box 33533, Charlotte, NC 28233, Tel. 704-494-0001, ext. 20
  www.centerforcommunitytransitions.org

- **Crossroads Reentry Ministries (CRM)**
  P.O. Box 861, Huntersville, NC 28070, Tel. 704-499-1332
  www.crossroadsreentry.org

- **CSI Resource Center Without Walls**
  1830-B Tillery Place, Raleigh, NC 27604, Tel. 919-715-0111,
  ext. 216, http://communitysuccess.org

- **Durham Reentry Program**
  Durham County Criminal Justice Resource Center,
  326 East Main St., Durham, NC 27701, Tel. 919-560-0500
  http://dcone.gov/government/departments-a-e/criminal-
  justice-resource-center

- **Eureka House**
  P.O. Box 11396, Winston Salem, NC 27116, Tel. 336-761-8407
  www.eurekahouse.org

- **Exodus Foundation.org**
  13016 Eastfield Rd., Suite 200-222, Huntersville, NC 28078,
  Tel. 704-947-9090, www.exodusfoundation.org

- **Exodus Homes**
  122 8th Avenue Dr. SW, Hickory, NC 28602-3351,
  Tel. 828-324-4870, www.exodushomes.com

- **Going Home Initiative**
  Department of Correction – Research and Planning,
  2020 Yonkers Rd., 4221 MSC, Raleigh, NY 27699,
  Tel. 919-716-3080, www.doc.state.nc.us/rap/goinghome.htm

- **Goodwill Industries of Northwest North Carolina, Inc.**
  2701 University Parkway, Winston-Salem, NC 27115,
  Tel. 336-724-3621, www.goodwillnwnc.org/work/

- **GORE Community Development Corporation**
  2118 Breezewood Dr., Charlotte, NC 28262, Tel. 704-549-0634
  www.gorecdc.org

- **LINC, Inc. (Leading into New Communities): Residential
  ReEntry Program**
  LINC, Inc., Re-Entry Office, 222 Division Dr., Wilmington,
  NC 28401, Tel. 910-332-1132, www.lincnc.org

- **Mecklenburg County Sheriff's Office Reentry Programs**
  700 E. 4th St., Charlotte, NC 28202, Tel. 704-336-8210
  www.mecksheriff.com/reentryprograms.asp

- **North Carolina Department of Public Safety: Re-Entry**
  Office of Transition Services
  www.docstate.nc.us/rap/OTS.htm

- **North Carolina Justice Center**
  224 S. Dawson St., Raleigh, NC 27601, Tel. 919-856-2570
  www.ncjustice.org

- **Passage Home**
  513 Branch St., Raleigh, NC 27601, Tel. 919-834-0666

  100 Shannon Dr., Zebulon, NC 27597, Tel. 919-834-0666,
  ext. 237, www.passagehome.org

- **Substance Abuse Treatment and Recidivism Reduction (STARR)**
  Durham County Detention Facility, 219 S. Mangum St.,
  Durham, NC 27701, Tel. 919-560-0972
  http://dconc.gov/government/departments-a-e/criminal-justice-resource-center

NORTH DAKOTA

- **Bismarck Transition Center**
  2001 Lee Ave., Bismarck, ND 58504, Tel. 701-222-3440, ext. 101
  www.cccscorp.com/btc.htm

- **Centre Inc.** (Re-entry centers (halfway houses) and transition
  programs in Fargo, Grand Forks, and Mandan)
  Residential Transitional Re-entry Center: 123 15th St. North,
  Fargo, ND 58102, Tel. 701-237-9340

  Residential Transition Program: 201 S. 4th St., Grand Forks, ND
  58201, Tel. 701-775-2681

  Residential Transitional Re-entry Center: 100 6th Ave. SE,
  Mandan, ND 58554, Tel. 701-663-8120, centreinc.org/location/

- **Job Service North Dakota**
  P.O. Box 5507, Bismarck, ND 58506, Tel. 701-328-2825
  www.jobsnd.com

- **Lake Region Residential Reentry Center**
  225 Walnut St. W., Devils Lake, ND 58301, Tel. 701-662-0735

- **Mission River Correctional Center: Transitional Facilities**
  1800 48th Ave., SW, P.O. Box 5521, Bismarck, ND 58506,
  Tel. 701-328-9696, www.nd.gov/docr/adult/missouri.html

- **North Dakota Department of Corrections: Reentry/ Transitional Facilities**
  3100 Rail Road Ave., Bismarck, ND 58501, Tel. 701-328-6390
  www.nd.gov/docr/adult/transfacs/centre.html

- **Northlands Rescue Mission**
  420 Division Ave., Grand Forks, ND 58201, Tel. 701-772-6600
  http://northlandsrescuemission.org

- **SHARE Network: Job Service North Dakota**
  P.O. Box 5507, Bismarck, ND 58506-5507, Tel. 701-328-2825
  www.jobsnd.com

- **Tompkins Rehabilitation and Corrections Center**
  2605 Circle Dr., Jamestown, NC 58401, Tel. 701-253-3755
  www.nd.gov/docr/adult/transfacs/trcc.html

OHIO

- **AGAPE/Community Reentry Program**
  1378 Loretta Ave., Columbus, OH 43211, Tel. 614-477-4931

- **Alvis: 180 Degree Impact**
  2100 Stella Ct., Columbus, OH 43215, Tel. 614-252-8402
  alvis180.org

- **Cincinnati-Hamilton County CAA Fresh Start**
  MidPointe Crossing, 1740 Langdon Farm Rd., Cincinnati,
  OH 45237, Tel. 513-924-2031, www.cincy-caa.org/2014/03/ex-offender-fresh-start.html

- **Cleveland Eastside Ex-Offender Coalition**
  8003 Broadway Ave., Cleveland, OH 44105, Tel. 216-641-9012
  www.clevelandeastside.info

- **Columbus Area Integrated Health Services:**
  Re-Entry Programs
  1515 E. Broad St., Columbus, OH 43205, Tel. 614-252-0711
  http://209.190.40.254/programs-services/prison-re-entry-programs

- **Columbus Urban League**
  788 Mount Vernon Ave., Columbus, OH 43203, Tel. 614-257-6300
  www.cul.org

- **Community for New Directions**
  993 East Main St., Columbus, OH 43205, Tel. 614-257-0305
  http://cndonline.org/contact

- **Community Linkage Program**
  Ohio Department of Mental Health and Addiction Services,
  30 East Broad St., 8th Fl., Columbus, OH 43215-3430,
  Tel. 614-466-1325, mha.ohio.gov

- **Community Re-entry: Lutheran Metropolitan Ministry**
  The Richard Sering Center, 4515 Superior Ave., Cleveland,
  OH 44103, Tel. 216-696-2715
  www.lutheranmetro.org/Community-Re-entry

- **Cuyahoga County Office of Reentry**
  Courthouse Square, 310 West Lakeside Ave., Suite 550,
  Cleveland, OH 44113, Tel. 216-699-3437
  reentry.cuyahogacounty.us

- **The Exit Program**
  897 Oakwood Ave., Columbus, OH 43206, Tel. 614-253-8969
  www.theexitprogram.com

- **Franklin County Reentry Coalition**
  373 South Hight St., 25th Fl., Columbus, OH 43215,
  Tel. 614-525-5577, www.franklincountyohio.gov/reentry/

- **Goodwill Industries of Greater Cleveland and**
  East Central Ohio, Inc.
  408 Ninth St., SW, Canton, OH 44707, Tel. 800-942-3577
  www.goodwillgoodskills.org

- **Hamilton County Office of Reentry**
  Hamilton County Administration Building, 138 E. Court St.,
  Rm. 101, Cincinnati, OH 45202, Tel. 513-946-4304
  www.hamiltoncountyohio.gov/das/Reentry/

- **Impact Community Action – Re-Entry Program**
  700 Bryden Rd., Columbus, OH 43215, Tel. 614-252-2799
  www.impactca.org

- **Montgomery County Office of Ex-Offender Reentry**
  1133 S. Edwin C. Moses Blvd., Rm. 370, Dayton, OH 45408,
  Tel. 937-225-6460
  www.mcohio.org/departments/ex-offender_reentry/index.php

- **New Home Islamic Re-Entry Society**
  2302 Putnam Ave., Toledo, OH 43620, Tel. 419-283-2290
  http://newhomeislamicreentry.weebly.com/index.html

- **North Star Neighborhood Reentry Resource Center**
  1834 East 55th St., Cleveland, OH 44103, Tel. 216-881-5440
  www.northstarrentry.org

- **Ohio Community Corrections Association**
  Alvis House Administrative Building, 2100 Stella Ct.,
  Columbus, OH 43215, Tel. 614-252-8417
  www.occaonline.org

- **Ohio Ex-Offender Reentry Coalition**
  Ohio Department of Rehabilitation and Correction, Court and
  Community, Adult Reentry, 770 W. Broad St., Columbus, OH
  43222, Tel. 614-752-0627
  www.reentrycoalition.ohio.gov/

- **OhioMeansJobs Centers**
  jfs.ohio.gov/owd/wia/wiamap.stem

- **Ohio Justice and Policy Center**
  215 E. 9th St., Suite 601, Cincinnati, OH 45202, Tel. 513-421-1108
  www.ohiojpc.org

- **Ohio Reentry Collaborative**
  1133 S. Edwin C. Moses Blvd., Rm. 370, Dayton, OH 45408,
  Tel. 937-496-7047, www.mcohio.org/departments/ex-offender_
  reentry/reentry_collaborative.php

- **Ohio Reentry Resource Center**
  Ohio Department of Rehabilitation and Correction,
  770 West Broad St., Columbus, OH 43222, Tel. 614–387-0588
  www.drc.ohio.gov/web/offenderrentry.htm

- **Providing Real Opportunities for Ex-Offenders to Succeed (PROES)**
  Employment Connection, 1020 Bolivar Rd., Cleveland,
  OH 44115, Tel. 216-664-4673

- **Re-Entry/STAR (Successful Transitions-Accelerated Reentry) Program**
  www.ohnd.uscourts.gov/home/u-s-pretrial-services-probation-office/district-initiatives/re-entry-star- program/

- **Reentry Bridge Network, Inc.**
  P.O. Box 9491, Canton, OH 44711, Tel. 530-209-7683
  http://reentrybridgenetwork.org

- **Reentry Circles of Dayton**
  Think Tank, Inc., 20 S. Limestone St., Springfield, OH 45502,
  Tel. 937-322-4970, www.thinktank-inc.org

- **2nd Chances 4 Felons Resource Listing**
  Tel. 214-900-4265
  www.2ndchances4felons.com/ohio.php

- **Solid Opportunities for Advancement and Retention (SOAR) Program**
  Greater Cincinnati Urban League, 3458 Reading Rd.,
  Cincinnati, OH 45229, Tel. 513-281-9955, www.gcul.org/solid-opportunities-for-advancement-and-retention-soar

- **Stark County Re-Entry Court**
  201 Cleveland Ave., SW, Suite 105, Canton, OH 44702,
  Tel. 330-451-7186, www.starkcountyohio.ogv/common-pleas/re-entry-program

- **Summit County Reentry Coalition**
  OhioMeansJobs Center, 1040 E. Tallmadge Ave., Akron,
  OH 44310, Tel. 330-633-1050, summitcountyreentrynetwork.org

- **Teaching Opportunity Unity by Connecting Hearts (T.O.U.C.H.)**
  37 Robinwood Ave., Whitehall, OH 43213, Tel. 614-338-8733
  mcstouch.org

- **Towards Employment**
  1255 Euclid Ave., Suite 300, Cleveland, OH 44115,
  Tel. 216-696-5750, www.towardsemployment.org

- **Transitions Program: Akron Urban League**
  250 E. Market St., Akron, OH 44308, Tel. 330-434-3101
  www.akronurbanleague.org/employment/transitions-program

- **Urban League of Greater Cincinnati**
  Urban League of Greater Southwestern Ohio,
  3458 Reading Rd., Cincinnati, OH 45229, Tel. 513-281-9955
  www.gcul.org

- **Women's Re-Entry Network**
  4515 Superior Ave., Cleveland, OH 44103, Tel. 216-696-2715
  www.lutheranmetro.org/womens-re-entry.html

OKLAHOMA

- **Big Five Community Services**
  Bryan County Big Five, 1502 North 1st St., Durant, OK 74702,
  Tel. 580-924-5331, www.bigfive.org

- **Bridges to Life Program**
  City Rescue Mission, 800 West California Ave., Oklahoma City,
  OK 73106, Tel. 405-232-2709, https://cityrescue.org

- **Casa Recovery Ministry/New Starts Prison Ministry**
  P.O. Box 19353, Oklahoma City, OK 73144, Tel. 405-387-2052
  http://prisonministry.net/casa

- **Center for Employment Opportunities**
  228 Robert S. Kerr, Suite 600, Oklahoma City, OK 73102,
  Tel. 405-488-8200

  803 S. Peoria, Tulsa, OK 74120, Tel. 918-894-6561
  ceoworks.org

- **City Care**
  City Care's Pershing Center, 2400 General Pershing Blvd.,
  Oklahoma City, OK 73107, Tel. 405-609-2400
  http://citycareinc.org

- **Community Action Project (CAP) of Tulsa County**
  4606 South Garnett, Suite 100, Tulsa, OK 74146,
  Tel. 918-382-3200, captulsa.org

- **Exodus House**
  2624 E. Newton St., Tulsa, OK 74110, Tel. 918-382-0905
  433 NW 25th4 St., Oklahoma City, OK 73103, Tel 405-525-2300
  www.okumcministries.org/cjamm/exodus_house.htm

- **Female Offenders Committed to Ultimate Success (FOCUS)**
  1608 S. Elwood Ave., Tulsa, OK 74119, Tel. 918-587-3888

- **Genesis One**
  1830 N. 106th E. Ave., Tulsa, OK 74116, Tel. 918-388-1882
  www.genesisonenetwork.com

- **Kay County Reentry Coalition**
  P.O. Box 322, Ponca City, OK 74602
  www.kaycountyreentryhelp.com

- **Living Faith Ministries**
  1404 E. I-44 Service Rd., Oklahoma City, OK 73111,
  Tel. 405-607-0928, http://lfmok.publishpath.com

- **Living Hope Ministries**
  P.O. Box 22564, Oklahoma City, OK 73123, Tel. 405-473-8412
  www.livinghopeok.org

- **OKC Compassion, Inc.**
  2132 W. Park Place, Oklahoma City, OK 73147,
  Tel. 405-473-8412, www.okccompassion.net

- **Oklahoma Collaborative Mental Health Reentry Program**
  oraline.net/site/headline/49

- **Oklahoma – CURE (Citizens United for Rehabilitation of Errants)**
  P.O. Box 9741, Tulsa, OK 74157-0741, Tel. 918-744-9857
  www.okcure.org

- **Oklahoma Partnership for Successful Reentry, Inc.**
  P.O. Box 60433, Oklahoma City, OK 73146-0433,
  Tel. 405-202-4930, www.okreentry.org

- **Oklahoma Reentry: Transitional Services and Resources**
  2901 Classen Blvd., Suite 200, Oklahoma City, OK 73118,
  Tel. 405-962-6135, www.ok.gov/re-entry/

- **Out of the Rutz**
  New Hope Christian Fellowship, 400 S. Lincoln, Ponca City, OK
  74601, Tel. 580-763-5939, http://nhcfpc.com

- **Passport to the Future**
  Little Dixie Community Action Agency, Inc., 609 SW "B" St.,
  Antlers, OK 75423, Tel. 580-298-2921, www.littledixie.org

- **Ponca Tribal Social Development Center**
  Tribal Affairs Building, 20 White Eagle Dr., Ponca City,
  OK 74601, Tel. 580-762-6617, www.ponca.com

- **Prisoner Re-Entry Initiative: Tulsa County**
  Community Service Council, 16 East 16th St., Suite 202,
  Tulsa, OK 74119-4402, Tel. 918-585-5551, www.csctulsa.org

- **Reentry: George Kaiser Family Foundation**
  www.gkff.org/areas-of-focus/female-incarceration/reentry/

- **Resonance Center for Women, Inc.**
  1608 S. Elwood Ave., Tulsa, OK 74119, Tel. 918-587-3888
  www.resonancetulsa.org

- **She Brews Coffee House Reentry Program**
  414 West Will Rogers Blvd., Claremore, OK 74017,
  Tel. 918-923-6020, www.shebrewscoffeehouse.org

- **Tulsa Reentry One-Stop**
  533 East 36th St. North, Tulsa, OK 74106, Tel. 918-938-6141
  www.csctulsa.org/content.php?p=316

- **Turning Point Job Readiness**
  Community Action Agency of Oklahoma City, 319 SW 25th St.,
  Oklahoma City, OK 73109. Tel. 405-232-0199
  www.caaofokc.org

- **Upward Transitions**
  1134 W. Main St., Oklahoma City, OK 73106, Tel. 405-232-5507

- **Workforce Oklahoma**
  1120 Frisco Ave., Clinton, OK 73601, Tel. 580-323-1341
  oklahomaworks.gov

- **Work Ready Oklahoma Reentry Services**
  3 E. Main St., Oklahoma City, OK 73104, Tel. 405-418-3923
  workreadyoklahoma.com

OREGON

- **ARCHES Project**
  1164 Madison St., NE, Salem, OR 97301, Tel. 503-399-9080
  www.mwvcaa.org/CRP/ARCHES_project.html

- **Better People**
  P.O. Box 19435, Portland, OR 97280, Tel. 503-462-3593
  www.betterpeople.org

- **Community Action Reentry Service (CARS)**
  2475 Center St., NE, Salem, OR 97301, Tel. 503-585-6232
  www.mwvcaa.org

- **Goodwill Industries of Lane and South Coast Counties**
  1010 Green Acres Rd., Eugene, OR 97408, Tel. 541-345-1801
  www.goodwill-oregon.org

- **Helping Hands Reentry**
  1010 3rd Ave., Suite A, Seaside, OR 97138, Tel. 503-738-4321
  www.helpinghandsreentry.org

- **Mercy Corp: Reentry Transition Center (RTC)**
  1818 NE Martin Luther King Blvd.., Portland, OR 97202,
  Tel. 971-255-0547, ext. 206
  www.mercycorpsnw.org/reentry/transition-center/

- **Northwest Regional Re-entry Center (NERRC)**
  6000 NE 80th Ave., Portland, OR 97218, Tel. 503-546-0470
  nw-rrc.org

- **Oregon Reentry**
  oregonreentry.wikidot.com

- **Partnership for Safety and Justice**
  825 NE 20th Ave., #250, Portland, OR 97232, Tel. 503-335-8449
  www.safetyandjustice.org

- **Prisoner Reentry Employment Program (PREP)**
  7916 SE Foster Rd., Suite 104, Portland, OR 97206,
  Tel. 503-772-2300, seworks.org/job-seekers/resources-for-ex-offenders/prisoner-reentry-employment-program

- **Red Lodge Transition Services**
  P.O. Box 55157, Portland, OR 97238, Tel. 503-245-4175
  redlodgetransition.org/services/

- **Road to Success Re-Entry Program**
  oregonreentry.wikidot.com/road-to-success-re-entry-program

- **ROAR Alliance: Reentry Organizations and Resources**
  www.roaralliance.org

- **Sponsors: A New Beginning**
  Sponsors, Inc., 338 Highway 99 North, Eugene, OR 97402,
  Tel. 541-485-8341, sponsorsinc.org

- **Step Ahead**
  Minnesota Department of Corrections, 651-361-7200
  www.iseek.org/exoffenders/

- **Steps to Success East**
  1415 SE 122nd Ave., Portland, OR 97233, Tel. 503-256-0432

- **Volunteers of America**
  3910 SE Stark St., Portland, OR 97214, Tel. 503-235-8655
  www.voaor.org

- **Washington County Reentry Council**
  P.O. Box 463, Hillsboro, OR 97123
  siteadmin@washingtoncoreentry.org, washingtoncoreentry.org

- **Worksource Oregon**
  www.worksourceoregon.org

PENNSYLVANIA

- **Accelerated Support Services for Older Adults**
  2038 Bedford Ave., Pittsburgh, PA 15219, Tel. 412-392-4450
  www.hillhouse.org

- **Allegheny County Jail Re-Entry Program**
  Family Services of Western Pennsylvania, U-PARC Bldg. A-3,
  3230 William Pitt Way, Pittsburgh, PA 15238, Tel. 724-834-7830,
  ext. 701, fswp.org/services/allegheny-county-jail-re-entry-program

- **Alumni Ex-Offenders Association**
  Reconstruction, Inc., P.O. Box 7691, Philadelphia, PA 19101,
  Tel. 215-223-8180, www.reconstructioninc.org

- **Amiracle4sure, Inc.**
  1625 N. Front St., Harrisburg, PA 17102, Tel. 717-238-1523
  www.amiracle4sure.com

- **Baker Industries, Inc.**
  184 Pennsylvania Ave., Malvern, PA 19355, Tel. 610-296-9795
  www.bakerindustries.org

- **Beginning in the Right Direction (B.I.R.D.) Ministries**
  739 Spruce Road, New Holland, PA 17557
  www.birdministries.org

- **Career and Workforce Development Center East**
  YMCA of Greater Pittsburgh - Homewood Branch,
  7140 Bennett St., Pittsburgh, PA 15208, Tel. 412-241-2811, ext. 35

- **Center for Alternatives in Community Justice**
  411 South Burrowes St., State College, PA 16801,
  Tel. 814-234-1059, www.cacj.us

- **Center for Returning Citizens: The Friend's Center**
  1501 Cherry St., Philadelphia, PA 19102, Tel. 215-305-8793
  http://tcrcphilly.org

- **Community Action Association of Pennsylvania (CAAP)**
  222 Pine St., Harrisburg, PA 17101, Tel. 717-233-1075
  www.thecaap.org

- **Community Renewal for Sex Offenders (CR-SO)**
  New Person Ministries, Inc., P.O. Box 223, Reading, PA 19607,
  Tel. 610-777-2222, www.newpersonministries.org

- **Capital Region Ex-offender Support Coalition, Inc. (CRESC)**
  CareerLink, 100 N. Cameron St., Harrisburg
  (meet every third Thursday, 3-4pm)
  www.reentrynow.org

- **Christian Recovery Aftercare Ministry (CRAM)**
  509 Division St., Harrisburg, PA 17110, Tel. 717-234 -3664
  www.craminc.org

- **Divine Intervention Ministries**
  2203 Centre Ave., Pittsburgh, PA 15213, Tel. 412-621-0622
  www.divineinterventionministries.org

- **Domestic Outreach Center**
  6207 Brownsville Rd., Finleyville, PA 15332, Tel. 412-559-1197
  http://domesticoutreach.com

- **Ex-Offender Re-Entry Program of Monroe County, Inc.**
  P.O. Box 1251, Stroudsburg, PA 18360, Tel. 570-421-3280
  http://ex-offender.com

- **GEO Reentry Centers**
  Allegheny County Reentry Services Center: 357 N. Craig St.,
  Pittsburgh, PA 15217, Tel. 412-578-0513

  Cambria County Reentry Services Center: 499 Manor Dr.,
  Ebensburg, PA 15931, Tel. 814-471-1801

  Dauphin County Reentry Services Center: 2151 Greenwood St.,
  Harrisburg, PA 17104, Tel. 717-561-9600

  Franklin County Reentry Services Center: 550 West Loudon St.,
  Chambersburg, PA 17201, Tel. 717-263-0450

  Lancaster County Reentry Services Center: 439 E. King St.,
  Lancaster, PA 17601, Tel. 717-391-8202

  Luzerne County Reentry Services Center: 125 N. Wilkes Barre
  Blvd., Suite #4, Wilkes Barre, PA 18702, Tel. 570-208-4858

Lycoming County Reentry Services Center: 330 Pine St., Williamsport, PA 17702, Tel. 570-323-1274

Philadelphia County Reentry Services Center: 1 Reed St., Suite 10, Philadelphia, PA 19147, Tel. 215-463-1260

York County Reentry Services Center: 1 E. Market St., Suite 204/301, York, PA 17401, Tel. 717-848-4448
www.georeentry.com/locations and www.reentrypa.com

- **God's Treasure House Ministries**
P.O. Box 5, Schwenksville, PA 19473, Tel. 215-723-7499
www.godstreasurehouse.org

- **Goldring Reentry Initiative (GRI)**
University of Pennsylvania, School of Social Policy and Practice, 3701 Locust Walk, Philadelphia, PA 19104, Tel. 215-898-5512
www.sp2.upenn.edu/degree-programs/certificate-programs-specializations/goldring-reentry-initiative-gri/home/

- **Goodwill Industries of Southwestern Pennsylvania**
Robert S. Foltz Building, 118 52nd Street, Pittsburgh, PA 15201, Tel. 412-481-9005, www.goodwillswpa.org

- **I'm FREE – Females Reentering Empowering Each Other**
4700 Wissahickon Ave., Suite 126, Bldg. A, Philadelphia, PA 19144, Tel. 215-951-0330, www.imfreeonline.org

- **Jewish Employment and Vocational Service**
JEVS Prison Program, Philadelphia Industrial Correctional Center, 8301 State Rd., Philadelphia, PA 19136, Tel. 215-685-7114, www.jevs.org

- **Jubilee Ministries**
235 S. 12th St., Lebanon, PA 17042, Tel. 717-274-7528
www.jub.org

- **Justice and Mercy**
P.O. Box 187, Hopeland, PA 17533, Tel. 717-733-5130
www.justicemercy.org

- **Lancaster County Reentry Management Organization (RMO)**
  313 West Liberty St., Suite 114, Lancaster, PA 17603,
  Tel. 717-735-0333, http://lancastercountyreentry.org

- **Lydia's Place, Inc.**
  700 Fifth Ave., 4th Fl., Pittsburgh, PA 15219, Tel. 412-697-0880
  http://lydiasplace.org

- **Mayor's Office of Reintegration Services (RISE)**
  990 Spring Garden St., 7th Fl., Philadelphia, PA 19123,
  Tel. 215-683-3370, rise.phila.gov

- **Metropolitan Career Center/STRIVE Philadelphia**
  Philadelphia, PA Public Health Management Corporation,
  100 S. Broad St., Suite 830, Philadelphia, PA 19110,
  Tel. 215-568-9215
  theworkforce-institute.org or striveinternational.org

- **New Start II at Jackson Street**
  Resources for Human Development, 5000 Jackson St.,
  Philadelphia, PA 19124, Tel. 215-537-0119, www.rhd.org

- **Next Step Recovery Housing**
  637 Broadway Ave., 2nd Fl., McKees Rocks, PA 15136,
  Tel. 412-331-2887, www.nextstepfoundation.com

- **Offender Reentry**
  Pennsylvania Board of Probation and Parole, 1101 S. Front St.,
  Suite 5400, Harrisburg, PA 17104, Tel. 717-787-5699
  www.pbpp.state.pa.us

- **Opportunity House**
  430 N. 2nd St., Reading, PA 19601, Tel. 610-374-4696
  http://opphouse.org/looking-for-help/housing.aspx

- **Pennsylvania Prison Society**
  245 North Broad St., Suite 200, Philadelphia, PA 19107-4775,
  Tel. 215-564-4775, www.prisonsociety.org

- **People for People: Project Fresh Start**
  800 N. Broad St., Philadelphia, PA 19130, Tel. 215-235-2340
  www.peopleforpeople.org/index.html

- **Philadelphia Ready4Work**
  Connection Training Services (CTS), 2243 West Allegheny Ave., Philadelphia, PA 19132, Tel. 215-320-5557, http://ctstraining.org

- **Philadelphia Workforce Development Corporation**
  1617 John F. Kennedy Blvd., 13th Fl., Philadelphia, PA 19103-1813, Tel. 215-557-2625
  www.philaworks.org/about-us

- **Philadelphia Youth Network**
  400 Market St., Suite 200, Philadelphia, PA 19106, Tel. 267-502-3800

- **Program for Female Offenders**
  1515 Derry St., Harrisburg, PA 17104, Tel. 717-238-9950

- **Promise Place**
  381 S. Second St., Steelton, PA 17113, Tel. 717-948-6440
  http://home.epix.net/~theprogram/promise.htm

- **Ready, Willing & Able**
  1211 Bainbridge St., Philadelphia, PA 19147, Tel. 215-795-3255
  www.rwaphiladelphia.org

- **Re-Entry One Stop Satellite Center**
  Impact Services Corporation, 1952 E. Allegheny Ave., Philadelphia, PA 19134, Tel. 215-423-2944, ext. 193 (Re-entry Programs), www.impactservices.org

- **Reentry Services at the Berks County Community Reentry Center**
  BCPS/Berks Connections Pretrial Services, 633 Court St., 16th Fl., Reading, PA 19601, Tel. 610-478-6920
  www.berksconnections.org/reentry

- **Reentry Services for Chester County**
  Probation, Parole, and Pretrial Services, 201 West Market St., Suite 2100, West Chester, PA 19380-0989, Tel. 610-344-6290
  www.chesco.org/1146/Reentry-Services

- **Reentry Services Map (Interactive) for Pennsylvania**
  Pennsylvania Department of Corrections, interactive map for finding re-entry services in 67 counties
  reentrymap.cor.pa.gov

- **Renewal, Inc.**
  601 Grant St., 5th Fl., Pittsburgh, PA 15219, Tel. 412-690-2445
  www.renewalinc.com

- **Restorative Justice**
  City of Philadelphia Mural Arts Program, 1729 Mt. Vernon St, Philadelphia, PA 19130, Tel. 215-685-0726, http://muralarts.org

- **Safe Haven Re-Entry Program (ShaRP)**
  2509 North 30th St., Philadelphia, PA 19132, Tel. 215-740-5157
  www.sharpphilly.org

- **Southwestern Pennsylvania Reentry Project**
  Mon Valley Initiative, 303 East 8th Ave., Homestead, PA 15120, Tel. 412-464-4000, www.monvalleyinitiative.com

- **STAR Re-Entry Court**
  U.S. Probation Office Eastern District of Pennsylvania Federal Building, 504 W. Hamilton St., Allentown, PA 18101, Tel. 610-434-4062

  William J. Green Federal Building, 600 Arch St., Philadelphia, PA 19106, Tel. 215-597-7950

  The Madison Building, 400 Washington St., Reading, PA 19601, Tel. 610-320-5253, www.paep.uscourts.gov/re-entry-court

- **Stephen's Place, Halfway House**
  729 Ridge St., Bethlehem, PA 18015, Tel. 610-861-7677, http://stephens-place.org

- **Womanspace East, Inc.**
  P.O. Box 3826, Pittsburgh, PA 15230, Tel. 412-765-2661, Tel. 717-985-6440, www.wseinc.org

- **X-Offenders Empowerment**
  X-Offenders for Community Empowerment, 2227 N. Broad St., Philadelphia, PA 19132, Tel. 215-668-8477
  http://x-offenders.org

RHODE ISLAND

- **The Blessing Way**
  70 Pemberton St., Providence, RI 02908, Tel. 401-709-3697
  http://theblessingway.org

- **Caritas Women's Program**
  Caritas, Inc.-Eastman House, 166 Pawtucket Ave., Pawtucket, RI
  02860, Tel. 401-722-4644, caritasri.com

- **Crossroads**
  Crossroads Rhode Island, 106 Broad St., Providence, RI 02903,
  Tel. 401-521-2255, www.crossroadsri.org

- **Department of Corrections: Statewide Reentry Initiative**
  Dix Building, Cranston, RI 02920, Tel. 401-462-1129
  www.doc.ri.gov/reentry/index.php

- **Family Resources Community Action**
  245 Main St., Woonsocket, RI 02895, Tel. 401-766-0900
  800 Clinton St., Woonsocket, RI 02895, Tel. 401-765-5797
  www.communitycareri.org

- **netWORKri Center**
  One-Stop Career Center System of the Rhode Island Department
  of Labor and Training, Central General Complex,
  1511 Pontiac Ave., Cranston, RI 02920, Tel. 401-462-8000
  www.networkri.org

- **Norfork House**
  TriHab: Division of Gateway Healthcare, 58 Hamlet Ave.,
  Woonsocket, RI 02895, Tel. 401-765-4040
  www.gatewayhealth.org/substance.asp

- **Northern Western Community Reentry**
  Community Care Alliance, P.O. Box 1700, Woonsocket,
  RI 02895, Tel. 401-235-7000
  www.communitycareri.org/Home.aspx

- **Open Doors**
  485 Plainfield St., Providence, RI 02909, Tel. 401-781-5808
  www.opendoorsri.org

- **Recovery Net**
  The Providence Center, 528 North Main St., Providence,
  RI 02904, Tel. 401-528-0123, https://providencecenter.org

- **Rhode Island Communities for Addiction Recovery
  Efforts, Inc. (RICARES)**
  243 Main St., Pawtucket, RI 02860, Tel. 401-475-2960
  http://ricares.org

- **Turning Around Ministries (TAM)**
  50 Dr. Marcus F. Wheatland Blvd., Newport, RI 02840,
  Tel. 401-846-8264, www.tamri.org

- **Westbay Probation Project**
  Westbay Community Action Partnership, 224 Buttonwoods Ave.,
  Warwick, RI 02886, Tel. 401-732-4660, ext. 124
  www.westbaycap.org

SOUTH CAROLINA

- **Aiken Center for Alcohol and Other Drug Services:
  Offender Based intervention Programs**
  The Aiken Center, 1105 Gregg Hwy., Aiken, SC 29801,
  Tel. 803-649-1900. www.aikencenter.org

- **Alston Wilkes Society**
  3519 Medical Dr., Columbia, SC 29203, Tel. 803-799-2490
  www.alstonwilkessociety.org/community-services.html

- **Angels Charge Ministry – A Way Out to a New Life** (for women)
  95 Ashley St., Spartanburg, SC 29307, Tel. 864-529-5472
  www.angelschargeministry.org

  Battered But Not Broken Ministry
  564 Old York Rd., Chester, SC 29706, Tel. 803-385-2290
  www.batteredbutnotbrokenministries.org

- **Deborah's House** (for women)
  418 East River St., Anderson, SC 29624, Tel. 864-260-0062

- **Guidebook for Incarcerated Veterans in South Carolina**
  www.va.gov/HOMELESS/docs/Reentry/09_sc.pdf

- **JumpStart Ministry**
  951 S. Pine St., Spartanburg, SC 29302, Tel. 864-423-4930
  www.newlifedeliveranceworshipcenter.com/#/resources/
  prisoner-re-entry-program

- **Lowcountry Rise**
  P.O. Box 40372, North Charleston, SC 29423, Tel. 843-810-4234
  lowcountryrise.org

- **Magdalene House of Charleston**
  P.O. Box 1286, Ladson, SC 29456, Tel. 843-834-6771
  magdalenehouseofcharleston.org

- **Prosperity Center – Berkeley County**
  325 E. Main St., Moncks Corner, SC 29461, Tel. 843-761-6033

- **Soteria Community Development Corporation**
  P.O. Box 6061, Greenville, SC 29606, Tel. 864-272-0681
  www.soteriacdc.org

- **South Carolina Correctional Association**
  P.O. Box 210603, Columbia, SC 29221, Tel. 803-896-3301
  www.myscca.org

- **South Carolina Reentry Programs**
  South Carolina Department of Probation, Parole, and Pardon
  Services, 2221 Devine St., Suite 600, Columbia, SC 29250
  Tel. 803-734-9220, www.dppps.sc.gov/Offender-Supervision/
  Supervision-Strategies/Reentry-Programs

- **South Carolina STRONG**
  2510 N. Hobson Ave., North Charleston, SC 29405,
  Tel. 843-554-5179, www.southcarolinastrong.org

- **Step by Step Ministry HOPE Project, Inc.**
  113 Mason St., Greenville, SC 29601, Tel. 864-315-3730
  www.stepbystephope.org

- **Women Reaching Out – Heart of Hannah Outreach Center**
  11400 Old White Horse Rd., Travelers Rest, SC 29690-9046,
  Tel. 864-834-5600, www.heartofhannah.com

SOUTH DAKOTA

- **Community Alternatives of the Black Hills (CABH) Re-Entry Program**
  5031 Highway 79, Rapid City, SC 57701, Tel. 605-341-4240
  www.cecintl.com

- **Center of Hope**
  225 E. 11th St., Suite 101, Sioux Falls, SD 57104,
  Tel. 605-334-9789, www.centerofhopesf.org

- **Fatherhood & Families LSS**
  Lutheran Social Services, 705 East 41st St., Suite 200,
  Sioux Falls, SD 57105, Tel. 605-866-4444
  www.lsssd.org/family_services/fatherhood/

- **Goodwill of the Great Plains**
  3100 West Fourth St., Sioux City, IA 51103, Tel. 712-258-4511
  www.goodwillgreatplains.org

- **Hope Center Re-Entry Program**
  615 Kansas City St., Rapid City, SD 57701, Tel. 605-716-4673
  www.hopecenterrapidcity.org

- **Offender Reentry: U.S. Probation and Pretrial Services, District of South Dakota**
  United States Probation Office, 314 S. Main Ave., Rm. 100,
  Sioux Falls, SD 57104, Tel. 605-977-8900
  www.sdp.uscourts.gov/offender-reentry

- **One-Stop Career Centers**
  South Dakota Department of Labor, Knelp Building,
  700 Governor's Dr., Pierre, SD 57501, Tel. 605-773-3101
  www.state.sd.us/dol/sdjob/js-home.htm

- **Pennington County Health & Human Services Rebound Program**
  725 N. LaCross St., Suite 200, Rapid City, SD 57701,
  Tel. 605-394-2156, www.pennco.org/HHS

- **Rapid City Offender Re-Entry Program**
  Community Development, City of Rapid City, 333 Sixth St.,
  Rapid City, SD 57701, Tel. 605-716-4005, www.rcgov.org

- **Reentry: South Dakota Department of Corrections**
  3200 East Highway 34, c/o 500 East Capitol Ave., Pierre,
  SD 57501, Tel. 605-773-3478, http://doc.sd.gov/about/reentry

- **South Dakota Employment**
  http://sd.gov/employment.aspx

- **Volunteers of America Dakotas**
  P.O. Box 89306, Sioux Falls, SD 57109, Tel. 605-334-1414
  www.voa-dakotas.org

TENNESSEE

- **Chattanooga Endeavors, Inc.**
  2007 E. 27th Street, Chattanooga, TN 37407, Tel. 423-266-1888
  www.chattanoogaendeavors.com

- **CONNECT Ministries**
  2340 Magnolia Ave., Knoxville, TN 37914, Tel. 865-851-8005
  www.connectministries.net

- **Corizon Health Tennessee Reentry**
  tennessee.corizonreentry.com

- **Doorways Reentry Program**
  915 East McLemore Ave., Suite 201, Memphis, TN 38106,
  Tel. 901-726-6191
  familiesofincarcerated.org/doorways_reentry_program.html

- **Families of Incarcerated Individuals, Inc.**
  915 East McLemore Ave., Suite 201, Memphis, TN 38106,
  Tel. 901-726-6191, www.familiesofincarcerated.org

- **Humility Understanding God Grace Spiritual Strength (HUGGS)**
  110 Glancy St., Suite 202, Goodlettsville, TN 37072,
  Tel. 615-262-0063, huggstn.org

- **John R. Hay House Brown Annex**
  427 E. Sullivan St., Kingsport, TN 37662, Tel. 423-578-3771
  hayhouseinc.org/services/brown-annex

- **Karat Place** (for women)
  P.O. Box 9092, Memphis, TN 38190, Tel. 901-525-4055
  karatplace.org

- **The Lighthouse: Safe Harbors of Memphis, Nashville, Clarksville, and Little Rock**
  4384 Stage Rd., 4th Fl, Memphis, TN 38128, Tel. 901-646-2273
  lighthousekeepers@lhmm.org, www.lhmm.org

- **Memphis and Shelby County Office of Reentry**
  1362 Mississippi Blvd., Memphis, TN 38106, Tel. 901-222-4550
  www.mscor.org

- **Men of Valor Aftercare/Re-Entry Program**
  1410 Donelson Pike, Suite B-1, Nashville, TN 37217,
  Tel. 615-399-9111, www.men-of-valor.org

- **Nashville Dismas House**
  1513 16th Ave. South, Nashville, TN 37212, Tel. 615-297-9287
  www.dismas.org/nashville

- **Project Return, Inc.**
  806 4th Ave. South, Nashville, TN 37210, Tel. 615-327-9654
  www.projectreturninc.org

- **Sobriety Rocks Outreach**
  P.O. Box 203, Bolivar, TN 38008, Tel. 731-658-5157
  www.sobrietyrocks.yolasite.com

- **Tennessee Career Center**
  Regional Offices Directory, Tel. 615-741-6642
  www.secareercenter.org/www/docs/9/staff.htm

- **Tennessee Rehabilitation Services**
  Tennessee Department of Correction, Rachel Jackson Building,
  6th Fl., Nashville, TN 37243-0465, Tel. 615-741-1000
  www.tngov/correction/sectoin/tdoc-rehabilitation

- **Transformation Project**
  P.O. Box 22908, Chattanooga, TN 37422-2908, Tel. 423-899-4770,
  ext. 105, www.transformationproject.org

- **Upper Cumberland Dismas House**
  1226 Byrne Avenue, Cookeville, TN 38501-1207,
  Tel. 931-520-8448

TEXAS

- **Austin/Travis County Reentry Roundtable (A/TCRRT)**
  3000 Oak Springs Dr., Austin, TX 78702, Tel. 512-926-5301
  http://reentryroundtable.net

- **Bexar County Re-Entry Program**
  Bexar County Office of the Commissioner, 222 South Comal,
  San Antonio, TX 78207, Tel. 210-335-8744
  http://gov.bexar.org/reentry

- **Bridges to Life (BTL): Rehabilitation, Reconciliation, and Community Safety**
  Bridges to Life, P.O. Box 570895, Houston, TX 77257,
  Tel. 713-463-7200, www.bridgestolife.org

- **Compassion Christian Counseling**
  1029 S. Main St., Lumberton, TX 77657, Tel. 409-832-5772
  http://hisclinic.org

- **C.O.O.L. Ministries, Inc.**
  5005 W. 34th St., Suite 103-C, Houston, TX 77092,
  Tel. 713-592-0134, http://coolministries.net

- **Cornerstone Assistance Network**
  3500 Noble Ave., Fort Worth, TX 76111, Tel. 817-632-6000
  www.canetwork.org

- **Creative Outreach Ministries**
  P.O. Box 1325, Montgomery, TX 77356, Tel. 936-441-5433
  www.creativeoutreach.com

- **Disciples 4 Christ Outreach**
  P.O. Box 1052, Caddo Mills, TX 75135, Tel. 214-230-3426
  http://disciples4christoutreach.org

- **Exodus Ministries, Inc.**
  4630 Munger Ave., #10, Dallas, TX 75204, Tel. 214-827-3772
  http://exodusministries.org

158   *The Ex-Offender's Re-Entry Assistance Directory*

- **Freedom House Discipleship**
  3542 Mercury Ave., Odessa, TX 79764, Tel. 432-381-5453
  www.agapedreamcenter.com

- **Front Steps: Restoring Hope to Austin's Homeless**
  500 East 7th St., Austin, TX 78701, Tel. 512-305-4100
  www.frontsteps.org

- **Goodwill Industries of Dallas**
  3020 N. Westmoreland Rd., Dallas, TX 75212, Tel. 214-638-2800
  www.goodwilldallas.org

- **Goodwill Industries of Houston**
  1140 West Loop North, Houston, TX 77055, Tel. 713-692-6221
  www.goodwillhouston.org

- **Goodwill Industries of Southeast Texas and Southwest Louisiana**
  460 Wall St., Beaumont, TX 77701, Tel. 409-838-9911
  www.goodwillbmt.org

- **His Father's Heart Ministries**
  5715 NW Central Dr., Suite F-109, Houston, TX 77092
  Tel. 713-996-0980, http://hisfathersheart.org

- **Hope Prison Ministries, Inc.**
  3515 Sycamore School Rd., Suite 125, PMB, 172, Fort Worth, TX 76133, Tel. 817-323-7686
  www.hopeprisonministries.org

- **House Where Jesus Shines**
  18320 Gholson Rd., Waco, TX 76705, Tel. 254-829-2100
  www.housewherejesusshines.org

- **Hungry for God Home**
  3504 Victorine Lane, Del Valle, TX 78617, Tel. 512-247-4942
  www.hungryforgodchurch.org

- **MentorCare Ministries**
  1808 Chattanooga Dr., Bedford, TX 76022, Tel. 817-688-4044
  www.mentorcare.org

- **One-Stop Centers**
  Employment and training helpline: 1-877-872-5627
  www.servicelocator.org

- **SEARCH Homeless Services**
  2505 Fanin St., Houston, TX 77002, Tel. 713-739-7752
  www.searchhomeless.org

- **Sharing Hope Ministry**
  P.O. Box 7160, Amarillo, TX 79114, Tel. 806-358-7803
  www.sharinghopeministry.org

- **Spirit Key Ministry**
  13617 Kaltenbrun Rd., Houston, TX 77086, Tel. 281-813-0093
  www.spiritkey.org

- **Tarrant County Reentry Coalition**
  www.tcreentry.org

- **Tarrant County Reentry Resource List**
  cornerstone.meettheneed.org/directory/print-all.php

- **Texas Criminial Justice Coalition Reentry Guide**
  www.criminaljusticecoalition.org/tools_for_re_entry/adult_services

- **Texas Department of Criminal Justice: Reentry and Integration**
  Reentry and Integration Division
  4616 W. Howard Lane, Suite 200, Austin, TX 78728,
  Tel. 512-671-2134, tdcj.state.tx.us/divisions/rid/index.html

- **Texas Prison Ministry**
  7520 Hillcroft St., Houston, TX 77081, Tel. 713-972-5789
  www.texasprisonministry.com

- **Texas ReEntry Services, Inc.**
  610 S. Jennings Ave., Fort Worth, TX 76104, Tel. 817-834-2833
  txrs.org

- **Texas Offenders Reentry Initiative (T.O.R.I.) of Bishop T.D. Jakes**
  P.O. Box 4386, Dallas, TX 75208, Tel. 214-941-1325, ext. 300
  P.O. Box 2645, Ft. Worth, TX 76113, Tel. 817-632-7437

1703 Gray, Houston, TX 77003, Tel. 713-650-0595

2803 E. Commerce St., San Antonio, TX 78205

www.medc-tori.org

- **Trinity Restoration Ministries (TRM)**
P.O. Box 363, Rowlett, TX 75030, Tel. 214-565-4260
http://trinintyrestoration.org

- **Unlocking DOORS Texas Reentry Network**
Reentry Brokerage Center, 1402 Corinth St., Suite 235, Dallas, TX 75215, Tel. 214-296-9258, www.unlockingdoors.org

- **Volunteers of America Texas, Inc.**
300 E. Midway Dr., Euless, TX 76039, Tel. 817-529-7300
www.voatx.org

UTAH

- **Active Reentry**
10 S. Fairgrounds Rd., Price, UT 84501, Tel. 435-637-4950
www.arecil.org

- **Adult Substance Abuse Treatment Program**
Volunteers of America Utah, 435 W. Bearcat Dr.,
Salt Lake City, UT 84115, Tel. 801-363-9414, www.voaut.org

- **Department of Workforce Services**
P.O. Box 45249, Salt Lake City, UT 84145, Tel. 801-526-9675
http://jobs.utah.gov

- **Foundation for Family Life**
Riverton, UT, Tel. 801-679-3821
www.fflut.org

- **The Genesis Project**
3525 Riverdale Rd., Ogden, UT 84405, Tel. 801-896-4370
www.genesisutah.com

- **Golden Spike Outreach**
1537 Saxon Circle, Springville, UT 84663, Tel. 801-489-9870

Golden Spike Treatment Ranch, Inc., 12000 South 73200 West, Lucin Valley, UT 84313, goldenspikeoutreach.com

- **Papilion House, Inc.** (for women)
  341 North 1100 East, American Fork, UT 84003,
  Tel. 801-473-3963, www.papilionhouse.com

- **Salt Lake County Criminal Justice Services**
  145 East 1300 South, Suite #501, Salt Lake City, UT 84115,
  Tel. 385-468-3500, slco.org/criminal-justice/

- **Treatment Resource Center**
  150 E. Center, Provo, UT 84603, Tel. 801-344-1200

  2445 South Water Tower Way, Ogden, UT 84401,
  Tel. 801-627-7810

  1225 W. Valley View Dr., Logan, UT 84321, Tel. 801-713-6240

  36 W. Fremont Ave., Salt Lake City, UT 84101,
  Tel. 801-239-2145 (women) or 801-239-2199 (men)

  835 East 300 North, #500, Richfield, UT 84701,
  Tel. 435-896-2770

  620 South 5300 West, Suite 247, Hurricane, UT 84737,
  Tel. 435-634-2800

  1365 S. Carbon Ave., Price, UT 84501, Tel. 435-636-2800, ext. 817,
  corrections.utah.gov

- **Utah County Reentry Resource**
  ucreentry.wordpress.com

- **YWCA Choices for Women**
  YWCA, 322 East 300 South, Salt Lake City, UT 84111,
  Tel. 801-537-8604, www.ywca.com

VERMONT

- **Battleboro Community Justice Center**
  230 Main St., Suite 302, Brattleboro, VT 05301,
  Tel. 802-251-8142, www.bcrj.org/programs

- **Burlington Offender Support Services**
  Burlington Community Justice Center, 200 Church St.,
  Burlington, VT 05401, Tel. 802-865-7155
  www.burlingtonvt.gov/CJC/Offender-Support-Services
  http://www.det.state.vt.us

- **Burlington Housing Authority**
  65 Main St., Burlington, VT 05401, Tel. 802-864-0538
  burlingtonhousing.org

- **Burlington Offender Re-entry Program**
  Offender Workforce Development Specialist,
  179 S. Winooski Ave., Burlington, VT 05401, www.vabir.org

- **Center for Restorative Justice**
  439 Main St., Suite 2, Bennington, VT 05201,
  Tel. 802-447-1595, www.bcrj.org/programs

- **Community Resource Centers**
  Vermont Department of Employment and Training,
  5 Green Mountain Dr., P.O. Box 488, Montpelier, VT 05601,
  Tel. 802-828-4000, www.det.state.vt.us

- **Circles of Support and Accountability (CoCSA)**
  Burlington Community Justice Center, 2000 Church St.,
  Burlington, VT 05401, Tel. 802-865-7155
  www.burlingtonvt.gov/CJC/Circles-of-Support-and-
  Accountability-COSA

- **Dismas of Vermont**
  103 E. Allen E. St., Winooski, VT 05404, Tel. 603-795-2770
  www.dismasofvermont.org

- **Essex Community Justice Center: Community
  Transition Program**
  137 Iroquois Ave., Suite 101, Essex Junction, VT 05452,
  Tel. 802-872-7690, www.essex.org

- **Franklin Grand Isle Restorative Justice Center**
  Offender Re-entry Specialist, 120 North Main St.,
  St. Albans, VT 05478 , http://cjnvt.org/center/st-albans-
  community-justice-center/

- **Greater Barre Community Justice Center**
  20 Auditorium Hill, Barre, VT 05641, Tel. 802-476-0276
  www.gbcjc.org

- **Judd Reentry Transitional Housing**
  NEKCA Community and Justice Programs, 70 Main St.,
  Newport, VT 05855, Tel. 802-334-7318
  www.nekcavt.org/index.php/community-and-justice-programs

- **Lamoille Restorative Center Reentry Program**
  221 Main St., P.O. Box 148, Hyde Park, VT 05755,
  Tel. 802-888-5871 and 802-888-0657, www.lrcvt.org

- **Mercy Connections Vermont Women's**
  Mentoring Program (VWMP)
  Mercy Connections, 255 South Chaplain St., Suite 8, Burlington,
  VT 05401, Tel. 802-846-7063
  http://mercyconnectoins.org/index.html

- **Newport Community Justice Center Offender Re-entry**
  Orleans County Restorative Justice Center, 55 Seymour Lane,
  Newport, VT 05855, Tel. 802-487-9327, www.kingdomjustice.org

- **RUNCJC Offender Reentry**
  Rutland's United Neighborhoods Community Justice Center, 128
  Merchant's Row, Suite 401, Rutland, VT 05701,
  Tel. 802-770-5364, www.runcjc.org

- **Saint Albans Community Justice Center**
  17 Lake St., #2, Saint Albans, VT 05478, Tel. 802-524-7006
  http://stalbansvt.com

- **Springfield Restorative Justice Center Community Re-entry**
  Historic Bank Block, 96 Main St., Suite 208, Springfield,
  VT 05156, Tel. 802-885-8707, www.springfieldrjc.org

- **South Burlington Community Justice Center:**
  Offender Reentry
  19 Gregory Dr., South Burlington, VT 05403, Tel. 802-846-4215
  www.sburl.com/cjc

- **Vermont Works for Women – Vocational Training for**
  Incarcerated Women
  51 Park St., Essex Junction, VT 05401, Tel. 802-655-8900,
  ext. 504, www.vtworksforwomen.org

- **Vermont Works for Women – Transitional Jobs Program**
  51 Park St., Essex Junction, VT 05401, Tel. 802-655-8900,
  ex. 504, www.vtworksforwomen.org

VIRGINIA

- **Adult Alternative Program**
  121 W. Brookland Park Blvd., Richmond, VA 23222,
  Tel. 888-323-1164, www.adultalternativeprogram.com

- **Assisting Families of Inmates**
  1 North Fifth St., Suite 416, Richmond, VA 23219,
  Tel. 804-643-2401, www.afoi.org

- **Boaz & Ruth**
  3030 Meadowbridge Rd., Richmond, VA 23222,
  Tel. 804-329-4900, www.boazandruth.com

- **Bridging the Gap in Virginia**
  5104 Roanoke Avenue, Newport News, VA 23605,
  Tel. 804-321-4421, www.bridgeingthegapinvirginia.org

- **Career Connect**
  Virginia Employment Commission, 703 E. Main St., Richmond,
  VA 23219, Tel. 804-786-1484, www.vec.state.va.us

- **Gemeinschaft Home**
  1423 Mt. Clinton Pike, Harrisonburg, VA 22802, Tel. 540-434-1690
  www.gemeinschafthome.com

- **Norfolk Prisoner Reentry Program**
  The City of Norfolk, Human Services, 741 Monticello Ave.,
  Norfolk, VA 23510, Tel. 757-664-6000
  www.norfolk.gov/index.aspx?NID=1938

- **Opportunities, Alternatives, and Resources (OAR)**
  10640 Page Ave., Suite 250, Fairfax, VA 22030,
  Tel. 703-246-3033, www.oarfairfax.org

- **Opportunity, Alliance, Reentry (OAR) of Richmond, Inc.**
  1 North 3rd St., Suite 200, Richmond, VA 23219, Tel. 804-643-2746
  www.oarric.org

- **Re-entry Program: Virginia Community Corrections**
  P.O. Box 26963, Richmond, VA 23261-6963, Tel. 804-674-3000
  vadoc.virginia.gov/community/default.shtm

- **Resource Information Help for the Disadvantaged (RIHD)**
  P.O. Box 55, Highland Springs, VA 23075, Tel. 804-426-4426
  www.rihd.org

- **Step-Up, Inc.**
  5900 East Virginia Beach Blvd., Suite 102, Norfolk, VA 23502,
  Tel. 757-588-3151, http://stepupincorporated.org/index.html

- **Virginia Beach Reentry Council**
  Human Services Building, 3432 Virginia Beach Blvd.,
  Virginia Beach, VA 23452, Tel. 757-385-3111
  www.vbgov.com/government/departments/human-services/Pages/
  VirginiaBeachReentryCouncil.aspx

- **Virginia Center for Restorative Justice: Reentry Program**
  3420 Pump Rd., Suite 188, Richmond, VA 23233,
  Tel. 804-313-9596, www.vcrj.org

- **Virginia CARES** (Community Action Re-entry System,
  12 sites throughout the state)

  Department of Community and Human Services:
  2355-A Mill Rd., Alexandria, VA 22314, Tel. 703-746-5919

  Capitol Area Partnership - Uplifting People: 3930 Anderson
  Highway, Powhatan, VA 23139, Tel. 804-598-3351

  Lynchburg Community Action Group: 915 Main St., Lynchburg,
  VA 24504, Tel. 434-455-1601, ext. 311

  New River Community Action: 110 Roanoke St., Christiansburg,
  VA 24073, Tel. 540-382-9382

  Office of Human Affairs: 2410 Wickham Ave., Newport News,
  VA 23607, Tel. 757-247-0379, ext. 305

  People, Inc.: 1173 W. Main St., Abingdon, VA 24210,
  Tel. 276-619-2204

  Pittsylvania County Community Action Agency:
  713 Piney Forest Rd., Danville, VA 24541, Tel. 434-793-5627

Support to Eliminate Poverty - Martinsville Office: East Main St., Martinsville, VA 24112, Tel. 276-638-8311

Support to Eliminate Poverty - Rocky Mount Office: 200 Dent St., Rocky Mount, VA 24151, Tel. 540-483-4901

Total Action Against Poverty - Covington Office: 118 South Lexington Ave., Covington, VA 24426, Tel. 540-962-6328

Total Action Against Poverty - Roanoke Office: 302 Second St., SW, Roanoke, VA 24011, Tel. 540-283-4901

Virginia CARES - Fredericksburg Office: 5620 Southpoint Centre Blvd., Fredericksburg, VA 22407, Tel. 540-710-2102, ext. 5031

www.vacares.org/sites.html and vacares.org/assets/docs/Client-Brochureupdates8-3-2015.pdf

- **Virginia CURE (Citizens United for the Rehabilitation of Errants)**
  P.O. Box 2310, Vienna, VA 22183, Tel. 703-272-3624

  Northern Virginia CURE: Arlington Unitarian Universalist Church, 4444 Arlington Blvd., Arlington, VA 2204

  Hampton Roads CURE: Norview Baptist Church, 1127 Norview Ave., Norfolk, VA 23515

  Richmond CURE: Friends Meeting House, 4500 Kensington Ave., Richmond, VA 23221, vacure.org

- **Virginia Department of Social Services: Prisoner Reentry & Human Services**
  801 E. Main St., Richmond, VA 23219-2901, Tel. 800-777-8293
  www.dss.virginia.gov/community/prisoner_reentry/

- **Virginia Interfaith Center**
  1716 East Franklin St., Richmond, VA 23223, Tel. 804-643-2474
  www.virginiainterfaithcenter.org

WASHINGTON

- **American Civil Liberty Union (ACLU): Second Chances**
  901 Fifth Ave., Suite 630, Seattle, WA 98164,
  Tel. 206-624-2184, aclu-wa.org/second-chances

- **Conviction Careers**
  P.O. Box 432, Lynnwood, WA 98046, Tel. 866-436-1960
  www.convictioncareers.org

- **Crossways Ministries**
  P.O. Box 1954, Auburn, WA 98071
  www.crosswaysministries.com

- **Fresh Start Jail and Prison Programs**
  Fresh Start Housing of Washington, 10924 Mukilteo Speedway,
  Suite 230, Mukilteo, WA 98275, Tel. 206-486-4493
  http://freshstarthousingwa.org/index1.html

- **Goodwill Industries Inland Northwest**
  130 E. Third Ave., Spokane, WA 99202, Tel. 509-838-4246
  www.discovergoodwill.org

- **The If Project** (links to local resources)
  www.theifproject.com/resources/recently-out-of-prison/

- **Incarcerated Veterans**
  Washington State Department of Veteran's Affairs,
  P.O. Box 41150, Olympia, WA 98504-1150, Tel. 1-800-562-2308
  www.dva.wa.gov/incarcerated_project.html

- **Institutions Project - Reentry Clinics**
  Columbia Legal Services, 101 Yesler Way, Suite 300, Seattle,
  WA 98104, Tel. 206-287-8625, http://columbialegal.org

- **King County Criminal Justice Initiatives Project**
  King County Mental Health, Chemical Abuse and Dependency
  Services Division, 401 5th Ave., Suite 400, Seattle, WA 98104,
  Tel. 206-263-8954
  www.kingcounty.gov/healthservices/MentalHealth.aspx

- **Mentally Ill Offender Services Program**
Sound Mental Health, 1600 E. Olive St., Seattle, WA 98122, Tel. 206-302-2300, http://smh.org

- **New Connections – Irma Gary House** (for women)
613 S. 15th St., Tacoma, WA 98405, Tel. 253-617-1405
www.nctacoma.org

- **Offender/Ex-Offender Resources for Washington State**
email: contact@4people.org
4people.org/Reentry/Reentry.html

- **Offender Re-entry Community Safety Program (ORCSP)**
Multiple locations throughout Island, San Juan, Skagit, Snohomish, and Whatcom counties, www.compasshealth.org/services/offender-re-entry-community-safety-program-orcsp

- **Offender Reentry: Department of Corrections**
801 88th Avenue SE, Tumwater, WA 98501, Tel. 360-725-9100
www.washingtonci.com/offender-reentry.html

- **Opportunity Council**
1419 Cornwall Ave., Bellingham, WA 98225, Tel. 360-734-5121
www.oppco.org

- **Oxford Houses**
List of contacts: wa.oxfordhouse.us/?page_id=113
wa.oxfordhouse.us

- **People for People**
309 E. Mountain View Ave., Ellensburg, WA 98926,
Tel. 509-925-3311, www.pfp.org

- **Pioneer Human Services**
7440 W. Marginal Way S., Seattle, WA 98108, Tel. 206-768-1990
www.pioneerhumanservices.org

- **Restorative Community Coalition**
P.O. Box 31026, Bellingham, WA 98228, Tel. 360-739-7493
http://whatcomrec.org/main.html

- **Seattle Goodwill/STRIVE Seattle**
700 Dearborn Place S., Seattle, WA 98144, Tel. 206-329-1000
www.seattlegoodwill.org

- **STAR's Mission**
  The STAR Project, 321 Wellington Ave., Walla Walla, WA 99362, Tel. 509-525-3612, www.thestarproject.us

- **Transforming Lives**
  Washington State Department of Social and Health Services, Box 11699, Tacoma, WA 98411-9905, www.dshs.wa.gov

- **Women's Re-entry Program**
  University of Washington Women's Center, Cunningham Hall, Box 353070, Seattle, WA 98185, Tel. 206-685-1090
  depts.washington.edu/womenctr/programs/re-entry-program/

- **WorkSource Center**
  Tel. 1-877-872-5627
  www.wa.gov/esd/work/localconnections.htm

WEST VIRGINIA

- **Covenant House**
  600 Shrewbury St., Charleston, WV 25301, Tel. 304-344-8053
  www.wvcovenanthouse.org

- **Liberty Center of Roark-Sullivan Life Way Center**
  Liberty Center, 509 & 611 Shrewsbury St., Charleston, WV 25301, Tel. 304-414-3114, http://rslwc.org

- **Northern Panhandle Reentry Program**
  Capitol Complex, 1900 Kanawha Blvd. East, Building One, Room E-100, Charleston, WV 25305-0830, Tel. 304-558-0145
  www.courtswv.gov/lower-courts/reentry.html

- **Rea of Hope, Inc.**
  1429 Lee St., Charleston, WV 25301, Tel. 304-344-5363
  www.reaofhope.org/index.php

- **Second Chance Mentoring Program**
  KISRA (Kanawha Institute for Social Research and Action, Inc.), 131 Perkins Ave., Dunbar, WV 25064, Tel. 304-768-8924
  www.kisra.org/#!employment/c1zy3

- **West Virginia Re-Entry Initiative**
  1409 Greenbrier St., Charleston, WV 25311, Tel. 304-558-2036
  www.wvdoc.com/wvdoc/OffenderReEntry/tabid/118/Default.aspx

- **Work4WV**
  112 California Ave., Charleston, WV 25305, Tel. 304-558-1138
  www.state.wv.us/scripts/bep/jobs/

WISCONSIN

- **Asha's Corrections Care Continuum (CCC)**
  ASHA Family Services, Inc., 3719 West Center St., Milwaukee,
  WI 53210, Tel. 414-875-1511, www.ashafamilyservices.org

- **ATTIC Correctional Services**
  601 Atlas Ave., P.O. Box 7370, Madison, WI 53707,
  Tel. 608-223-0017, www.correctionalservices.org

- **Circles of Support**
  Goodwill NCW Community Center, 1800 Appleton Rd.,
  Menasha, WI 54952, Tel. 920-968-6832
  www.goodwillncw.org

- **Circles of Support - Inmate Re-entry Program**
  AMOS, Inc., P.O. Box 1211, La Crosse, WI 54602,
  Tel. 608-606-9419
  www.amosadvocates.org/index.html

- **CLM Aftercare Program**
  Changing Lives Ministry, Inc., P.O. Box 250514,
  Milwaukee, WI 53225

- **Columbus House**
  Kenosha Human Development Services, Inc., 5407 8th Ave.,
  Kenosha, WI 53140, Tel. 262-657-7188, www.khds.org

- **Community Advocates Justice 2000**
  Community Advocates, 728 N. James Lovell St., Milwaukee,
  WI 53233, Tel. 414-270-2970, www.communityadvocates.net

- **The Demeter Foundation, Inc.**
  P.O. Box 259283, Madison, WI 53725, Tel. 608-298-3563
  www.thedemeterfoundation.com

- **EATA Re-Entry Program**
  1819 Aberg Ave., Madison, WI 53704, Tel. 608-242-7431
  www.eata.org/Re-Entry_Program.html

- **Fair Shake, Inc.**
  P.O. Box 63, Westby, WI 54667, Tel. 608-634-6363
  www.fairshake.net

- **Joshua Glover House: Federal Residential Reentry Center**
  Wisconsin Community Services, Inc., 2404 N. 50th St.,
  Milwaukee, WI 53210, Tel. 414-442-3700
  www.wiscs.org/programs/reentry/joshua_glover_house-1

- **Kenosha Programs and Services**
  Salvation Army Kenosha Corps Community Center,
  3116 75th St., Kenosha, WI 53142, Tel. 262-564-0286
  www.salvationarmywi.org/wum/kenosha

- **Madison Urban Ministries (MUM)**
  2300 S. Park St., Suite 2202, Madison, WI 53713,
  Tel. 608-256-0906, www.emum.org

- **New Song Prison Ministries**
  New Song Ministries, 3116 75th St., P.O. Box 2212, Kenosha,
  WI 53142, Tel. 262-818-2700, www.newsongministries.us

- **Opening Avenues to Reentry Success (OARS)**
  Wisconsin Department of Health Services, 1 West Wilson St.,
  Madison, WI 53703, www.dhs.wisconsin.gov/oars/index.htm

- **Federal Residential Re-Entry Center**
  2930 N. 25th St., Milwaukee, WI 53206, Tel. 414-445-3301
  www.wiscs.org/programs/reentry/parsons_house-4

- **Project 180**
  Center for Self-Sufficiency (CFSS) - Program Office,
  728 N. James Lovell St., Milwaukee, WI 53233, Tel. 414-270-2957
  www.centerinc.org/index.html

- **Project for Assistance in Transition from Homelessness (PATH)**
  Outreach Community Health Centers, 711 W. Capitol Dr.,
  Milwaukee, WI 53206, Tel. 414-374-2400
  www.orchc-milw.org

- **Project RETURN**
  2821 N. 4th St., Suite 202, Milwaukee, WI 53212,
  Tel. 414-374-8029, www.projectreturnmilwaukee.org

- **Racine Vocational Ministry**
  Second Chance Program, 214 7th St., Racine, WI 53403,
  Tel. 262-633-8660, www.rvmracine.org

- **Re-Entry Services at The Nehemiah Center
  for Justice and Reconciliation**
  Nehemiah Center for Urban Leadership Development,
  655 W. Badger Rd., Madison, WI 53713, Tel. 608-257-2453
  http://nehemiah.org

- **Restorative Community Service**
  The Benedict Center, 135 W. Wells St., Suite 700, Milwaukee,
  WI 53203, Tel. 414-347-1774, www.benedictcenter.org

- **TEAM Reentry Program: Justiceworks**
  1578 Strongs Ave., Stevens Point, WI 54481,
  Tel. 715-344-3677
  www.justiceworksltd.org/team-reentry-program/

- **Wisconsin Department of Workforce Development**
  Job Centers, Ex-Offender Toolkit, 201 E. Washington Ave.,
  Madison, WI 53702, Tel. 888-258-9966
  wisconsinjobcenter.org/exo

- **Wisconsin Reentry Program**
  Wisconsin Department of Corrections, P.O. Box 7925,
  Madison, WI 53707-7925, Tel. 608-240-5000, doc.wi.gov/about/
  doc-overview/office-of-the-secretary/reentry-unit

WYOMING

- **Adult Community Corrections (ACCs)**
  Wyoming Department of Corrections - Services and Programs
  http://corrections.wy.gov/services/index.html

- **Booth Hall Adult Re-Entry**
  VOA Northern Rockies-Booth Hall, 1299 Raymond St,
  P.O. Box 1346, Gillette, WY 82717, Tel. 307-682-8505
  www.voanr.org

- **Casper Re-Entry Center (CRC)**
  10007 Land Mark Lane, P.O. Box 2380, Casper, WY 82604,
  Tel. 307-268-4840, www.cecintl.com/facilities_rr_wy_001.html

- **Cheyenne Transitional Center**
  322 W. 17th St., Cheyenne, WY 82001, Tel. 307-632-9096
  www.avaloncorrections.com

- **Goodwill Industries of Wyoming**
  612 W. 17th St., Cheyenne, WY 82001, Tel. 307-634-0823
  www.goodwillwy.org

- **Interfaith-Good Samaritan**
  710 E. Garfield St., Suite 127, Laramie, WY 82070,
  Tel. 307-742-4240, www.interfaithgoodsam.com

- **Second Chance Ministries**
  706 Longmont St., Gillette, WY 82716, Tel. 307-682-3148
  www.secondchancegillette.org

- **Seton House - Family Transitional Housing**
  919 North Durbin St., P.O. Box 1557, Casper,
  WY 82601, Tel. 307-577-8026, www.setonhousecasper.org

- **Transitional Housing & Self-Sufficiency Program**
  Community Action of Laramie County, 211 W. 19th St.,
  Cheyenne, WY 82001, Tel. 307-635-9291, www.calc.net

- **Wyoming Offender Reentry and Community Resources**
  1934 Wyott Dr., Suite 100, Cheyenne, WY 82002,
  Tel. 307-777-3775, corrections.wy.gov/services/transition.html

5

Re-Entry Handbooks, Workbooks, Directories, Curricula, and Databases

I F YOU'RE INTERESTED IN DEVELOPING, acquiring, or simply surveying re-entry handbooks, workbooks, directories, and databases, you should first search for what's available online for free or a nominal fee rather than try to literally "reinvent the wheel" from scratch. Indeed, during the past decade, several organizations have developed useful re-entry resources to assist ex-offenders with the re-entry process. Many are sponsored by the re-entry or education sections of state departments of correction and are state-specific in terms of re-entry details. Others have been developed by nonprofit and volunteer groups, such as the United Way or publishers, such as Houghton Mifflin Harcourt and Impact Publications.

While some of this information may be found with the Federal Bureau of Prison's 230 Residential Reentry Centers (halfway houses), most will be part of pre-release programs in state prisons, which often begin 18 months prior to an inmate's release. The handbooks and participant workbooks typically run 100 to 300 pages in length and are facilitated by re-entry specialists who help inmates develop realistic re-entry or transition plans for life on the outside.

Standard Contents

Most of these re-entry resources cover similar ground. However, most also are customized to respond to each state's unique criminal laws, court orders, sentencing guidelines, and probation procedures. A typical handbook, for example, will have individual chapters and sections devoted to the following re-entry issues and activities:

- Documentation
- Housing
- Employment
- Transportation
- Food
- Clothing
- Health and wellness
- Mental health
- Substance abuse
- Education
- Life skills

- Parenting and child support
- Family and friends
- Personal finances
- Voting rights
- Parole issues
- Legal matters
- Restorative justice
- Veterans affairs
- Living under supervision
- Tattoo removal

Downloadable Re-Entry Guides and Online Databases

One of the best examples of a comprehensive re-entry guide is Colorado's 228-page *The Go Guide: Getting On After Getting Out, A Reentry Guide for Colorado* (www.ccjrc.org/find-help – paper version available for $10.00). Covering the following 20 chapters of customized content for Colorado, this book is literally a roadmap for re-entry success for Colorado inmates and their families:

Chapter 1: Info you need now...and later

Make good use of your time..1
Working with case managers... 2
Time computation..3
The Americans with Disabilities Act...7
Record keeping... 9
Restitution payments..10
Mentoring programs...12

Chapter 2: Planning for release

Why plan for release 14
Choosing a parole sponsor 17
Paroling or discharging homeless.. 20
Sex offense conviction/determination 21
Interstate Compact..22
Special needs parole 24
Presumption of parole 25
Appealing a denied parole plan..26

Chapter 3: Community corrections

An overview 28

The referral process 29
19 ways to succeed 32
Other information about community corrections 33

Chapter 4: Going before the parole board for release

Prison sentence for crime committed before July 1, 1993 39
Prison sentence for crime committed after July 1, 1993 39
Colorado Board of Parole 40
Factors considered by the parole board 40
What should be in a release plan 42
The hearing 42
Requesting a reconsideration of a parole decision 46
Parole suspension and rescission hearings 46
Waiving a parole hearing 47
Ordering a tape of the hearing 47

Chapter 5: Understanding parole

Parole basics 48
Intensive supervision program–parole (ISP-P) 52
19 Ways to succeed on parole 53
Advice for getting along with your parole officer 54
How to avoid revocation 55
Difficulty with your parole officer 56
DOC community re-entry program 56
Treatment accountability for safer communities (TASC) 57
Benefits and assistance 58
People convicted of a sexual offense 58
Absconding, escape, and association 60
Early discharge from parole 61

Chapter 6: Going before the parole board for a revocation

Filing of a parole complaint 63
Arrest or summons 63
Parole revocation hearing 64
Self-revocation 66
Possible outcomes of a revocation hearing 67
Options available to the parole board if parole is revoked 67
Community return-to-custody facilities (CRCF) 69
Administrative appeal of parole revocation 69
Appealing to a district court 69

Chapter 7: Legal matters

Old tickets and fines 70
Detainers for pending charges 71

Pending charges and warrants when no detainer
  has been filed 72
Detainers for unfinished and consecutive sentences 73
Detainers for Immigration and Customs Enforcement (ICE) 74
Dealing with warrants after release...74
Divorce and other family law matters..74

Chapter 8: Child support

Child support...76
How to ask for a lower child support order..78
Child support after your release from prison 81
Why you don't want to ignore your child support 81
Resources after release 82
Problems with a child support enforcement unit...................................82
Payment records of child support...82
Example letter to a child support enforcement unit 83

Chapter 9: Staying connected and reconnecting

Staying connected while you're in prison...84
Getting ready for release 85
Getting right with you 86
Reconnecting with your spouse or partner...86
Reconnecting with your children 87
Connecting with friends 88
New relationships...88
Resources for you and your family 89
Address confidentiality program 94

Chapter 10: The first days out

A letter from a friend...95
Getting off the bus...96
Contacting your parole officer..97
Using your release debit card 97
Changes in technology 98
Wanting it all NOW...99

Chapter 11: Places to find help

Denver metro area 101
Resources for the rest of the state..110

Chapter 12: Medical, substance abuse, and mental health treatment

Medical records while incarcerated..115
DOC medical records 115

Medical care after release 116
Substance abuse treatment services...............................126
Mental health treatment services...................................132

Chapter 13: Shelters and housing

Shelters, transitional housing, and long-term housing 137
Public Housing Program and Housing Choice
    Voucher Program 154
Renting a home...155
Buying a home 157

Chapter 14: Identification documents

State identification card or driver's license 160
Birth certificate 162
Social Security card..164
Marriage certificate/divorce decree...............................166
U.S. Passport 166
Veterans: DD-214...166
Getting help...167

Chapter 15: Employment

Networking and other job search strategies 168
Employment and parole: working together.....................169
Applications 170
The interview..174
Background checks 177
Day labor and temporary agencies.................................178
Apprenticeship programs 178
Employment with state agencies and
    professional licensing 179
Work Opportunity Tax Credit and the Federal
    Bonding Program..180
Small business rumors and information...........................181
Where to find help..181
Professional clothing...188
Sealing an arrest or conviction record.............................189
Expungement..192
Executive clemency...192

Chapter 16: Continuing your education

General Education Development (GED)..............................194
College 194
Financial aid information 199
Outstanding school loans and grants...............................202

Chapter 17: Applying for benefits and assistance

Applying for Social Security benefits and Medicaid
   prior to release 204
Interview advice 205
Social Security Administration (SSA) benefits 206
Department of human/social services: benefits
   and assistance..209

Chapter 18: Veterans

U.S. Department of Veterans Affairs...................................213
Information about health care benefits.................................214
Disability compensation or pension benefits........................215
Other resources for veterans...216

Chapter 19: Money matters

Taking care of loose financial ends 218
Saving for release..219
Checking and savings accounts...220
Individual development accounts...220
Budgeting 221
Credit report 222
Income taxes..222
Wage garnishment 224
Don't get stuck with high fees..225
Places to get help, information, and classes 225

Chapter 20: Voting information

Who can and cannot vote in Colorado 227
Frequently asked questions 228
Current information..228

Another useful reentry handbook, designed with both nationwide and state content, is the ***Essential Reentry Sourcebook: Resources and Assistance for Individuals, Families, and Communities, 2ⁿᵈ Edition,*** edited by Terrell M. Hall and Shawn R. Pelly (Ray Brook Reentry Initiative, Federal Bureau of Prisons, Federal Correctional Institutions, Ray Brook, NY, 2015). It includes over 3,500 local, state, and national listing relating to ex-offender re-entry. You can download a PDF version of this resource at:

www.fairshake.net/reentry-resources/search-for-a-resource

(click onto "Essential Reentry Sourcebook" link)

One of the best online search databases for identifying state and local re-entry resources is found in Florida: ***FDOC Reentry Resources Directory*** (Florida Department of Corrections):

www.dc.state.fl.us/resourceDirectory/Search.aspx

Many institutions also use Impact Publications's 16 re-entry books, workbooks, journal, and pocket guides (see the ads and order form at the end of this book). Sample pages of these resources can be previewed by accessing the titles at www.impactpublications.com:

- **Journal**
  99 Days to Re-Entry Success Journal

- **Pocket Guides**
  The Anger Management Pocket Guide
  The Re-Entry Employment and Life Skills Pocket Guide
  The Re-Entry Personal Finance Pocket Guide
  The Re-Entry Start-Up Pocket Guide
  Re-Imagining Life on the Outside Pocket Guide

- **Workbooks**
  Best Jobs for Ex-Offenders
  The Ex-Offender's 30/30 Job Solution
  The Ex-Offender's Job Interview Guide
  The Ex-Offender's Quick Job Finding Guide
  The Ex-Offender's Re-Entry Success Guide

- **Books**
  Best Resumes and Letters for Ex-Offenders
  The Ex-Offender's Guide to a Responsible Life
  The Ex-Offender's New Job Finding and Survival Guide
  Overcoming 101 More Barriers to Employment
  Overcoming Employment Barriers

Several re-entry preparation resources, similar in scope to Colorado's ***To Go Guide***, are available online and most can be downloaded for free. Start with the following websites for developing your own rich inventory of re-entry handbooks, training resources, and databases. If you're unable to find a resource directory on a particular state or geographic location (the remainder of this chapter includes 29 states and the District of Columbia), access the United Way's 2-1-1 (www.211.org), which is one of the most comprehensive gateways to local resources relevant to many aspects of ex-offender re-entry. Also, as recommended in the last section of this chapter, with examples of Virginia's re-entry curricula, contact your state's re-entry or education office within the Department of Corrections to inquiry about the availability of similar free resources.

NATIONWIDE

- ***Building Career Facilitation Skills – Module 6: Helping Offenders Secure Employment Facilitator's Curriculum***
  National Institute of Corrections. Download PDF version here:
  www.ncda.org/aws/NCDA/asset_manager/get_file/72608

- ***Employment Information Handbook***
  Federal Bureau of Prisons, Inmate Transition Branch, 2011.
  Download PDF version here:
  www.bop.gov/resources/pdfs/emp_info_handbk.pdf

- ***Essential Reentry Sourcebook: Resources and Assistance for Individuals, Families, and Communities, 2nd Edition***
  Edited by Terrell M. Hall and Shawn R. Pelly, Ray Brook Reentry Initiative, Federal Bureau of Prisons, Federal Correctional Institutions, Ray Brook, NY, 2015. This nearly 350-page re-entry resource directory represents one of the most comprehensive treatments of the subject. Includes over 3,500 local, state, and national listing for overcoming re-entry challenges. Download PDF version here:
  www.fairshake.net/reentry-resources/search-for-a-resource
  (click onto "Essential Reentry Sourcebook)

- ***Fair Shake Reentry Resource Center***
  Fair Shake, Inc. Includes a wealth of linkages to important re-entry information and services. Access online here:
  www.fairshake.net

- ***OES (Offender Employment Specialist): Building Bridges, A National Institute of Corrections Training Program***
  National Institute of Corrections. A 120-page training manual, with onsite activities combined with five hours of DVD segments

(divided into 72 short video segments), feature practitioners in the field sharing a variety of tools, strategies, and best practices for ex-offender re-entry focused on the employment process. Download PDF version here: www.uaa.alaska.edu/centerforhumandevelopment/servingoffend ersconfences/upload/OES-Training-Manual.pdf

- *Offender Transition Program: Resource Manual*
  Federal Bureau of Prisons, 2010. Download PDF version here: www.uaa.alaska.edu/centerforhumandevelopment/servingoffender sconfences/upload/Offender-Transition-Program-Resource-Manu al.pdf

- *Prisoners' Assistance Directory*
  National Prison Project of the American Civil Liberties Union Foundation, 17th Edition, 2012. Download PDF version here: www.aclu.org/files/assets/2012_pad_final_1.pdf

- *Reentry Services Directory*
  National Reentry Resource Center, Justice Center, The Council of State Governments. Access state-by-state directory to local reentry services for ex-offenders and their families here: csgjusticecenter.org/reentry/reentry-services-directory/

- *Thinking for a Change: Integrated Cognitive Behavior Change Program. Version 4.0*
  Jack Bush, Barry Glick, and Juliana Taymans. Washington, DC: National Institute of Corrections, 2016. This new version of this popular curriculum is to be released in 2016. Request it by completing this online form: info.nicic.gov/t4c/node/11

- *TPC Reentry Handbook: Implementing the NIC Transition from Prison to the Community Model*
  U.S. Department of Justice, National Institute of Corrections, 2008. Presents the TPC (Transition from Prison to the Community) model that was piloted in eight states (Georgia, Indiana, Michigan, Missouri, New York, North Dakota, Oregon, Rhode Island). Download PDF version here: info.nicic.gov/nicrp/?q=system/ files/022669.pdf

- *United Way 2-1-1*
  Operated by the United Way, this is a free and confidential service that helps anyone find local resources they need. Searchable online by zip code, city, or state. Specialty areas include: human trafficking, crisis and emergency, disaster assistance, food, health, housing and utilities, jobs and support, reentry, and veterans. Can also call (211) to speak with a trained local United Way service professional. Access this directory online at:
  www.211.org

ALABAMA

- *Re-Entry Resources*
  Alabama Department of Corrections. Online directory of service providers accessed through:
  www.doc.state.al.us/ReentryResources.aspx

ALASKA

- *Reentry Manual*
  Alaska Department of Corrections, 2012. This 50+ page interactive manual includes many useful forms. Download PDF version here:
  www.correct.state.ak.us/TskForce/documents/Re%20Entry%20All%20edited%20pg%2040.pdf

ARKANSAS

- *Little Rock Re-Entry Service Directory*
  Online directory accessed through:
  www.arkansasreentry.com/resources

- *Re-Entry Handbook: Road to Re-Entry – Going Home to Stay*
  Arkansas Department of Correction. An 89-page re-entry directory. Download PDF version here:
  adc.arkansas.gov/reentry/Documents/ReEntryHandbook.pdf

CALIFORNIA

- ***Community Resources Directory***
  California Department of Corrections and Rehabilitation. Online directory accessed through:
  www.cdcr.ca.gov/Community_Partnerships/resource_directory.aspx

- ***Insight Prison Project***
  One-page directory of re-entry resources in California. Online directory accessed through:
  www.insightprisonproject.org/resources.html

COLORADO

- ***The Go Guide: Getting On After Getting Out, A Reentry Guide for Colorado***
  Carol Peeples and Christie Donner. Colorado Criminal Justice Reform Coalition, 2012. See table of contents on pages 175-179. While this is not a free or downloadable publication, you can order the 228-page paper version for a nominal fee of $10.00 (plus $3 shipping) by following the order instructions here:
  www.ccjrc.org/find-help/go-guide/

  Alternatively, you can call 303-825-0122, fax 303-825-0304, or email info@ccjrc.org your order or complete the online order form and your $13.00 (check, money order, or major credit card) to:

      Colorado Criminal Justice Reform Coalition
      1212 Mariposa St., Suite 6, Denver, CO 80204
  A downloadable and printable PDF version of the order form is available here:
  www.ccjrc.org/wp-content/uploads/2016/03/ReEntry_Guide_Order.pdf

DISTRICT OF COLUMBIA

- ***Reentry Resources***
  CSOSA – Court Services and Offender Supervision Agency for the District of Columbia. Listing of various resources and services rel-

evant to ex-offenders in Washington, DC, including links to PDF directories, such as the 307-page *Starting Out, Starting Over, Staying Out: A Guide for District of Columbia Ex-Offenders: Housing, Food, Employment and Other Resources* (www.csosa.gov/reentry/resources/dc-cure.pdf). Access database here: www.csosa.gov/reentry/resources.aspx

FLORIDA

■ *FDOC Reentry Resources Directory*
Florida Department of Corrections. A comprehensive online directory to different types of re-entry services that can be searched by county, city, zip code, and keyword phrase. Access this directory through:
www.dc.state.fl.us/resourceDirectory/Search.aspx

GEORGIA

■ *Reentry Handbooks*
State Board of Pardons and Paroles. Four different handbooks (*Reentry Skills Handbook in English, Reentry Skills Handbook in Spanish, Parole Handbook, Inmate Handbook*). Download PDF version here:
pap.georgia.gov/reentry-handbooks

■ *Reentry Skills Building Handbooks*
Georgia Department of Corrections and State Board of Pardons and Paroles, 2015. Download PDF versions in English and Spanish here:
www.dcor.state.ga.us/pdf/ReentrySkillsBuildingHandbook-English.pdf (English)

www.dcor.state.ga.us/pdf/ReentrySkillsBuildingHandbook-Spanish.pdf (Spanish)

HAWAII

- *Offender Reentry Guides*
  Hawaii Department of Public Safety. Four separate reentry guides designed for four separate islands: Oahu, Big Island, Maui, and Kauai. Download PDF version here:
  dps.hawaii.gov/about/divisions/corrections/about-corrections

IDAHO

- *Pre-Release Handbook: Reentry and Community Transition Guide*
  Idaho Department of Correction, 2009. Download PDF version here:
  www.idoc.idaho.gov/content/document/pre_release_manual

ILLINOIS

- *Re-Entry Illinois*
  Corporation for Supportive Housing. This website functions as a gateway to re-entry resources, with emphasis on housing, in numerous counties throughout the state. Access it online here:
  www.reentryillinois.net

- *RED (Re-Entry Directory) Chicago*
  Designed for inmates preparing for release and for ex-offenders on the outside, this directory links ex-offenders to service providers in the Chicago area. Much of the material in this directory is borrowed with permission from the Colorado Criminal Justice Reform Coalition's *The GO Guide: Getting on After Getting Out*. Download PDF version here: www.redchicago.info and underthedoor.org/red-chicago/current-edition

INDIANA

- *Inmate Aid Re-entry Resources*
  Online directory to prison and re-entry resources for ex-offenders and their families. Access online here:
  inmateaid.com/pages/details/re-entry-resources-indiana-department-of-corrections-537

KENTUCKY

- **Re-Entry Directory**
  Kentucky Protection and Advocacy. Online resource directory to service providers offering assistance to those with disabilities (especially mental health) and formerly incarcerated. Includes links to counties throughout the state. Access online here:
  www.kypa.net/Re-Entry_Directory.html

LOUISIANA

- **Community Re-Entry Resource Map**
  Louisiana Department of Public Safety and Corrections, Corrections Services. Offers a map of counties in nine regions which include re-entry services. Access online here:
  www.doc.la.gov/pages/reentry-initiatives/community-resource-map

- **Louisiana 100-Hour Reentry Prerelease Program**
  Houghton Mifflin Harcourt, 2013. Five 40-page participant workbooks available at $3.45 each – Personal Development; Problem Solving & Decision Making; Anger Management; Values Clarification, Goal Setting & Achieving; Victim Awareness & Restitution: www.hmhco.com/shop/education-curriculum/adult-education/la-reentry-preparation-program

MASSACHUSETTS

- **Coming Home Directory: A Resource Directory of Offender Reentry Services in Greater Boston**
  Crime and Justice Institute at Community Resources for Justice. A searchable online directory for ex-offenders and their families, which can be accessed at: cominghomedirectory.org
  A limited number of printed directories are available upon request: Coming Home Directory Crime and Justice Institute at Community Resources for Justice

  355 Boylston St., Boston, MA 02116-3313
  Tel. 617-482-2520, ext. 128, Fax 617-362-8054
  Email: cominghomedirectory@crj.org

MINNESOTA

- *Adult Pre-Release Handbook: Pre-Release Information for an Informed Re-Entry and a Successful Transition. 5th Edition*
  Minnesota Department of Corrections, 2010. Download PDF version here:
  www.doc.state.mn.us/PAGES/files/large-files/Publications/Pre ReleaseHandbook.pdf

- *STEP AHEAD Workbook – Assess Yourself, Create a Plan and Set Goals, Find a Job, and Manage Your Career*
  This 68-page workbook was developed by Goodwill-Easter Seals Minnesota and iSeek. Download PDF version here:
  www.iseek.org/exoffenders/workbook.html
  www.iseek.org/iseek/static/STEP-AHEAD-Workbook.pdf

MISSISSIPPI

- *Mississippi Reentry Guide*
  Foundation for the Mid South. Offers links to a variety of national, state, and county re-entry resources:
  www.msreentryguide.com

MISSOURI

- *Start Here St. Louis Area Resource Directory*
  Inside Dharma. Download PDF version here:
  www.startherestl.org

NEW JERSEY

- *A Guidebook for Reentry Veterans in New Jersey*
  U.S. Department of Veterans Affairs. Download PDF version here: www.nj.gov/parole/docs/veterans/USVA GuidebookforReentryVeteransinNewJersey.pdf

- *New Jersey Smartbooks*
  New Jersey Department of Corrections, Office of Transitional Services. Includes smartbooks for eight counties that list re-entry service providers and resources.

www.state.nj.us/corrections/pdf/OTS/SmartBooks/Bergen
CountySmartBook.pdf

www.state.nj.us/corrections/pdf/OTS/SmartBooks/
BurlingtonCountySmartBook.pdf

www.state.nj.us/corrections/pdf/OTS/SmartBooks/Camden
CountySmartBook.pdf

www.state.nj.us/corrections/pdf/OTS/SmartBooks/Essex
CountySmartBook.pdf

www.state.nj.us/corrections/pdf/OTS/SmartBooks/Gloucester
CountySmartBook.pdf

www.state.nj.us/corrections/pdf/OTS/SmartBooks/Middlesex
CountySmartBook.pdf

www.state.nj.us/corrections/pdf/OTS/SmartBooks/Passaic
CountySmartBook.pdf

www.state.nj.us/corrections/pdf/OTS/SmartBooks/Union
CountySmartBook.pdf

NEW MEXICO

- *Offender Re-Entry Resource Manual for Bernalillo County*
  A 232-page resource guide. Download PDF version here:
  cd.nm.gov/apd/rr/resource_manual.pdf

NEW YORK

- *Bronx Reentry Working Group*
  Bronx Reentry Working Group. Includes nearly 200 re-entry service providers in the Bronx area. Access online here:
  bronxreentry.org/directory/all-resources-by-name

- *Inside Books Project*
  Functions as both a searchable online resource and downloadable
  PDF resources for inmates and ex-offenders in transition: Access
  online and as a PDF here:
  insidebooksproject.org/resource-guide

NORTH CAROLINA

- *County Resource Guide*
  North Carolina Department of Public Safety, Office of Research
  and Planning/Office of Transition Services. Offers a searchable
  database of community re-entry resources in each of North Carolina's 100 counties. Access online here:
  randp.doc.state.nc.us/scripts/htmSQL.exe/docs/hsql/CM/
  CountyResourceGuide-Rptindex.hsql

- *Guidebook for Incarcerated Veterans in North Carolina*
  A 24-page handbook for formerly incarcerated veterans in North
  Carolina. Download PDF version here:
  www.va.gov/homeless/docs/reentry/09_nc.pdf

OKLAHOMA

Resource List for Oklahoma City
Download PDF version here:
www.strategicreentrygroup.com/Websites/srgroup/images/
resource_list_rev34.pdf

OREGON

- *Transition Support Directory*
  Partnership for Safety and Justice. Includes a listing of support services for ex-offenders in transition. Download PDF version here:
  www.safetyandjustice.org/files/2011%20Transition%20
  Support%20Directory.pdf

PENNSYLVANIA

- *Interactive Reentry Services Map*
  Pennsylvania Department of Corrections. An interactive map for
  finding re-entry services in 67 counties through the state:
  reentrymap.cor.pa.gov

■ *Preparing for Your Return to the Community: What Offenders and Their Families Need to Know*
Pennsylvania Board of Probation and Parole. Downloadable booklet with tips on survival and parole experience. Download PDF version here:
www.pbpp.pa/gov/information/Documents/Publications/What%20Offenders%20 and %20Their%20Families%20Need%20To%20Know%20%20May%202015.pdf

■ *Reintegration Services (RISE)*
The Mayor's Office of Reintegration Services in Philadelphia. Includes links to numerous local resources and services for assisting ex-offenders with community re-entry:
rise.phila.gov

SOUTH CAROLINA

■ *Guidebook for Incarcerated Veterans in South Carolina*
A 22-page handbook for formerly incarcerated veterans in South Carolina. Download PDF version here:
www1.va.gov/homeless/docs/reentry/09_sc.pdf

TEXAS

■ *Bexar County Reentry Program*
County of Bexar, 2016. Resource directory for locating ex-offender services within the county – by geographic location and type of service. Download PDF version here:
home.bexar.org/reentry/docs/CommunityReEntryResourceDirectory.pdf

■ *Reentry Resource Guide*
TDCJ's Reentry and Integration Division. County-by-county compilation of resources to assist ex-offenders with re-entry. Access database here:
tdcj.state.tx.us/documents/rid/RID_Reentry_Resource_Guide.pdf

- ***Tarrant County Ex-Offender Reentry Resources***
  Tarrant Cares and the Tarrant County Reentry Coalition. A searchable online database for locating local services relevant to ex-offender re-entry. Access database here:
  tarrant.tx.networkofcare.org/pr/

- ***Travis County Reentry Success Guide: A Guide to Travis County Area Resources for People Leaving Jail or Prison***
  Travis County Justice and Public Safety Division, Criminal Justice Planning Department, 2013. Download PDF version here:
  www.reentryroundtable.net/wp-content/uploads/2013/01/Resource-Guide-January-20131.pdf

VIRGINIA

- ***Local Resource Directory to Community Corrections***
  Virginia Department of Corrections. Download PDF version here:
  vadoc.virginia.gov/community/western.shtm (western region)

  vadoc.virginia.gov/community/central.shtm (central region)

  vadoc.virginia.gov/community/eastern.shtm (eastern region)

- ***A Re-entry Roadmap for Veterans in Virginia***
  Virginia Department of Corrections. Download PDF version here:
  vadoc.virginia.gov/documents/reentry-roadmap-for-veterans-virginia.pdf

In-House Curricula and Resources

The referenced re-entry guides and databases that are listed in this chapter represent a growing transparency trend – make such information available to the public via the Internet. While most of the information represents public-funded re-entry projects that are not proprietary nor copyrighted and thus can be downloaded and printed for personal use, other re-entry guides and databases function as in-house resources for ongoing re-entry programs. Unfortunately, these guides and databases cannot be easily accessed since they have not yet been made available for public consumption over the Internet. Therefore, in order to locate and review such materials, you'll need to check with individual state departments of correction, usually the re-entry office or division, and inquiry about the availability of such materials. These offices may send you copies of their resources via downloadable email attachments.

An example of an excellent curriculum, including a 190-page participant workbook and a 185-page instructor's guide, can be found in Virginia's Department of Corrections, Offender Workforce Development Program. Developed in 2012 by the state's Offender Workforce Development Specialist, Dr. Vicki Mistr, and pioneered at The Virginia Correctional Center for Women as part of the "Thinking for a Change" program, this training program consists of the following materials:

- ***Ready to Work: Tools for Success – Participant Workbook***
- ***Ready to Work: Tools for Success – Facilitator's Guide***

In 2013 Dr. Mistr also developed a related curriculum called ***Resources for Successful Living***, which is available in two versions:

- ***Resources for Successful Living: Participant Book***
- ***Resources for Successful Living: Facilitator's Guide***

While not available in printable PDF form through a website, these curricula can be acquired as downloadable PDFs by contacting Virginia's re-entry office:

> Offender Workforce Program Manager
> Virginia Department of Corrections
> 6900 Atmore Drive
> Richmond, VA 23225
> Tel. 804-887-8267
> vadoc.virginia.gov

Many other states may have developed, or are in the process of developing, similar re-entry curriculum materials that are available in Virginia. You are well advised to contact your relevant state correctional educational and/or re-entry office to inquire about current resources that can be made available to you as downloadable PDF files.

Appendices

A Collateral Consequences of Convictions:
State-by-State Restrictions 196

B Your Re-Entry Success IQ...199

C Re-Entry Preparation Checklist 208

D Weekly Goal Setting and Achievement Activities 213

E My Re-Entry Success Contract 216

F Weekly Job Search Performance and Planning Report 219

G Recommended Re-Entry Resources 221

Appendix A

Collateral Consequences
of Convictions:
State-by-State Restrictions

WHEN YOU RECEIVE A SENTENCE for a criminal conviction, you may be shocked to discover that you also face a variety of life-long sentences – restrictions on what you can and cannot do in reference to employment, licensing, certification, education, finance, housing, government benefits, voting rights, and travel. Indeed, you may quickly discover that you will never be completely free, since your conviction comes with "conditions." Known as "collateral consequences of convictions," these restrictions are something most ex-offenders are not aware of until they are released from jails and prisons and encounter the street-level realities of being an ex-con.

Employment remains the single most important accelerator for re-entry success. Without a decent job, life on the outside for ex-offenders can be very difficult. Therefore, it's extremely important that newly released inmates quickly find a job that enables them to succeed at re-entry – acquire affordable housing and transportation, minimize debt, become "banked" and financially stable, and acquire a variety of important support services relating to food, clothing, physical and mental health, substance abuse, and education.

However, many ex-offenders face employment and related barriers based upon the nature of their convictions. If, for example, you have been convicted for fraud, your job options relating to financial institutions will be limited. If you've been convicted of a sex crime, you'll be prohibited from acquiring jobs that deal with the care of children and the elderly. Indeed, various states prohibit convicted felons from acquiring jobs relating to finance, health care, education, children, and law enforcement. Knowing which states prohibit ex-offenders from entering certain occupations can be difficult for many ex-offenders who don't know where to find such information.

A great deal of employment misinformation, including urban legends, affects ex-offenders who wish to re-enter the work world . . . until now. The good news is that the **American Bar Association** has created a very useful interactive tool for identifying employment and other restrictions on ex-offenders. Known as the **National Inventory of Collateral Consequences of Convictions**, this website should be used by all ex-offenders who need to be aware of legal restrictions affecting their futures:

www.abacollateralconsequences.org

It includes an interactive state map (www.abacollateralconsequences.org/map/) for identifying and searching multiple jurisdictions on a variety of restrictive criteria. Its search feature enables users to simultaneously explore ABA's database by three different **consequences**: categories, types, and offenses:

www.abacollateralconsequences.org/search/?jurisdiction=15

Consequence categories include restrictions relating to:
- Employment
- Occupational and professional license and certification
- Business license and other property rights
- Government contracting and program participation
- Government loans and grants
- Judicial rights
- Government benefits
- Education
- Political and civic participation

Consequence types include restrictions by:
- Mandatory/Automatic
- Discretionary
- Discretionary (waiver)
- Background Check
- N/A General Relief

Consequences offenses include restrictions by:

- Any offense (including felony, misdemeanor, and lesser offense)
- Any felony
- Any misdemeanor
- Crime of moral turpitude
- Crimes involving fraud, dishonesty, misrepresentation, or money-laundering
- Crimes of violence, including "person offenses"
- Weapons offenses
- Controlled substances offenses
- Sex offenses
- Public corruption offenses
- Election-related offenses
- Motor vehicle offenses
- Child support offenses
- Other
- N/A (background check, general relief)

Appendix B

Your Re-Entry Success IQ

HOW WELL PREPARED ARE EX-OFFENDERS FOR re-entering and succeeding in the free world? There are no right or wrong answers to the following exercise. Be aware that it is a very long and thorough exercise – it may take 30 minutes to complete. Most of the issues included here relate to the re-entry success process, which is outlined in another book – *The Ex-Offender's Re-Entry Success Guide* (Impact Publications, 2016). The exercise is designed to give ex-offenders useful feedback by measuring their current level of re-entry information, skills, and strategies as well as identifying those they need to develop and improve. They identify their level of **re-entry competence**, or how well prepared they are for re-entry, by completing the following exercise:

INSTRUCTIONS: Respond to each statement by circling which number at the right best represents your situation.

SCALE: 1 = Strongly disagree   4 = Agree
            2 = Disagree   5 = Strongly agree
            3 = Maybe, not certain

Getting Ready for Freedom Day

1. I know my release date.   1 2 3 4 5
2. I've been preparing myself for release.   1 2 3 4 5
3. I have a written re-entry plan that covers the first 180 days after my release.   1 2 3 4 5
4. I have someone waiting to help me on the outside.   1 2 3 4 5
5. I've changed a lot for the better since I first came here.   1 2 3 4 5

6. I'm confident I can make it on the outside.   1 2 3 4 5
7. I've stayed out of trouble while incarcerated.   1 2 3 4 5

Responsibility and Forgiveness

8. I know why I'm here; I've come to terms with
    my situation.   1 2 3 4 5
9. I've taken responsibility for my actions.   1 2 3 4 5
10. I plan to never lie, make excuses, or blame
    others for my problems.   1 2 3 4 5
11. I've taken responsibility for turning my
    life around.   1 2 3 4 5
12. I've asked for and received forgiveness from
    myself and others.   1 2 3 4 5
13. I've decided to change my life so that I'll never
    again end up here.   1 2 3 4 5
14. I've committed myself in writing (personal
    contract spelling out what I need to do by
    specific dates) to change my life.   1 2 3 4 5
15. I usually take responsibility for my own
    actions rather than blame other people for
    my situation or circumstance.   1 2 3 4 5

Anger, Rage, and Stress

16. I seldom get angry with others.   1 2 3 4 5
17. I avoid getting into verbal or physical
    confrontations.   1 2 3 4 5
18. If I get angry at anyone, it's usually myself.   1 2 3 4 5
19. No one is angry with me.   1 2 3 4 5
20. I keep my stress under control.   1 2 3 4 5
21. I regularly exercise both my body and my mind.   1 2 3 4 5

Purpose and Goals

22. I believe I have a purpose in life.   1 2 3 4 5
23. I know what I both like and dislike about
    my life.   1 2 3 4 5
24. I try to live a purposeful life by being of value
    to others.   1 2 3 4 5

25. I volunteer to help others.   1 2 3 4 5

26. I've achieved many things in life.   1 2 3 4 5

27. I know what I want to achieve in the next
10 years.   1 2 3 4 5

28. I'm a spiritual person who acknowledges a
higher power.   1 2 3 4 5

Character and Trustworthiness

29. I'm a person of good character.   1 2 3 4 5

30. I have high moral standards.   1 2 3 4 5

31. I usually know the difference between right
and wrong and act accordingly.   1 2 3 4 5

32. I always tell the truth.   1 2 3 4 5

33. I'm an honest person who can be trusted.   1 2 3 4 5

34. I usually do what I say I'll do.   1 2 3 4 5

35. I've learned to trust others.   1 2 3 4 5

36. I usually see good qualities in other people.   1 2 3 4 5

Self-Esteem

37. I generally like myself and want to do good.   1 2 3 4 5

38. I feel both confident and competent in
what I do.   1 2 3 4 5

39. I can laugh at myself.   1 2 3 4 5

40. I have a healthy sense of self respect.   1 2 3 4 5

41. I understand how I can be whatever I
want to be.   1 2 3 4 5

42. I know I need to make some changes in
my life.   1 2 3 4 5

Motivation, Self-Discipline, and Personality

43. I know what motivates me to do what I do.   1 2 3 4 5

44. I have good common sense.   1 2 3 4 5

45. I'm very well organized and use my time well.   1 2 3 4 5

46. I usually think things through before
taking action.   1 2 3 4 5

47. I'm sensitive to other people's feelings.   1 2 3 4 5

48. I'm a "person of light" rather than a "person of heat."   1 2 3 4 5
49. I usually know what to do without having to be told.   1 2 3 4 5
50. I'm in better control of my impulses.   1 2 3 4 5
51. I generally have a positive attitude.   1 2 3 4 5
52. I'm not a self-centered or selfish person.   1 2 3 4 5
53. I understand my personality and how it affects others.   1 2 3 4 5

Decision-Making and Leadership

54. I consider myself to be a very mature person who makes good decisions for myself and others.   1 2 3 4 5
55. I'm very good at making quick and correct decisions.   1 2 3 4 5
56. Other people look up to me for advice and assistance.   1 2 3 4 5
57. I'm a team player who gets along well with others on the team.   1 2 3 4 5
58. I know what's right and wrong and usually tryto do what's right.   1 2 3 4 5

Communication and Etiquette

59. I usually think before I speak.   1 2 3 4 5
60. I'm good at giving speeches before a group.   1 2 3 4 5
61. My English is very good.   1 2 3 4 5
62. I enjoy writing and I'm a good writer.   1 2 3 4 5
63. I know bad language – words, grammar, diction – when I hear it.   1 2 3 4 5
64. I use positive language with correct grammar and diction.   1 2 3 4 5
65. I avoid using rough street language.   1 2 3 4 5
66. People enjoy talking with me and listening to what I say.   1 2 3 4 5
67. I'm a good listener who wants to learn from others.   1 2 3 4 5

68. I make good eye contact with people.   1 2 3 4 5
69. I know proper etiquette, including showing
    up on time, greeting people, expressing
    gratitude, dressing, grooming, eating, and
    table manners.   1 2 3 4 5
70. I have a polite and likable manner; I frequently
    use the words and phrases "please," "excuse
    me," "thank you," "would it be possible to."   1 2 3 4 5

Friends and Relationships

71. I tend to associate with people of good
    character.   1 2 3 4 5
72. I tend to associate with positive people
    and avoid those with negative thinking
    and bad language.   1 2 3 4 5
73. I tend to run with winners rather than losers.   1 2 3 4 5
74. I have many good friends.   1 2 3 4 5
75. I find it easy to make friends.   1 2 3 4 5
76. I have a few very close friends who will
    stand by me during difficult times.   1 2 3 4 5
77. I have, or can gain, the support of family and
    friends for my re-entry.   1 2 3 4 5
78. I have a mentor to help with re-entry.   1 2 3 4 5
79. I have someone waiting for me on the outside
    who will assist me with re-entry.   1 2 3 4 5
80. I get along well with authority figures.   1 2 3 4 5

Family

81. I come from a stable and loving family.   1 2 3 4 5
82. My relatives tend to live a long life.   1 2 3 4 5
83. I get along well with my family.   1 2 3 4 5
84. Both parents are alive and married to each other.   1 2 3 4 5
85. My family is willing to help me with re-entry.   1 2 3 4 5
86. I'm a good parent. (Don't respond if you're
    not a parent.)   1 2 3 4 5
87. I've been a good son or daughter.   1 2 3 4 5

Re-Entry Basics

88. I know where I'll be staying the first 90 days
    after release.   1 2 3 4 5
89. I don't anticipate a problem with transportation. 1 2 3 4 5
90. All my important documents are in order.   1 2 3 4 5
91. I already have a job lined up.   1 2 3 4 5
92. If I have any problems, I know where to
    go for help.   1 2 3 4 5
93. I have addiction or anger problems under
    control.   1 2 3 4 5
94. I plan to meet all my probation/parole
    obligations according to the book, including
    showing up on time.   1 2 3 4 5
95. I plan to avoid alcohol.   1 2 3 4 5
96. I plan to avoid drugs.   1 2 3 4 5
97. I plan to avoid people and situations that
    could lead to trouble.   1 2 3 4 5
98. I plan to never lie, make excuses, or blame
    others for my problems.   1 2 3 4 5
99. I am good at budgeting and saving money.   1 2 3 4 5
100. I know how to get the best deal on a car.   1 2 3 4 5

Education, Training, and Interests

101. I have my high school diploma or GED
     certificate.   1 2 3 4 5
102. I enjoy reading and do so frequently.   1 2 3 4 5
103. I have taken advantage of self-help programs
     (anger management, addiction, etc.) while
     incarcerated.   1 2 3 4 5
104. I've taken advantage of vocational training
     and skill development programs while
     incarcerated.   1 2 3 4 5
105. I'm eager to learn new things and acquire
     new skills.   1 2 3 4 5
106. I admire educated people.   1 2 3 4 5
107. I know where and how to get more education
     and training on the outside.   1 2 3 4 5

108. I enjoy making music – singing or playing an
     instrument.   1 2 3 4 5
109. I have hobbies that I enjoy and could turn
     into a job.   1 2 3 4 5

Mental Health and Disabilities

110. I know what's both wrong and right about me.   1 2 3 4 5
111. I seldom get depressed.   1 2 3 4 5
112. I've not received psychological counseling.   1 2 3 4 5
113. I've never been on medication for
     psychiatric issues.   1 2 3 4 5
114. My mental state is very good.   1 2 3 4 5
115. I'm in control of my feelings and emotions.   1 2 3 4 5
116. I'm a quick learner.   1 2 3 4 5
117. I don't experience mood swings.   1 2 3 4 5
118. I have no disabilities.   1 2 3 4 5
119. Other people feel I have my act together.   1 2 3 4 5

Jobs and Careers

120. I know what type of job or career I want
     to pursue.   1 2 3 4 5
121. I have the knowledge and skills to pursue
     that job or career.   1 2 3 4 5
122. I have a resume that clearly communicates to
     potential employers what I have done, can do,
     and will do for them in the future.   1 2 3 4 5
123. I know how to best look for jobs.   1 2 3 4 5
124. I know which jobs are best suited for
     ex-offenders.   1 2 3 4 5
125. I know where to look for these jobs.   1 2 3 4 5
126. I know what to say when a potential employer
     asks about my conviction and incarceration.   1 2 3 4 5
127. I can specify why employers should hire me
     despite red flags in my background.   1 2 3 4 5
128. I can list my major accomplishments.   1 2 3 4 5
129. I can develop a job referral network.   1 2 3 4 5

130. I know how to find job leads.   1 2 3 4 5
131. I can use the telephone to develop prospects
     and get referrals and interviews.   1 2 3 4 5
132. I can persuade employers to interview me.   1 2 3 4 5
133. I have a list of at least 10 questions about
     the company I want to ask during interviews.   1 2 3 4 5
134. I know the best time to talk about salary
     with an employer.   1 2 3 4 5
135. I have little difficulty in making cold
     calls and striking up conversations
     with strangers.   1 2 3 4 5
136. I know how to best follow up a job interview.   1 2 3 4 5
137. I would like to start my own business.   1 2 3 4 5

Dealing With Setbacks and Rejections

138. I'm generally a very positive person.   1 2 3 4 5
139. I always try to keep a positive attitude.   1 2 3 4 5
140. I approach new situations with enthusiasm.   1 2 3 4 5
141. I'm a very persistent person who does not
     give up easily.   1 2 3 4 5
142. I'm used to dealing with rejections in a
     positive manner.   1 2 3 4 5
143. I don't take rejections personally.   1 2 3 4 5
144. I'm a very resilient person who quickly
     bounces back from adversity.   1 2 3 4 5
145. If someone rejects me for a job, I'll be even
     more motivated to continue looking for
     another job.   1 2 3 4 5
146. When I get discouraged, I find strength in
     knowing that tomorrow can be a better day
     if only I make it happen.   1 2 3 4 5
147. I have the power within me to shape my future.   1 2 3 4 5

TOTAL [   ]

Calculate your potential for re-entry success by adding the numbers you circled and add them up for an overall score. If your total is less than 500 points, you need to work on developing your re-entry skills. If you score under 400, your future on the outside is likely to be tough and you may not make it for long. You need to do some serious work in preparing yourself for the free world.

If your overall score is more than 600 points, you are well on your way toward re-entry success.

In fact, how you scored each item will indicate to what degree you need to work on improving a specific indicator of re-entry success. Some things, such as changing your mindset, developing a written plan, and writing a resume, can be done immediately whereas others are things you'll need to work on over the coming months or years.

If your overall score is more than 600 points, you are well on your way toward re-entry success. Focus on improving those things that appear to be re-entry weaknesses.

Appendix C

Re-Entry Preparation Checklist

Name: _____ Date: _____

INSTRUCTIONS: Check those boxes that are most relevant to your situation as well as include any details for each item checked.

Identification

- ❏ Social Security number   (# _____)
- ❏ Driver's license   (# _____)
- ❏ Birth certificate
- ❏ State ID card
- ❏ CDIB (Certificate of Degree of Indian Blood) card
- ❏ U.S. passport or passport card
- ❏ U.S. military ID
- ❏ Marriage certificate
- ❏ Court order or judgments
- ❏ Other ID   (# _____)

Housing

- ❏ Need assistance with housing
- ❏ Housing already arranged
- ❏ Location:
  Address _____
  City_____ State____ Zip code_____

Contact/Communication

❏ Phone number(s):
Personal:_____
Emergency:_____
❏ Email:_____
❏ Mailing address:
Address _____
City_____ State____ Zip code_____

Clothing

❏ Have street clothes to wear leaving institution
❏ Have access to clothing sources
❏ Have clothing suitable for a job interview
❏ Know where to find free or inexpensive clothes and accessories

Food/Drink

❏ Have sufficient income to feed myself
❏ Know where to find food pantries and soup kitchens
❏ Consume healthy foods and beverages

Transportation

❏ Arranged transportation from institution
❏ Arranged daily transportation

Personal Finance

❏ Primary financial supporter (name: _____)
❏ Debts/payments:
Rent/mortgage: $ _____
Utilities: $ _____
Alimony: $ _____
Child support: $ _____
Loans: $ _____
Restitution: $ _____
Court costs/fines: $ _____

Civil judgments: $ _____

Tickets: $ _____

Telephone: $ _____

Cable TV: $ _____

Internet: $ _____

Insurance: $ _____

Food/groceries: $ _____

Alcohol/drugs: $ _____

Hair/make-up: $ _____

Memberships/fees: $ _____

Clothes/accessories: $ _____

Entertainment/recreation: $ _____

Other: $ _____

❑ Financial assets (List: _____)

❑ Valid ID for cashing checks

❑ Credit/debit cards: _____

❑ Bank accounts:

Checking: _____

Savings: _____

Other: _____

❑ Investments: _____

Medical

❑ Medical needs: _____

❑ Medical providers:

Name/address: _____

Name/address: _____

Name/address: _____

❑ Dental

❑ Eye care

❑ Insurance

❑ ACA

❑ Medicaid

❑   Medicare
❑   Medication: _____
❑   Mental health _____
❑   Substance abuse_____
❑   Monthly out-of-pocket medical costs: $_____
❑   Monthly out-of-pocket medication costs: $_____

Legal

❑   Legal obligations:_____
❑   Supervision required (supervisor:_____)
❑   Special parole or probation conditions: _____

Offender Registration (Violent, Sex, or Methamphetamine)

❑   Committed offense under the Sex Offender Registration Act
❑   Committed offense under the Violent Offender Registration Act
❑   Committed drug-related offense relating to the possession, dis-
    tribution, manufacturing, or trafficking of methamphetamines
    or illegal amounts of or uses of pseudoephedrine
❑   Registration of your address with local law enforcement re-
    quired within three days of release

Programs

❑   Completed treatment program(s) while incarcerated: _____
❑   Received referral for aftercare:
    Name:_____
    Address: _____
    Phone number:_____
    Aftercare plan (specify: _____)

Family/Children

❑ Spouse (name: _____)
❑ Partner (name: _____)
❑ Living with spouse
❑ Living with partner
❑ Living with children
❑ Living with parents
❑ Who you prefer living with: _____
❑ Children (#_____ ; ages: _____)
❑ Contact with children (frequency: _____)
❑ How well you get along with family members:
  (circle level of relationship)

Spouse:	Great	Good	So-So	Not Good	Terrible
Partner:	Great	Good	So-So	Not Good	Terrible
Children:	Great	Good	So-So	Not Good	Terrible
Mother:	Great	Good	So-So	Not Good	Terrible
Father:	Great	Good	So-So	Not Good	Terrible
Brother(s):	Great	Good	So-So	Not Good	Terrible
Sisters(s):	Great	Good	So-So	Not Good	Terrible
Grandparents:	Great	Good	So-So	Not Good	Terrible

Mentor

❑ Participated in mentor program (when/where: _____)
❑ My mentor: _____
❑ Interested in finding a mentor: _____
❑ Interested in becoming a mentor: _____

Appendix D

Weekly Goal Setting and Achievement Activities

YOUR FIRST 99 DAYS ON THE OUTSIDE will be critical to your long-term re-entry success. Indeed, you need to hit the ground running with a clear plan of action for every day during an initial 14-week period. For example, what exactly do you plan to do – from making telephone calls and meeting with specific people – on days 2, 11, 25, 41, 68, and 92 that contributes to your success? By all means **keep yourself very busy** doing things that get you established in a community with a new set of **supportive relationships**. Your major concerns will most likely relate to housing, transportation, food, clothing, finances, and a job.

Use the following form (make 14 copies for completing 14 weeks of goals and activities) as a starting point for developing your own large planning calendar. Start by setting **three major goals** for each of the weeks in your 99-day journey to re-entry success. Within each of the weeks, identify specific **daily activities** that will contribute to achieving your **weekly goals**. For example, your major goals for Week #1 might be to:

- find affordable housing
- renew your driver's license
- open a bank account
- locate a temporary job

Try to focus on at least **three goals** each week. Each goal should be translated into **specific activities** – who, what, when, where, and how – that can be **measured** in terms of success or failure. Identify exactly what you will do on each day of the week.

Always remember that **re-entry is a full-time job**. Plan accordingly by spending at least eight hours each day translat-

> *Re-entry should be your full-time job!*

ing your plans into **activities and outcomes**. Start each morning by reviewing and revising what you plan to do for the day. Then spend the next eight hours taking the necessary actions that contribute to your desired outcomes.

When you finish, be sure to **evaluate your progress** by completing the evaluation form that accompanies each weekly goal setting and activities form. Then reflect on your progress – what did you do right, what could you do better, and what changes do you need to make to better accomplish your goals? This evaluation and feedback exercise may prove to be the most important routine activity for transforming your life in the next 99 days!

My 3 major goals for Week #_____ are to:

1. _____

2. _____

3. _____

Monday activities: _____

_____

_____

Tuesday activities: _____

_____

_____

Wednesday activities: _____

_____

_____

Thursday activities: _____

_____

_____

Friday activities: _____

_____

_____

Saturday activities: _____

_____

_____

Sunday activities: _____

_____

_____

Evaluating My Weekly Progress

On a scale of 1 to 10, how well did I achieve my three goals for the week? Circle the number that best represents how well I did:

	Poorly				*So-So*			*Outstanding*		
Goal #1:	1	2	3	4	5	6	7	8	9	10
Goal #2:	1	2	3	4	5	6	7	8	9	10
Goal #3:	1	2	3	4	5	6	7	8	9	10

What things did I do that were responsible for my success?

_____

_____

_____

What did I do that contributed to the lack of success in achieving my goals?

_____

_____

_____

What changes do I need to make to better accomplish my weekly goals?

_____

_____

_____

Appendix E

My Re-Entry Success Contract

1. I'm committed to changing my life and staying out for good. Today's date is_____.

2. I will effectively manage my time so that I can successfully complete each step in the re-entry process as summarized on page 218.

3. I will make contacts with at least 10 key organizations that can help me with various aspects of re-entry by this date: _____.

4. I will contact at least three people who might be willing to help me with re-entry by this date: _____.

5. I will begin acquiring all necessary re-entry documents on this date:_____.

6. I'll complete my transportation plan by this date:_____.

7. I will secure transitional housing by this date:_____.

8. I will spend at least one week conducting research on different jobs, employers, and organizations. I will begin this research during the week of_____.

9. I will complete my job objective by_____.

10. I will complete my resume by_____.

11. I will put together my new job search/interview wardrobe by _____.

12. Each week I will make_____ new job contacts.

13. I understand the importance of rejections and how to best handle them.

14. My first job interview will take place during the week of_____.

15. I will begin my new job by_____.

16. I will make a habit of learning one new skill each year.

Signature:_____

Date: _____

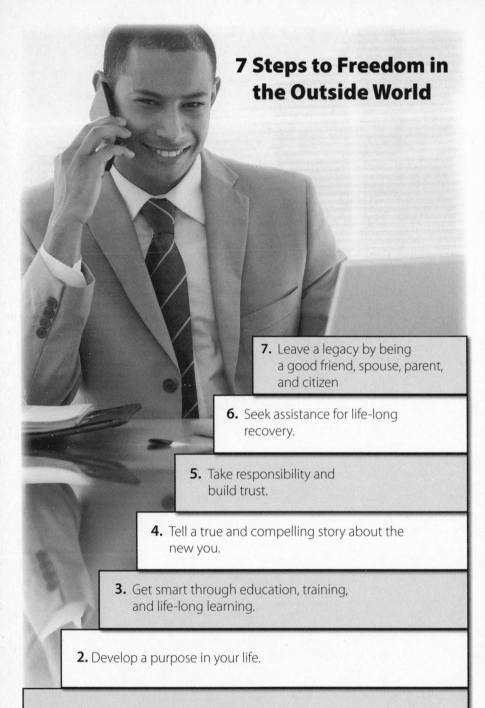

7 Steps to Freedom in the Outside World

7. Leave a legacy by being a good friend, spouse, parent, and citizen

6. Seek assistance for life-long recovery.

5. Take responsibility and build trust.

4. Tell a true and compelling story about the new you.

3. Get smart through education, training, and life-long learning.

2. Develop a purpose in your life.

1. Change your attitudes and motivation.

Appendix F

Weekly Job Search Performance and Planning Report

1. The week of:_____.

2. This week I:
   - wrote_____job search letters.
   - sent_____resumes and_____letters to potential employers.
   - completed_____applications.
   - made_____job search telephone calls.
   - completed_____hours of job research.
   - set up_____appointments for informational interviews.
   - conducted_____informational interviews.
   - received_____invitations to a job interview.
   - followed up on_____contacts and_____referrals.

3. Next week I will:
   - write_____job search letters.
   - send_____resumes and_____letters to potential employers.
   - complete_____applications.
   - make_____job search telephone calls.
   - complete_____hours of job research.
   - set up_____appointments for informational interviews.
   - conduct_____informational interviews.
   - follow up on_____contacts and_____referrals.

4. Summary of progress this week in reference to my Re-Entry
   Success Contract commitments: _____

   _____

   _____

   _____

   _____

   _____

   _____

   _____

   _____

   _____

   _____

   _____

   _____

   _____

   _____

   _____

   _____

   _____

   _____

   _____

   _____

   _____

   _____

Appendix G

Recommended Re-Entry Resources

RE-ENTRY RESOURCES ARE constantly changing – old ones disappear, new ones surface, and current ones move around from one location and website to another. While I have tried to make this directory as accurate as possible as of April 2016, I fully expect several of the names, addresses, telephone numbers, and websites will change in the coming months and years (see page x). This is especially true for many nonprofit organizations that operate on shoestring budgets. Many of these re-entry groups are dependent on public funding and donations. Indeed, while conducting research for this directory, I frequently heard a similar story: *"We've moved because our funding has been cut."*

Please share any additional resources you feel would be useful for ex-offender re-entry success. Future editions of this directory will reflect reader recommendations. Please email, fax, or mail your recommendations to:

Ron Krannich
IMPACT PUBLICATIONS
9104-N Manassas Drive
Manassas Park, VA 20111
Fax 703-335-9486
Email: ron@impactpublications.com

I recommend including the following re-entry resource(s):

_____

_____

_____

_____

_____

Re-Entry Success Resources

THE FOLLOWING RE-ENTRY RESOURCES are available from Impact Publications. Full descriptions of each as well as downloadable catalogs and video clips can be found at www. impactpublications.com. Complete the following form or list the titles, include shipping (see formula on page 227), enclose payment, and send your order to

IMPACT PUBLICATIONS
9104 Manassas Dr., Suite N
Manassas Park, VA 20111-5211
1-800-361-1055 (orders only)
Tel. 703-361-7300 or Fax 703-335-9486
Email: query@impactpublications.com
Quick & easy online ordering: www.impactpublications.com

Orders from individuals must be prepaid (check, money order, credit card). Pricing and availability current as of May 2016. Visit www.impactpublications.com for updated product information.

Qty.	TITLES	Price	TOTAL
Featured Title (GSA Schedule – Contract #GS-02F-0146X)			
_____	Ex-Offender's Re-Entry Assistance Directory (page 228)	$29.95	_____
Re-Entry Pocket Guides (GSA Schedule – Contract #GS-02F-0146X)			
_____	The Anger Management Pocket Guide	$2.95	_____
_____	The Quick Job Finding Pocket Guide	2.95	_____
_____	Re-Entry Employment & Life Skills Pocket Guide	2.95	_____
_____	Re-Entry Personal Finance Pocket Guide	2.95	_____
_____	Re-Entry Start-Up Pocket Guide	2.95	_____
_____	Re-Imagining Life on the Outside Pocket Guide	2.95	_____
Re-Entry and Survival for Ex-Offenders (GSA Schedule – Contract #GS-02F-0146X)			
_____	99 Days to Re-Entry Success Journal (page 228)	$4.95	_____
_____	Best Jobs for Ex-Offenders	11.95	_____
_____	Best Resumes and Letters for Ex-Offenders	19.95	_____
_____	Ex-Offender's 30/30 Job Solution	11.95	_____
_____	Ex-Offender's Guide to a Responsible Life	15.95	_____
_____	Ex-Offender's Job Interview Guide	11.95	_____
_____	Ex-Offender's New Job Finding and Survival Guide (page 228)	19.95	_____
_____	Ex-Offender's Quick Job Hunting Guide	11.95	_____
_____	Ex-Offender's Re-Entry Success Guide	11.95	_____
_____	A Map Through the Maze	11.95	_____
_____	Overcoming 101 More Employment Barriers	19.95	_____
_____	Overcoming Employment Barriers	19.95	_____
More Re-Entry and Survival Books			
_____	9 to 5 Beats Ten to Life	$20.00	_____
_____	99 Days and a Get Up	9.95	_____
_____	Bars and Books	34.95	_____
_____	Beyond Bars	14.95	_____
_____	Chicken Soup for the Prisoner's Soul	14.95	_____
_____	Dedicated Ex-Prisoner's Life and Success on the Outside	19.95	_____
_____	Houses of Healing	15.00	_____
_____	How to Do Good After Prison	19.95	_____
_____	Jobs for Felons	7.95	_____
_____	Letters to an Incarcerated Brother	16.00	_____
_____	Life Beyond Loss	20.00	_____

_____	Life Without a Crutch	7.95 _____
_____	Locked Down, Locked Out	18.95 _____
_____	Man, I Need a Job	7.95 _____
_____	No One is Unemployable	29.95 _____
_____	Orange is the New Black	16.00 _____
_____	Picking Up the Pieces (for Women)	20.00 _____
_____	A Question of Freedom	16.00 _____
_____	Quick Job Search for Ex-Offenders	7.95 _____
_____	Re-Entry Support Programs for Ex-Offenders	40.00 _____
_____	Serving Productive Time	14.95 _____
_____	What Works and Why? Effective Approaches to Re-Entry	35.00 _____

Attitude, Motivation, and Inspiration

_____	7 Habits of Highly Effective People	$17.00 _____
_____	30 Lessons for Living	16.00 _____
_____	100 Ways to Motivate Yourself	15.99 _____
_____	Attitude Is Everything	16.99 _____
_____	Awaken the Giant Within	17.99 _____
_____	Better Than Before	16.00 _____
_____	Bouncing Back: Rewiring Your Brain	17.95 _____
_____	Can I Get a Do Over?	14.95 _____
_____	Change Your Attitude	16.99 _____
_____	Change Your Questions, Change Your Life	19.95 _____
_____	Change Your Thinking, Change Your Life	22.00 _____
_____	Eat That Frog	15.95 _____
_____	The Element: How Finding Your Passion Changes Everything	16.00 _____
_____	Finding Your Own North Star	15.00 _____
_____	Free At Last: Daily Meditations By and For Ex-Offenders	15.95 _____
_____	Get Out of Your Own Way: Overcoming Self-Defeating Behavior	15.00 _____
_____	Get the Life Your Want	19.95 _____
_____	Goals!	19.95 _____
_____	How to Save Your Own Life	14.00 _____
_____	Making Good Habit, Breaking Bad Habits	15.00 _____
_____	Making Hope Happen	16.00 _____
_____	Magic of Thinking Big	15.99 _____
_____	The Power of Habit	16.00 _____
_____	The Power of Positive Thinking	15.99 _____
_____	Reinventing Your Life	17.00 _____
_____	The Secret	23.95 _____
_____	The Success Principles	19.99 _____
_____	Think and Grow Rich	18.95 _____
_____	What Should I Do With My Life?	18.00 _____
_____	Wishcraft: How to Get What You Really Want	16.00 _____

Reimagining Your Life With Purpose

_____	Claiming Your Place At the Fire	$16.95 _____
_____	Life Reimagined: Discovering Your New Life Possibilities	16.95 _____
_____	Man's Search for Meaning	9.99 _____
_____	The Power of Purpose	17.95 _____
_____	Repacking Your Bags	17.95 _____
_____	Something to Live For	16.95 _____
_____	Work Reimagined: Uncover Your Calling	16.95 _____
_____	Your Life Calling: Reimagining the Rest of Your Life	16.00 _____

Mindfulness

_____	Mindfulness: A Practical Guide to Awakening	$25.95 _____
_____	Mindfulness for Beginners	21.95 _____

_____	Mindfulness for Dummies	26.99 _____
_____	The Mindfulness Solution	16.95 _____
_____	One-Minute Mindfulness	15.95 _____
_____	The Power of Now	15.00 _____
_____	Stillness Speaks	17.00 _____

Career Exploration

_____	50 Best Jobs for Your Personality	$19.95 _____
_____	150 Best Jobs for a Secure Future	17.95 _____
_____	150 Best Jobs for Your Skills	17.95 _____
_____	200 Best Jobs for Introverts	16.95 _____
_____	200 Best Jobs Through Apprenticeships	24.95 _____
_____	300 Best Jobs Without a Four-Year Degree	20.95 _____
_____	Best Jobs for the 21st Century	19.95 _____
_____	Occupational Outlook Handbook	19.95 _____
_____	Top 100 Health-Care Careers	28.95 _____

Finding Jobs and Getting Hired

_____	The 2-Hour Job Search	$12.99 _____
_____	Guerrilla Marketing for Job Hunters 3.0	21.95 _____
_____	Job Hunting Tips for People With Hot and Not-So-Hot Backgrounds	17.95 _____
_____	Knock 'Em Dead: The Ultimate Job Search Guide	16.99 _____
_____	No One Will Hire Me!	15.95 _____
_____	The Quick 30/30 Job Solution	14.95 _____
_____	Unemployed, But Moving On!	13.95 _____
_____	What Color is Your Parachute? (annual edition)	19.99 _____

Career Assessment

_____	Career Match	$15.00 _____
_____	Discover What You're Best At	15.99 _____
_____	Do What You Are	18.99 _____
_____	Everything Career Tests Book	15.99 _____
_____	Go Put Your Strengths to Work	16.00 _____
_____	Pathfinder: How to Choose or Change Your Career	17.95 _____
_____	What Type Am I?	17.00 _____

Resumes and Cover Letters

_____	201 Dynamite Job Search Letters	$19.95 _____
_____	Best Keywords for Resumes, Letters, and Interviews	19.95 _____
_____	Best Resumes for People Without a Four-Year Degree	19.95 _____
_____	Blue-Collar Resume and Job Hunting Guide	15.95 _____
_____	Creating Your First Resume	12.95 _____
_____	Damn Good Resume Guide	11.99 _____
_____	Gallery of Best Resumes for People Without a Four-Year Degree	18.95 _____
_____	High Impact Resumes and Letters	19.95 _____
_____	Knock 'Em Dead Cover Letters	14.99 _____
_____	Knock 'Em Dead Resumes	14.99 _____
_____	Modernize Your Resume	18.95 _____
_____	Nail the Cover Letter	17.95 _____
_____	Nail the Resume!	17.95 _____
_____	Resumes for Dummies	18.99 _____

Networking and Social Media

_____	How to Find a Job on LinkedIn, Facebook, Twitter, and Google+	$20.00 _____
_____	Job Searching With Social Media for Dummies	19.99 _____
_____	Know 'Em Dead Social Networking	15.99 _____
_____	Networking for People Who Hate Networking	17.95 _____

_____	The Power Formula for LinkedIn Success	16.95 _____
_____	Savvy Networker	16.95 _____

Interviewing

_____	101 Dynamite Questions to Ask At Your Job Interview	$13.95 _____
_____	101 Great Answers to the Toughest Interview Questions	14.99 _____
_____	101 Smart Questions to Ask on Your Interview	13.99 _____
_____	Best Answers to 202 Job Interview Questions	17.95 _____
_____	I Can't Believe They Asked Me That!	17.95 _____
_____	Job Interview Tips for People With Not-So-Hot Backgrounds	14.95 _____
_____	KeyWords to Nail Your Job Interview	17.95 _____
_____	Knock 'Em Dead Job Interviews	14.95 _____
_____	Nail the Job Interview	14.95 _____
_____	Job Interview for Dummies	17.99 _____
_____	Savvy Interviewing (Krannich)	10.95 _____
_____	Sweaty Palms	13.95 _____
_____	Win the Interview, Win the Job	15.95 _____
_____	You Should Hire Me!	15.95 _____

Addiction

_____	12 Smart Things to Do When the Booze and Drugs Are Gone	$15.95 _____
_____	12 Stupid Things That Mess Up Recovery	15.95 _____
_____	Chicken Soup for the Recovering Soul	14.95 _____
_____	Denial Is Not a River in Egypt	13.95 _____
_____	Ending Addiction for Good	14.95 _____
_____	Free At Last	15.95 _____
_____	How to Get and Stay Sober	14.95 _____
_____	Life Without a Crutch	7.95 _____
_____	Now What? An Insider's Guide to Addiction and Recovery	15.95 _____
_____	Painkillers, Heroin, and the Road to Sanity	15.95 _____
_____	Passages Through Recovery	15.95 _____
_____	The Recovery Book	17.95 _____
_____	Rein in Your Brain	14.95 _____
_____	Stop the Chaos	15.95 _____
_____	The Truth About Addiction and Recovery	17.00 _____

Anger Management

_____	Anger Control Workbook	$21.95 _____
_____	Anger Management for Dummies	22.99 _____
_____	Anger Management for Everyone	17.95 _____
_____	Anger Management Sourcebook	18.95 _____
_____	Angry Men	14.95 _____
_____	Angry Women	14.95 _____
_____	Beyond Anger: A Guide for Men	15.99 _____
_____	Cage Your Rage for Women	20.00 _____
_____	Cage Your Rage Workbook	25.00 _____
_____	Forgiveness: How to Make Peace With Your Past...	16.00 _____
_____	Managing Anger and Rage: The Niagara Falls Metaphor Video Workbook Program	$139.00 _____
_____	Managing Teen Anger and Violence	19.95 _____
_____	New Cage Your Rage Program	769.95 _____
_____	Pathways to Peace Anger Management Workbook	29.95 _____
_____	Pulling Punches: A Curriculum for Rage Management	495.00 _____
_____	Violent No More	24.95 _____

Family, Parenting, and Manhood Skills

_____	52 Things Kids Need From a Dad	$12.99 _____
_____	Do Fathers Matter?	15.00 _____

_____	Fathering: What It Means to Be a Dad DVD	79.95 _____
_____	How to Be a Responsible Father: Instructor's Manual	$50.00 _____
_____	How to Be a Responsible Father: Workbook for Offenders	$30.00 _____
_____	How to Be a Responsible Mother: Instructor's Manual	$50.00 _____
_____	How to Be a Responsible Mother: Workbook for Offenders	$30.00 _____
_____	Parenting From the Inside Out	16.95 _____
_____	Parenting From the Inside Out Kit for Incarcerated Fathers	739.95 _____
_____	Parenting From the Inside Out Kit for Incarcerated Mothers	729.95 _____
_____	Parenting Skills Collection (6 DVD programs)	1,425.00 _____
_____	Power Source Parenting	15.00 _____
_____	The Responsible and Effective Father Kit	218.95 _____
_____	The Responsible and Effective Mother Kit	133.95 _____
_____	The Story of Fathers and Sons DVD	149.00 _____
_____	The Story of Mothers and Daughters DVD	149.00 _____

Special Value Kits

_____	72 Re-Entry Success Books for Ex-Offenders	$1,199.95 _____
_____	Attitude, Purpose, and Passion Are Everything Kit	912.95 _____
_____	Cage Your Anger, Rage, and Violence Kit	899.95 _____
_____	Discover What You're Best At Kit	441.95 _____
_____	Effective Face-to-Face and Online Networking Kit	889.95 _____
_____	Ex-Offender's Re-Entry Success Library	331.95 _____
_____	Helping Ex-Offenders Achieve Re-Entry Success	377.95 _____
_____	Job Finding With Social Media and Technology Kit	$282.95 _____
_____	Learning From Successes and Failures Kit	1,050.95 _____
_____	Mindfulness for Refocusing Your Life Kit	297.95 _____
_____	New Attitudes, Goals, and Motivations Kit	412.95 _____
_____	Overcoming Barriers to Employment Kit	583.95 _____
_____	Overcoming Self-Defeating Behaviors and Bouncing Back Kit	247.95 _____
_____	Prison Ministries and Chaplaincies	176.95 _____
_____	Reimagining Life: Discovering Your Meaning and Purpose in Life Kit	203.95 _____
_____	Start Your Own Business Kit	316.95 _____
_____	Substance Abuse, Addictive Behaviors, and Recovery Kit	1,115.95 _____
_____	The Ultimate Habit Change Kit	579.95 _____
_____	The Ultimate Prison Survival Kit	589.95 _____

Survival and Re-Entry Curriculum Programs

_____	99 Days and a Get Up Training Program	$2,500.00 _____
_____	From the Inside Out Curriculum	395.00 _____
_____	Co-occurring Disorders Program (CDP)	829.00 _____
_____	Life Skills Series for Parolees and Inmates	1,085.00 _____
_____	Life Without a Crutch Training Program	995.00 _____
_____	Now What? Project: A Map Through the Maze Prison Intake, Orientation, and Adjustment Program for Inmates	399.95 _____
_____	A New Direction for Ex-Offenders: A Curriculum	4,995.00 _____
_____	Ultimate Re-Entry Success Curriculum Starter Kit	1,795.00 _____

Re-Entry and Survival DVDs

_____	9 to 5 Beats Ten to Life	$95.00 _____
_____	Barriers to Communication and How to Overcome Them	129.95 _____
_____	Breaking and Entering...Into a Better Life	199.95 _____
_____	Construction Trade Options for Ex-Offenders	2,149.00 _____
_____	Countdown to Freedom (for men or women)	695.00 _____
_____	Day of Release and Beyond	129.00 _____
_____	Digital Communication Skills	129.95 _____
_____	Down But Not Out	149.00 _____

_____	Ex-Offenders CAN Ace the Job Interview	230.00 _____
_____	Ex-Offender's Guide to Job Fair Success	129.00 _____
_____	Expert Job Search Strategies for the Ex-Offender (3 DVDs)	$399.00 _____
_____	From Prison to Home	169.95 _____
_____	From Parole to Payroll (3 DVDs)	299.85 _____
_____	From Prison to Paycheck (8 DVDs)	999.00 _____
_____	In Your Hands: Life After Prison	169.95 _____
_____	Life After Prison	99.95 _____
_____	Living Free	149.00 _____
_____	New Ex-Offender Re-Entry DVDs for 2016	729.00 _____
_____	The Now What? DVDs: Inmate and Staff Versions	199.95 _____
_____	Parole: Getting Out and Staying Out	69.95 _____
_____	Power Source DVD Series (4 DVDs)	289.00 _____
_____	Putting the Bars Behind You	99.00 _____
_____	Resumes, Cover Letters, and Portfolios for Ex-Offenders	108.00 _____
_____	Soft Skills in the Workplace	149.00 _____
_____	Starting Fresh With a Troubled Background Series	299.95 _____
_____	Stop Recidivism, Now! (3 DVDs)	275.00 _____
_____	Tough Questions, Straight Answers	95.00 _____
_____	Why Bother? Finding the Will to Go On	119.95 _____

Life Skills/Personal Finance DVD/CD Programs

_____	Buying the Basics	$199.00 _____
_____	Life Skills for Independent Living CD Program	1,319.00 _____
_____	Life Steps DVD Series	799.95 _____
_____	Managing Your Personal Finances	540.00 _____
_____	On Your Own: Independent Living Skills	99.95 _____
_____	On Your Own Coast-to-Coast	99.00 _____

Addiction, Recovery, and Relapse Programs

_____	Addiction Recovery for Ex-Offenders DVD Series	$999.00 _____
_____	Co-Occurring Disorders Program	829.00 _____
_____	Substance Abuse and Addictive Behaviors Kit	557.95 _____

TERMS: Individuals must prepay; approved accounts are billed net 30 days. All orders under $100.00 should be prepaid.

RUSH ORDERS: fax, call, or email for more information on any special shipping arrangements and charges.

SUBTOTAL _____

Virginia residents add 6% sales tax _____

California residents add ____% sales tax _____

Shipping ($5 +8% of SUBTOTAL) _____

TOTAL ORDER _____

Bill To:

Name_____ Title _____
Address_____
City _____ State/Zip _____
Phone ( )_____ (daytime)
Email_____

Ship To: (if different from "Bill To;" include St. del. address).

Name_____ Title _____
Address_____
City _____ State/Zip _____
Phone ( )_____ (daytime)
Email_____

PAYMENT METHOD: ❏ **Purchase Order** #_____ *(attach or fax with this order form)*
❏ **Check** – Make payable to IMPACT PUBLICATIONS .
❏ **Credit Card**: ❏ Visa ❏ MasterCard ❏ AMEX ❏ Discover

Card #											Expiration Date		
Signature					Name on Card (print)								

Re-Entry Companion Guides

The Ex-Offender's New Job Finding and Survival Guide:
10 Steps for Successfully Re-Entering the Work World (2nd Edition)
Ronald L. Krannich, Ph.D.

#9218 What should ex-offenders do in order to land a good job? This book provides important answers to many re-entry questions facing ex-offenders. Beginning with an examination of 20 myths/realities and 22 principles for success, it reveals 10 steps to job and career success:

1. Examine and change your attitudes
2. Seek assistance and become proactive
3. Select appropriate job search approaches
4. Assess your skills and identify your motivational pattern
5. State a powerful objective
6. Conduct research on jobs and communities
7. Write effective resumes and letters
8. Network for information, advice, and referrals
9. Develop winning job interview skills
10. Negotiate salary and benefits like a pro

Includes two special chapters – (1) how to survive and prosper on the job as well advance your career, and (2) how to best navigate the electronic world after spending so much time behind a prison firewall. Rich in insights and filled with practical examples, exercises, self-tests, and resources. 240 pages. Copyright © 2016. ISBN 978-1-57023-362-3. **$19.95. SPECIALS: 10 copies for $159.60; 100 copies for $998.00; 1,000 copies for $7,980.00.**

---

99 Days to Re-Entry Success Journal: (2nd Edition)
Ronald L. Krannich, Ph.D.

#7679 This handy journal assists ex-offenders in dealing with key transition issues during their first 99 days, or 14 weeks, in the free world. It requires users to:

♦ specify three major objectives each week
♦ identify specific supporting daily activities
♦ anticipate related outcomes
♦ evaluate their progress at the end of each week
♦ make key adjustments for the next week

Users record exactly what they plan to do each day (a daily "To Do" list) and then evaluate their progress on a scale of 1 to 10 in accomplishing their goals for the week. The journal also includes important sections on:

♦ commitment   ♦ budgeting
♦ key contacts   ♦ personal information
♦ appointments   ♦ documentation
♦ financial planning ♦ re-entry resources

Helps ex-offenders focus on those things they need to do on a daily basis to develop a new pattern of behavior for achieving success in the free world. 64 pages. Copyright © 2016. ISBN 978-1-57023-372-2. **$4.95. SPECIALS: 10 copies for $39.80; 100 copies for $297.00; 1,000 copies for $2,227.00.**

The Ex-Offender's Re-Entry Assistance Directory:
Public and Private Support Programs for Making It on the Outside

Order #243

Quantity Discounts
Per unit discounts/costs

1-9 copies	0% ($29.95)
10-49 copies	10% ($26.97)
50-99 copies	15% ($25.46)
100-499 copies	20% ($23.96)
500-999 copies	25% ($22.46)
1,000-4,999 copies	30% ($20.97)

Quantity costs

10 copies	$269.70
25 copies	$674.25
50 copies	$1,348.50
100 copies	$2,396.00
500 copies	$11,230.00
1,000 copies	$20,970.00